THE SERVICE OF GLORY

THE SERVICE OF GLORY

The *Catechism of the Catholic Church*
on Worship, Ethics, Spirituality

Aidan Nichols, O.P.

T&T CLARK
EDINBURGH

T&T CLARK LTD
59 GEORGE STREET
EDINBURGH EH2 2LQ
SCOTLAND

First published 1997

ISBN 0 567 08555 4

British Library Cataloguing-in-Publication Data
A catalogue record for this book is available from the British Library

Typeset by Trinity Typesetting, Edinburgh
Printed and bound in Great Britain by Biddles Ltd, Guildford

God of power and mercy,
by whose grace your people give you praise and
    worthy service;
save us from faltering on our way
to the joys you have promised.

Oratio **of the Roman rite for the**
Thirty-first Sunday of the Year

Contents

Part Three
THE TREASURES OF MERCY
Spirituality

PART ONE

THE COVENANT OF RECONCILIATION

WORSHIP

Almighty, ever-living God,
you offer the covenant of reconciliation to mankind
in the mystery of Easter.
Grant that what we celebrate in worship,
We may carry out in our lives.

Oratio **of the Roman rite for**
the Friday of the Easter Octave

I

Introduction *

To those who suspect they are displaced persons in a universe of chance oblivious to their fate, the news of the self-involvement of the divine Trinity with the human race is not only good but the best possible news there can be. It is from this point that, its exposition of the Creed completed,[1] the *Catechism of the Catholic Church* resumes its task of initiating believers into the whole of faith in all its aspects. The Liturgy of the Church – our next stop on the *Catechism*'s journey – is the celebration of that trinitarian economy at work in the world, and first and foremost, of the mystery of Christ, the divine Son made human, who reveals the Father in the Holy Spirit. Beginning from the extremely high doctrine of the Liturgy found in the Dogmatic Constitution of the Second Vatican Council on that subject, the text we are to study in this book finds in liturgical celebration – and notably in the Sacrifice of the Mass – the actuation of the work of our redemption. And because our redemption does not – of its nature *cannot* – leave us unchanged, ethical, spiritual and even missionary consequences follow. In her Liturgy the Church proclaims and celebrates the mystery of Christ, with the events of the paschal *triduum* at its heart, so that the faithful may draw life from the copious stream and gives testimony to its revitalising power. In this sense all that the

---

*See p. 5 *Catechism*, Paragraphs 1066–1068.
[1]See A. Nichols, O.P., *The Splendour of Doctrine. The Catechism of the Catholic Church on Christian Believing* (Edinburgh 1995) for an account of the *Catechism*'s first 'book'.

3

Catechism will later say about moral life in Christ and growth in holiness through prayer issues from its treatment of the Liturgy as our appropriation, in the Church, of the death and resurrection of the humanised Word of God.

II

---

*The Nature of the Liturgy**

Not for the first time, the *Catechism* shows its remarkable power to synthesise disparate data in its comments on the *origins* of the word 'liturgy' (*leitourgia*) and the *use* of that term and its cognates in the New Testament. In the Greek *polis* a citizen's 'liturgy', a duty at once secular and sacred since the duality between the two had not yet dawned, was his contribution to the common weal. In Christianity, where it is divine action that secures human flourishing, with human 'praxis' playing its part only by way of response to God's initiative, such 'public works' will necessarily take the form of a sharing in the 'works of God' – an allusion to the opening of Jesus' High Priestly Prayer (John 17:4) where the Lord gives testimony that he has accomplished the 'work' the Father sent him on earth to perform. But how are we then to explain the fact that in the New Testament the language of 'liturgy' is used not only for celebration of the divine cultus, where the Redeemer makes present that finished work of his, but also for the preaching of the gospel and for active charity? The *Catechism*'s answer is that the Liturgy incorporates both the preaching of the gospel and its call to caritative action – what else *is* the *Ite missa est* of the Roman Mass but a dismissal in order to go forth and witness to the gospel in word and deed?

But a deeper explanation is also forthcoming, and a subtle one. Since she shares in the threefold office of Christ, at once *priestly* or sanctifying, *prophetic* or proclamatory and *royal* or set

*=*Catechism*, Paragraphs 1069–1102.

5

at the service of charity (for, to a Messiah borne by the foal of
an ass, he who *serves* reigns), the Church naturally shows forth
all these dimensions of her Christ-derived being when, in the
Liturgy, she presents herself as the servant and image of him
who is the only true 'Liturgist', the one Mediator between God
and man.

In its opening statement of what the Liturgy is the *Catechism*
focusses on three aspects – the Liturgy as *fount of life*, as *prayer*,
and as locus of what ought to be the deepest *catechesis* of all. A
word about each will be in order here. The Liturgy is a *fount of
life* because it launches the faithful on the new life of 'coinherence' (in the useful word coined by the Anglo-Catholic
lay theologian Charles Williams) where each finds his or her 'I'
only in the 'we' of the Church. Not of course that this takes
place by way of submission to a purely human institution: such
a proceeding would be totalitarian, fascistic. It is only because
the Church is the visible sign of a new communion between
God and humankind in Jesus Christ that all the virtualities of
personal and interpersonal identity are realised in her. In
celebrating the Liturgy by way of a diaconal ('serving') and
iconic ('imaging') collaboration with Christ, the Church
becomes more fully what she already is: the sign of salvation set
up before the nations. This happens, however, in no automatic
way. Whether in this or that person's life the ground has been
truly fertilised by the reception of the gospel through faith and
conversion, those indispensable preliminaries of liturgical
participation, will soon be shown by the litmus test of his or
her subsequent behaviour. The fruitfulness of liturgical
celebration is shown in personal renaissance of an ethical
and religious kind (the 'fruits' of the Spirit, as listed by Paul
in Galatians 5:22, range from charity to chastity), as well as
in a missionary impulse to spread the faith, and in the
building up of the Church-body's unity.

Within its own being as a fount of life in Christ, the Liturgy
is, first and foremost, *prayer*: a sharing in the prayer of Christ as,
in the Holy Spirit, that is directed to the Father. Here the
prayer of the Christian man takes its rise and finds its goal. And
yet the *Catechism* shows its awareness of a false liturgio-centrism
which would foreshorten the Christian hope and deprive the

Liturgy of its true glory: namely, to be a window onto the eternal trinitarian love. If the Liturgy serves, in the words of the Letter to the Ephesians, to root and found the inner man, through the Holy Spirit, in his only Son (cf. Ephesians 2:4 and 3:16–17), then it must also point on beyond itself to our final sharing in the life of the Trinity. As the Swiss theologian Hans Urs von Balthasar has evoked that hope, in a manner which simultaneously calls to mind its liturgical anticipation:

> Through the glory of the Son we shall see appear the abyss of the invisible Father, and this in the twofold figure [a reference to Balthasar's theology of the Spirit as at once the subjective relation of Father and Son and that relation's objective fruit] of the Holy Spirit of love. As those born of the Son we shall exist in the fire of that love where Father and Son meet. In that way, together with the Spirit, we shall be at the same time that same love's witnesses and its doxologists.[1]

But we are still on earth and so need education – literally, a 'drawing out' and in this context to the infinite dimensions of the mystery we would enter. So secondly, after describing the Liturgy as prayer, the authors of the *Catechism* consider it as a place of *teaching*. They are right to set the didactic goal of the Liturgy second to that of adoration and communion, for the former goal is really only means to the latter end. Liturgical catechesis (other forms of instruction in the Church are, evidently, not ruled out: the *Catechism* itself is one!) aims at our introduction into the mystery of Christ. Here we realise how misplaced is all preaching that would confine itself to the offer of homely wisdom about daily life, or comment on public policy, or the need for funding ecclesiastical projects (though all of these may have their place in the wider discourse of the Church). Liturgical preaching has a mystagogic rôle – to draw us from the visible to the invisible, from the signifier to the signified, from the signs that eye can see and ear hear (the 'sacraments') to the realities which those signs signify (the

---

[1] H. U. von Balthasar, *Theologik III. Der Geist der Wahrheit* (Einsiedeln 1987), p. 410.

'mysteries'). Conscious that the liturgical life of the Church unfolds not only in the midst of a variety of cultures but also in a diversity of ritual families (of which the Western and Eastern are simply the two largest groups), the *Catechism* will offer an understanding of the Liturgy which underpins such preaching by a resolute attention to what is 'fundamental and common'. This leads it to divide up its subsequent remarks under two main headings: the Liturgy as celebration of the paschal mystery[2] and the Liturgy of the seven sacraments and their ancillary rites.[3]

In setting the scene for its account of the Liturgy as the sacramental celebration of the saving events of Easter, the *Catechism* may presume that the reader has made his own what it had to say earlier on the economy of the Son and his atoning work. It begins therefore from the moment of Pentecost, which is the inauguration of the 'time of the Church'. The Church, prepared as she was in Israel, as well as by the teaching and institution-founding activity of the pre-Easter Jesus, and born on the cross, is manifested to the world at the first Pentecost: that is, Christ then begins to act through her by his distinctive *modus operandi* in the economy of the Spirit – through signs filled with the power that comes from cross and resurrection. Exalted crucified Son and outpoured Spirit of his love act together to communicate the fruits of the paschal mystery in the liturgical 'sign-system' of their co-mission from the Father.

It is with the *Father* – curiously, at first sight – that the *Catechism* begins its explanation of the 'Paschal Mystery in the Time of the Church'. Yet not so curiously, for, as the title of its first article affirms, the Liturgy, like the saving divine action it encapsulates, is the work of the entire holy Trinity, where the Father is, for Son and Spirit, both (in the relations of origin) Source, and (in the relations of communion), beloved Goal. The *Catechism*'s 'paterological' account of the Liturgy where the Father, is, likewise, beginning and end, turns out to be a miniature theology of *blessing*. Some Catholics find it

[2]Paragraphs 1076–1209.
[3]Paragraphs 1210–1300.

understandably confusing that, whereas the primary subject of blessing in Scripture is the God from whom all blessings flow, the same literature can also speak of human beings (and even the subrational creation) blessing God as object, while the Church includes in her ritual numerous prayers in which the priest, as her representative, blesses persons (such as the bride and groom at a nuptial Mass) or things (made either for sacred use, like rosary beads, or for frankly secular, such as a motor car). In making use of the multivalent – yet not for that reason internally incoherent – concept of blessing to throw light on what we are doing in the Liturgy, the *Catechism* incidentally sorts out these difficulties as well.

Blessing is a life-giving action typical of the Father. From the beginning of time his work has always been, most characteristically, blessing. Between the primal creation, hymned in the poem which opens the Book of Genesis, where God pours out benediction on all living creatures, but on man and woman in particular, and the New Jerusalem, the definitive co-presence of God and man in a renewed creation, where all the singing is of the wonderful works of him who sits upon the throne, blessing is, we can say, the Father's signature-tune. Reception of ever-fuller blessings marks the defining stages of the history of salvation. If the covenant with Noah confirms for the whole animal creation the blessing of fertility, despite man's sin, then the covenant with Abraham shows the divine blessing penetrating beyond cosmic nature into human history itself. And while, for Israel, exodus and the gift of the land, the Davidic dynasty, the temple presence and the return from exile are themselves divine blessings manifested in marvellous actions, the whole process comes to its climax for (in principle) the entire human race with the incarnation, death and resurrection of the Father's Word. That is when God overwhelms his human creatures with blessing and, through that nexus of actions, spreads abroad in our hearts the Spirit who so encloses all gifts in himself that Augustine will call his name quite simply *Donum*, '*the* Gift' *par excellence*.

And here comes the inversion of terms. In the Liturgy, loving faith, inspired by the Spirit, acknowledges the Father as the fount of such great blessings. In reproducing, doxologically, the movement of blessing, it necessarily traces that blessing from its term to its source. By adoration, thanksgiving and praise it ascribes all blessing to the Father, thus 'blessing' him in turn.

At the same time, and so as to bring the Father's work to completion the Church presents for his blessing herself and her (eucharistic) offerings, her faithful and the whole world – imploring, through her own benediction of the Father, that he will send the Spirit of his Son 'epicletically' upon a creation still groaning in travail. Thus even in the Old Testament, according to the Roman Benedictional:

> The God from whom all blessings flow favoured many persons – particularly the patriarchs, kings, priests, Levites, and parents – by allowing them to offer blessings in praise of his name and to invoke his name, *so that other persons or the works of creation would be showered with divine blessings.*[4]

That *Book of Blessings* notes further how this state of affairs is supremely enhanced when the Father sends the Word into the creation to make all things holy by his incarnation. Here, then, is the theological meaning of those varied blessings which the ministers of the Liturgy pronounce during the celebration of both sacraments and sacramentals, and whose scope can stretch from icons to iguanas.[5]

But if the Liturgy is the work of the Father, it is no less the work of the *Son* also. And here the *Catechism* treats the paschal mystery of Jesus Christ as that historically-achieved reality which is now both signified and communicated through the Liturgy of the Church. Mindful, perhaps, of Pope Leo the Great's celebrated statement that *all* that is visible in the life of the Redeemer has passed over into his sacraments, it feels obliged, accordingly, to treat the Saviour's teaching and (other) actions as essentially an anticipatory notice of this central event of man's redemption.

---

[4]'General Introduction', *Book of Blessings* (E.t. Collegeville, MN 1989), p. xxiv. Italics added.

[5]For how the redemptive incarnation might be said to affect the inanimate creation, see R. Potter, O.P., 'The Hallowing of Creatures. An Exegetical and Theological Inquiry', *Dominican Studies* VI (1953), pp. 21–41, especially at p. 31.

The *Catechism* affirms the unique status, *vis-à-vis* time, of the
Lord's death and resurrection. Albeit truly historical, they
alone of all such events are not swallowed up by the past. Since
by his dying Christ has conquered death, that event in which
transience is overcome endures for ever, thus enabling him to
take into the divine eternity all he achieved and underwent for
mortal man. And so the paschal mystery can embrace all ages
and be rendered present to each. In its abiding reality it draws
all to itself, or rather towards the life which the living God is and
which he makes available in his Christ who once declared
himself to be life, as well as way and truth (John 14:6). In this
bold statement of the metahistorical reality of the paschal
mystery – not being in any normal sense temporally bounded
– the Easter triumph can be *and is* re-presented in the Liturgy
of the Church, the *Catechism* betrays an allegiance to the
Mysterientheologie of the German Benedictine Odo Casel. Casel
wrote:

> It is Christ's will that this spring should always be running
> in the Church. Not just faith in the once dead Prince is to
> save the faithful; his saving act is to be a continual, lasting,
> mystical and yet concrete presence in the Church, from
> which the power of his Blood is to flow daily to give life and
> healing to the faithful.

And lest there were any doubt that he is speaking of the sacred
Liturgy, *Das christliche Kultmysterium* continues by describing
how, on the night of his betrayal Christ

> gave to his disciples this mystical celebration of his
> redeeming deed... As the Church grew out of the Lord's
> Blood, she is to live and grow in his strength. Still in
> heaven with his Father, each day he wills to sacrifice
> himself with her fighting and suffering on earth, wills to
> celebrate his death with her in the world by a mystical and
> symbolic act, and so to waken her to a new life, in and with
> God. Christ has given his mystery to the Church's care;
> she acts it out, and thereby fulfils his action, which has
> become hers. So Christ and the Church become one in

act and passion: the mystery is made a new and eternal covenant.[6]

Yet the mysteric is not at the expense of the institutional. The *Catechism* has no mind to attempt an overleaping of the apostolic succession of duly ordained ministers, which throughout historical time properly so called validates the sacramental signs of each new ecclesial generation by reference to the single origin, the generation of Jesus and his – precisely, *original* – apostles. The metahistorical reality, the mystery of Easter, is rendered present, in the eucharistic Sacrifice, with the other sacraments and liturgical rites in constellation round this sun, by the sign which is *the apostolic succession itself.*

> Thus the risen Christ, by giving the Holy Spirit to the apostles, entrusted to them his power of sanctifying: they became sacramental signs of Christ. By the power of the same Holy Spirit they entrusted this power to their successors. This 'apostolic succession' structures the whole liturgical life of the Church and is itself sacramental, handed on by the sacrament of Holy Orders.[7]

But though, without the sacrament of Order, the fulness of the paschal mystery in its liturgical expression is unavailable to Christians, the ministerial priest in his consecration of the eucharistic Gifts hardly exhausts the modalities of Christ's presence in the Church's worship. Christ is present in his Word when the Church preaches; in his power as the humiliated Pantocrator in the other sacraments; in his Name where two or three are gathered together for his sake. And these are all, as the *Catechism*'s closing citations from the Conciliar Liturgy Constitution make clear, gifts of the Lord Jesus to his Church-Bride, which look forward, then, to his transparent presence to his people in the nuptial joy of heaven. In the *Russian Primary Chronicle* the envoys of the Prince of Kiev, after they had witnessed the celebration of the holy Liturgy at Hagia Sophia,

---

[6]O. Casel, *The Mystery of Christian Worship, and Other Writings* (E.t. London 1962), pp. 58–59.

[7]Paragraph 1087.

in Constantinople, confessed themselves unable to say whether they had been in heaven or on earth, but knew they would never forget that beauty. Though the authors of the *Catechism* are too discreet to say so, it is a lesson that liturgical philistines in the modern Western church would do well to relearn.

And so to the relation between the Liturgy and the *Holy Spirit*. The *Catechism* presents the sacred Liturgy as a collaborative work of Spirit and Church. Because the foundation of the Church's life is faith and the sacraments of faith, the Spirit who establishes that life in relation to the Son, must be the 'tutor' of faith and the 'artifex' of those signs in which faith is aroused, expressed and brought to practical effect – the sacraments. The Spirit must be – in that key Balthasarian vocabulary we have already encountered – both *subjective* Spirit enabling our faith response to God in his outreach to us, and *objective* Spirit, turning what would otherwise be no more than human symbolic activity, a topic for anthropologists, into a sharing in the gestures of the risen Christ, a topic for theologians if ever there was one. But since none of this would be possible without the willingness of human freedom to be thus engaged, or at the least (on the severe Thomistic construal) by divine 'premotion' not to pose an obstacle to grace, the work of the Spirit requires the co-working of the human members of the Church.

If Irenaeus of Lyons could speak of Son and Spirit as the 'two hands' of the Father, the *Catechism* presents the mystagogical rôle of the Spirit in a conscious symmetry with the liturgical activity of the Son. The Spirit prepares the Church to meet and welcome Christ; he calls to mind and manifests the mystery of Christ to the worshipping assembly; and he makes that mystery present and actual by his transforming power. In sum, and by way of issue of all of these, he gives the Church a communion – an intimate share – in the life and mission of Christ. Thus in the condensed form of the liturgical action, the Holy Spirit continually hands over to the Church the content of the economy of the Son. In the Liturgy we see the entire drama of salvation in Old and New Testaments unfold before our eyes.

In speaking of the Spirit as preparing the Church to welcome Christ, the authors of the *Catechism* have in mind the abiding way in which the Spirit actualises the Old Testament as an

intrinsic part of the message of the gospel. As the Johannine
Christ tells the Samaritan woman, 'Salvation is from the Jews'
(John 4:22). The marvellous preparation of the Church in
Israel is reflected in three features of the Liturgy: the solemn
reading of the Old Testament Scriptures, the public praying of
the Psalms and the memory of those events of Hebrew history
which prefigure the fulfilment of world history in the mystery
of Christ. These features are, the *Catechism* insists, integral,
indispensable, and for this it gives the profound explanation
that

> It is on this harmony of the two Testaments that the
> Paschal catechesis of the Lord is built, and then that of the
> apostles and the Fathers of the Church.[8]

It is by the magnificent symphony of divine revelation in its two
great movements, the covenant with Israel, and the covenant
in Christ that the music of the Word of God is played. From the
discourse of the risen Christ on the road to Emmaus in St
Luke's Gospel, to the catechesis of the great Fathers, no other
form of initiation is known.

The *Catechism* can presuppose the scholarly work of such
students of early 'typological' symbolism (in both literature
and art) as Jean Daniélou and Hugo Rahner when it singles out
for special mention the Hebrew Bible's prefiguration of the
salvific (and not least sacramental) signs of the New Testament:
flood and ark, cloud and Red Sea crossing for Baptism, the
manna in the desert for the Mass. In the seasons of Advent (the
'Winter Lent') and Lent itself (the 'Great Lent') the Church
relives the story of the Israelite spring-time (the literal meaning
of the Anglo-Saxon word 'lent') which precedes the mid-
summer of Christ's coming. Catechists have a duty to unlock
the riches of a spiritual – which means above all a *Christological*
– reading of the Old Testament. Modelled on the Liturgy, such
an approach is inspired by the example of the Christian
Scripture themselves. Not for nothing does the closing book of
the Church's canon, the Apocalypse of St John, take in both
covenants in a single grand sweep, where the still moment of

---

[8]Paragraph 1094.

the worship of heaven, around which the bloody conflict of the spiritual battle swirls, finds twenty-four elders – twelve for Israel, and twelve for the apostles – casting their crowns simultaneously before the throne of God and of the Lamb.

Simultaneously: this raises the question of the continuing validity of the Word of God in the Old Testament, or as some English-speaking Christians would now have it, not without reason, the *Elder* Testament. In its present liturgical context the *Catechism* takes the opportunity to recall the high significance of Jewish worship for the evolution of the forms of the Catholic Liturgy in both East and West, though at the same time it does not fall to record the great difference of content for such a feast as Passover, the Christian *Pascha* (Easter), which the consummation of the hope of Israel brings in Jesus Christ. And this thought leads to another, that of the universality of the liturgical assembly of the *Catholica* meant as this is to embrace and transcend all this-worldly affinities, ethic or elective.

Not that all the relevant preparatory work for the celebration of the Christian Liturgy is Jewish. There remains, the *Catechism* warns its readers, the urgent personal obligation of due preparation for worship by a stirring up of the adhesion of faith in a conversion of heart. This too is the Spirit's gift.

But the pedagogic Spirit is also the remembering Spirit who brings to mind whatever Christ has said and done. Noting the fact that his work in the Liturgy is to memorialise the mystery of our salvation, the *Catechism* calls him, audaciously, 'the living memory of the Church'. The Spirit makes the worshipping Church mindful of the mighty deeds of God for humankind's redemption: in the Liturgy of the Word through rendering the Scriptures full of meaning for believers' lives, and in the Liturgy of the (eucharistic) Sacrifice by representing the atoning work of the Word made flesh, which of all remembering is best suited to elicit the doxological response of thanks and praise.

But in the biblical concept of remembering (in Greek, *anamnēsis*) events are not simply the object of mental recall. Rather are they by divine action called up, evoked, into the present in all their saving significance and power. In the formula of eucharistic consecration, for instance, the words

'Do this in memory of me', could as well be translated 'Do this to bring me into your present'. The Spirit, then, in calling to mind the mystery of Christ makes it manifest here and now, albeit under the signs of the sacramental economy characteristic of the 'time of the Church'. To the Western stress on the *anamnēsis* (understood inclusively of the dominical words at the Last Supper) as, *par excellence*, the consecrating moment when, implicitly, the Spirit transforms the oblations 'for our good and that of all [God's] Church', the *Catechism* counterposes the Eastern emphasis on the *epiklēsis* or explicit invocation of the Holy Spirit so that the eucharistic gifts and their recipients may be filled with his fulness. *Mutatis mutandis* the same is true of all the sacraments, for each has a crucial moment of making and a characteristic grace. This epicletic descent of the Spirit in the holy Liturgy 'hastens the coming of the Kingdom and the consummation of the mystery of salvation',[9] a thought familiar from such Eastern Orthodox theologians of worship as Alexander Schmemann.[10] The neo-Byzantine feel of the *Catechism*'s comments on the Spirit as 'actualiser' of the mystery of Christ persists in its very next statement. In the hope generated by so marked an intensification of man's movement toward the Kingdom, the members of the Church really taste by anticipation the full communion of the divine Trinity. The Spirit, sent by the Father who hears favourably the Church's epicletic prayer, brings about in the worshippers, inasmuch as they truly receive him, the first-fruits of their eternal inheritance. This is definitely, then, a *mystical theology of Catholic worship*.

Were any doubt to remain on that point it is dispelled in the *Catechism*'s closing remarks by way of introduction to the Liturgy. Here the Spirit is seen as fruitful Grace, coursing through the Vine of the Father – the whole Christ, Head and members – in the liturgical action. Through the Liturgy, the fraternal communion of the Church is inserted into the divine

---

[9]Paragraph 1106.

[10]See especially his *The Eucharist. Sacrament of the Kingdom* (E.t. Crestwood, NY, 1988).

communion of the Trinity. Or, better, since there can be no human communion in nature raised up by grace unless there be simultaneously participation in the communion of the Trinity, that human intercommunication is itself created by the fellowship of the Holy Spirit as he makes of the Church a sacrament of the reciprocal knowing and loving by Father and Son which he, the Spirit, personally is.

III

---

*The Sacraments at Large**

How does this ecclesial sharing in the Trinity through the
paschal mystery of Christ take place in the seven sacraments,
the *Catechism*'s next topic? Each of the seven has its own
specificity, which must be taken into account. And yet all are
examples of a *genre*, and so something can be said about them
as a whole. The *Catechism* will consider the genre of the
sacraments – what the Latin theology of the early modern
period called *De sacramentis in genere* – before turning what it
has to say about sacramental *doctrine* into an account of
sacramental *celebration*. For what we teach in doctrine is always
an invitation to worship, by celebration.

First and foremost, the sacraments are sacraments of Christ:
they are the continued visibility of the 'mysteries' of his life,
that life's deployment in particular events or in certain repeated
kinds of action. Ambrose in his *Apology of the Prophet David*
wrote:

> You have shown yourself to me face to face,
> O Christ, I find you in your sacraments.[1]

Not for nothing does St Thomas place his treatise on the
sacraments immediately after his treatment of Christ's life and
glorious death. Though it is the divine person of the Word
incarnate who principally ministers them to us, it is the humanity
of Christ which has become, through his passion and

---

*=*Catechism*, Paragraphs 1113–1134.
[1]Ambrose, *Apology of the Prophet David*, 12.

resurrection, the principle of redeeming grace. In the sacraments that redemptive life and death become actual again – not of course in their physical and historical detail but in the sense that the saving acts the Word performed in his humanity become present again, and dynamically and effectively so. And here the *Catechism* can presuppose everything it has professed about the Lord Jesus in its credal 'sub-book': the sacraments are necessarily sacraments of *God* in Christ, since Christ is God's communication of his own inner life, the Word, and is this both totally, absolutely, and in an incarnate, tangibly human fashion. Accordingly, while the sacramental signs are humanly intelligible (were they not, they would be of no earthly use in our salvation), they are, ultimately, signs in the language of God. In them God speaks, communicating by way of humankind's manifold language, including there its vocabulary of gesture. And this divine origin of the sacraments is something we could not possibly know unless, as the *Catechism* echoes Trent in confessing, they were themselves instituted by Jesus Christ. No purely human symbolic creation could have this valency. Although the New Testament records 'words of institution' only for Baptism and Eucharist, the Catholic doctrine is that the other sacraments are not so much *created* by the Church as *recognised* by her.

> In those pregnant engagements of her faith which we call the sacraments, the Church became increasingly aware that she was both doing and encountering Jesus' human will as the human expression of the *mystērion* of God's eternal saving will, by analogy, then, with those engagements of her faith for which Jesus' command was explicitly given.[2]

For to furnish an 'account of the sacraments in their rôle as organs of grace which depends primarily on the Church ... and not primarily on Christ ... seems to misplace the proper emphasis'.[3]

[2]C. Ernst, O.P., 'Acts of Christ: Signs of Faith', in idem, *Multiple Echo. Explorations in Theology*, edited by F. Kerr, O.P. and T. Radcliffe, O.P. (London 1979), p. 113.

[3]Idem. Ernst was commenting on the German Jesuit Karl Rahner's *The Church and the Sacraments* (E.t. London 1963).

As if to confirm this thought, the authors of the *Catechism*, having established the Christological credentials of the sacraments, now consider them as sacraments *of the Church*. Though the Church's rôle in the making of the sacraments is not constitutive but discriminatory (just as it is with the canon of Scripture and the mysteries of faith outlined in the apostolic creeds), this does not mean they cannot be called truly *her* sacraments as well as Christ's. The *Catechism* regards them as the Church's in a twofold sense: the sacraments are *from and through* her (the official English translation has 'by' her), but these gifts of the Lord are also *for* her. They are *from and through the Church* not, however, as unfoldings of her essence but inasmuch as she is the sphere of Christ's covenanted action in the Holy Spirit. They are *for the Church* not, again, idealistically, as means whereby she takes hold of her identity (though this is not excluded), but by a thoroughgoing ecclesiological realism, as the continuous constitution of that identity, bringing her to be as a mystery of communion with the triune God. The sacraments are events in which the Church recognises her own deepest identity as the corporate sacrament of Christ, and events, moreover, by whose celebration she becomes more fully that sacrament.

In constantly receiving, through the sacraments, her own being, the Church comes to exist not only as a mystery of communion (which might be considered wholly interior and spiritual) but also as an institution, albeit a unique one, and so with an outward and social face. In the sacraments the Church acts as what the *Catechism* will cumulatively term an organically structured priestly community.

That this is so appears already from the first two rites that any account of sacramental existence must mention. Baptism and Chrismation (Confirmation) are initiation rites, not into an *ethnos*, another tribe, but into the *laos*, the incomparable sacred people drawn by God from the nations, the royal and universal priesthood of all Christ's faithful. Baptism and Confirmation, therefore, equip one for the 'liturgy' of the Christian life, and notably as a sharer in its public worship, that 'Liturgy' which we capitalise to show its pre-eminent dignity as the fount and goal of Christian living in the world. But the great mass of initiated believers, this vast throng of potential liturgists, is no mere *dēmos*, no amorphous huddle. Its communal life is structured, in locality, in region or nation, or on the scale of the planet as a whole, thanks to a sacrament of ministerial priesthood which serves the rest by ordering its life in matters of faith, through the ministry of the Word, in matters of worship, through the ministry of the sacraments, and in matters of discipline, through the ministry of pastoral care. Good order is of course a *desideratum* in itself; and, considered theologically, may be held to express in the Church the ordered way God communicates his own perfections to his creatures in a cosmos where being is both differentiated yet one. The *Catechism*'s emphasis, however, like that of the Catholic doctrine of the sacrament of Order at large, lies not on such *synchronic* ordering whereby Christians, whether individuals or groups, living in the same time are interrelated but on that *diachronic* ordering which binds them through the apostles to Jesus Christ.

Soon the *Catechism* will move on to consider the sacraments as signs of faith. Perhaps of set purpose, it pauses to underline the objectivity of sacramental reality, something which easily gets lost to view when sacraments are considered as manifestations of religious subjectivity. For such a task the concept of sacramental 'character' is peculiarly well-fitted. Following the common doctrine of the Fathers and mediaevals: Baptism, Confirmation and Order, in securing entry to the royal and universal priesthood, and to that diverse mode of sharing in Christ's high-priestly office which is the ministerial or serving priesthood, consecrate their subjects to Christ. They seal disciples for him in such a definitive, 'indelible', way that these three sacraments may never be, without sacrilege, repeated. The *Catechism* also 'receives' as theological doctrine a much less ubiquitous notion: since Christ, as the chaste priest of the sacrifice of the cross is never without his immaculate Bride – the Church for whom he gave himself, character *also consecrates the Christian to the Church* – and so constitutes an abiding, objective call not only to the worship of God but also to the Church's service.[4] At the same time, attention is drawn

[4] The view of the influential late nineteenth-century Rhenish theologian Matthias Joseph Scheeben. See his *Die Mysterien des Christentums* (Freiburg 1951),

to the way sacramental character, in specifying anew the very being of a Christian in relation to the divine covenant, disposes him or her in positive fashion to receive God's manifold grace in Jesus Christ, and promises – indeed, 'guarantees' – the divine protection won by the victorious Lamb. Though this last should not be taken in a Calvinistic sense of the 'amissibility' (unloseableness) of salvation, it has to be said that a more realist conception of the objectivity of the sacramental realm could hardly be imagined.

Nonetheless, all seven sacraments are rightly spoken of, as the *Catechism* now proceeds to do, as sacraments *of faith*. 'Faith' here is no generalised religious attitude, but that only which can count as the subjective correlate of the Word of God: it is the distinctive subjectivity born of and fed by the Word. And if, for St Thomas Aquinas, the sacraments are always *sacramenta fidei*, the *Catechism* can draw on a splendidly compendious statement from the Second Vatican Council's Constitution on the Sacred Liturgy to explain how this is so. The sacraments do not just presuppose faith: by language and ritual they feed faith, strengthen faith, express faith.[5] The sacraments are faith's opportunities.

> By the sacraments Christ comes close to us, just as he was near to the apostles in Galilee and in Judaea. It is the risen Lord who by the power of his Holy Spirit directly sanctifies us in and through the prayers and ritual actions of the priest in the Church. Christ's presence with his apostles during his earthly life did not by any means free them from making personal efforts of faith and trust.

And the author of these words, the Louvain Jesuit Piet Fransen, goes on to explain the 'felicitous distinction' drawn by Thomas

pp. 486–488: the 'mystery' of sacramental character both interiorly marks and exteriorly organises the Church as Christ's mystical body, showing us the supernatural sublimity of the sacramental order as it binds us to the great 'Sacrament' of the God-man. Scheeben develops a nuptial theology of character – as consecration to *Christ in his love for the Church* – when coming to deal with the foundation of sacramental marriage in Christian initiation.

[5] *Sacrosanctum Concilium*, 59.

in his Commentary on the Sentences, whereby the veracity (*veritas*) of the presence of the mysteries of Christ's humanity, sheerly given with a sacrament which bestows what it promises, opens onto a truth yet more perfect still (*verum simpliciter*) when

> the recipient *in virtue of the sacrament* and thus by grace, accepts Christ freely, though prompted by Christ's virtue, in faith and charity.[6]

Liturgy is falsified when people are discouraged from making a personal preparation or a personal thanksgiving for (say) eucharistic communion, on the grounds that the example of the ancient Church with its cultic objectivism counts against this. The final 'objectivity' of the sacramental life is the crucified and risen Lord, and who should meet *him* without reflective preparing and grateful lingering in wonderment thereafter?

In the Catholic universe, such faith, understood as the act of believing adherence to God of the individual human being, is never to be disassociated from faith as the content, founded on divine revelation, which the total body of the Church hands down – as the God-given context and medium whereby individuals are to come to him – from age to age. Or as the *Catechism* itself puts it: 'The Church's faith precedes the faith of the believer who is invited to adhere to it.'[7] And indeed this is already true of the basic act of faith (the *fides qua*) in the sacramental encounter, since

> whenever a sacrament is dispensed the Church receives it actually – we can almost say existentially, from the hands of her heavenly Bridegroom, and this by faith.[8]

It is still more perspicuously true of the content of that faith (the *fides quae*). The Liturgy, embodying as it does the faith of the Church in this further sense, functions, therefore, as a rule for the individual's faith, a yardstick with which to measure

[6]P. Fransen, S.J., *Faith and the Sacraments* (London 1958), pp. 19–20. The reference is to St Thomas, *In Libros Sententiarum* IV, dist.1, q.2, q.6, sol.2, ad iii.
[7]Paragraph 1124.
[8]Fransen, *Faith and the Sacraments*, p. 15.

personal believing: its dimensions, its equilibrium, its discourse. In the ancient adage, *Lex orandi, lex credendi*: 'The norm of praying is a norm for believing.' The Liturgy permits us to overhear the Church interpreting her own faith in the best way she knows how.[9]

The conclusions which the *Catechism* most immediately draws might be thought ill-assorted: they are rubrical and ecumenical. From the premise that the Liturgy is the intimate speech of the Church as Bride with her Lord the conclusion follows that no individual, be they layperson, priest or bishop has the right to tinker with the liturgical forms. Nor can a group sanctify here what the individual would profane. And if this seems an embarrassing descent from the sublime to the all-too particular and hence, in context, ridiculous, it must be said that post-conciliar Western Catholicism has witnessed enough ideological instrumentalisation of liturgical practice to be well aware of the far-reaching distortions of Christian consciousness which such tampering can cause. Not even pope or Ecumenical Council can make the Liturgy travel on other lines than those laid by doctrinal and liturgiological tradition. And to these seemingly marginal but in fact central considerations of rubrical self-discipline, the *Catechism* adds another of concern to Christian unity. Faithfulness to the *lex orandi* is a criterion for the authenticity of Catholic participation in the ecumenical movement and as such constitutes not just a just a negative restraint (nothing can be mortgaged of what is liturgically prayed) but also a positive offer of the riches of Christian believing which Catholic worship can pour forth.

As sacraments of faith, these signs sacramentalise – symbolically embody and in symbolising effect – the faith that saves. They are, then, sacraments of *saving* faith, sacraments of *salvation*. It is precisely through their expression of the faith of the Church that the sacraments, worthily celebrated, bestow the saving grace they mean.

---

[9] For the Liturgy as a *locus theologicus*, see A. Nichols, O.P., *The Shape of Catholic Theology. An Introduction to its Sources, Principles and History* (Edinburgh and Collegeville, MN 1991), pp. 181–187.

The Father always hears the prayer of his Son's Church
which, in the epiclesis of each sacrament, expresses her
faith in the power of the Spirit.[10]

As always in its theology of liturgy, the *Catechism* would
integrate the bare matter and form needful for sacramental
validity into a richly textured account of the trinitarian economy,
leading some to comment that this second section of the book
reads as though it had been written not in Rome but in
Constantinople! None the worse for that, the *Catechism*
concludes its remarks 'on the sacraments in general' by pointing
to the eschatological dimension of these seven crucial signs. In
every sacrament, though pre-eminently in the Holy Eucharist,
'a pledge of future glory is given us', as St Thomas stresses
thereby showing that the theme is not at all unknown in the
Latin West, even if the Oriental liturgies do it more justice. The
true eschatological Liturgy is in time endlessly postponed.

Unfortunately, much that the Liturgy can teach theological
doctrine is ruined if worship is celebrated in ritually
inappropriate ways. The principle *Lex orandi, lex credendi*, can
bear, alas, an ironic interpretation. A Liturgy whose idiom has
been affected by secularism, ideology or a misapprehension of
its own priorities, will soon come to infect theological culture
with its own virus.[11] Not surprisingly, then, it is to the question
of *rite* that the *Catechism* now turns.

---

[10]Paragraph 1127.
[11]See A. Nichols, O.P., *Looking at the Liturgy. A Critical View of its Contemporary
Form* (San Francisco 1996).

IV

---

*The Rôle of the Rite**

These considerations bring the *Catechism* to the topic of the liturgical celebration of the sacraments that is, their contextualisation in a web of signs and symbols by way of ritual action. In other words, prior to considering each of the seven sacraments, the authors pause to reflect on what it is for the sacraments at large to be embodied in a rite, in the ritual shape of the Liturgy of the Church. And as if reluctant to come down from the heights on which their account of the sacraments in general has culminated, they present the earthly Liturgy not primarily in sociological guise but rather as thoroughly dependent on the transcendent, heavenly Liturgy of which it is the colony or outcrop in this world. An uncharacteristic lapse into insensitivity on the part of the translators has slightly weakened the force of this tremendous opening assertion of the *Catechism*'s liturgiology. Those who participate in the heavenly worship are not celebrating the earthly liturgy's celestial counterpart and source '*without* signs' (as the English would have it) but '*beyond* the signs' (*au-delà des signes*), in that full reality of the Kingdom to which the signs of the Church's worship point and where, their work done, they terminate.[1] For the deepest reality of the temporal liturgy is its participation in the eternal Liturgy of the saints of the Old and New Covenants with the Woman of the Apocalypse – the Mother of God – at their centre, and surrounding them a multitude

---

*=*Catechism*, Paragraphs 1135–1209.
[1]Paragraph 1136.

whom no one could number (Apocalypse 7:9) and whom the *Catechism* would seem to identify with all those saved outwith the visible means of God's grace in Israel and the Church.

The *Catechism* has four questions to ask of the earthly Liturgy: who celebrates, how, when and where? To answer the first of these questions: the celebrant, for the *Catechism*, is the whole community of the Church as the mystical body of Christ. Notice how, in introducing this theme, no empirical limit is set to the extent of this corporate subject of worship; only after this vital point has been made does the text take the further step of speaking of the 'celebrating assembly'. The transcendent subject of the Liturgy, over and above those gathered for any particular celebration, is the whole Church, united as body to the mediatorial humanity of its Head, the high priest Jesus Christ. This affirmation is essential if the Liturgy is not to be falsely recategorised as a means for group expression and so expropriated from the total *Catholica*.

Nonetheless, of course, the Liturgy as a social action cannot eventuate without its social agents who are, normally speaking, a diversified yet unified gathering, most fully expressed in the Eucharist of the bishop, assisted by deacons and surrounded by a *corona* of presbyters, with the people of God playing their part, not least via the special services of, for example, choir, readers, servers. Speaking of the entire assembly as *leitourgos*, the corporate liturgist, the *Catechism* also insists on the irreplaceable 'iconic' rôle of the celebrating priest. It is a pity that no reference was made in this section to the venerable tradition of the Church that a hermit-priest may celebrate without even so much as a server present. That aspect of Catholic practice underlines the truth that the 'impressiveness' of the Mass-Liturgy in no way turns on the size of the assembly or skills of the priest (any comparison with a rally and its leader would be completely out of place), but depends entirely on its mysteric bonding with the heavenly intercession of Jesus Christ.

If we then move to ask *how* is the Liturgy celebrated, the answer is 'semiotically': through signs and symbols. In a notably comprehensive statement, the *Catechism* describes sacramental celebration as woven from symbolic signs in such a way that:

in keeping with the divine pedagogy of salvation, their meaning is rooted in the work of creation and in human culture, specified by the events of the Old Covenant and fully revealed in the person and work of Christ.[2]

Like the good teacher which, in salvation history, God shows himself to be, materials already familiar to us from our natural environment and enhanced in their meaning for human life through relocation in that complex interchange that is culture, become focal points of the divine communication of truth, goodness and beauty, first in Israel and then, at the climactic centre of God's self-involvement with the world, in the incarnation of his Word as Jesus Christ. It is an aspect of the missionary significance of the Liturgy – though the *Catechism* does not make this point in so many words – that its constituent signs and symbols fit perfectly with human anthropology, start bells ringing for human culture at large, and share resonances with the other great world religions, as well as maintaining a continuity with Christianity's parent religion, Judaism, for the integration of whose followers into the community of the Messiah Catholicism still hopes and prays. Yet were this all, the gospel would simply confirm what was already given in other modes, contributing nothing uniquely its own. The compilers of the *Catechism* were well aware that this is far from the mind of apostolic Christianity: one need only think of Irenaeus' question and answer in the *Adversus Haereses*

What, then, did the Lord bring to us by his advent? Know that he brought all novelty by bringing himself who had been announced![3]

Pagan signs, thoroughly transformed by the grace of the Old Covenant in becoming Jewish signs, thus await a more astounding transmogrification still, for the ultimate meaning of the signs of the Elder Dispensation turns out to be – Christ in person. The *Catechism*, then, presents the Liturgy as a Christocentric sign-system drawing proximately on a Jewish

[2]Paragraph 1145.
[3]*Adversus Haereses* IV. 34, 1.

and ultimately on a cosmic or universal 'vocabulary' or 'repertoire'.

Its signs come in a wide variety of packages, for they belong to different media, and principally: words and gestures, song and music, and, last but definitely not least, sacred images, the only genre of liturgical sign to be singled out for dogmatic defence by an Ecumenical Council of the Church. The *gestures* of the Liturgy are already a kind of language. In a celebrated passage of the *Treatise on Painting*, Leonardo advised the artist to observe

> the motions of the dumb, who speak with movements of their hands and eyes and eyebrows and their whole person, in the desire to express the idea that is in their minds.[4]

Or, in the words of the art-historian Moshe Barasch's study of Giotto: 'Gesticulation, natural or deliberate, ... pervades our life'.[5] In symbolically intense activity, in *rite*, we expect that feature to be yet more pronounced: the Mass, for this Jewish interpreter of Western Christian iconography as for the *Catechism* itself, has a 'gestural character'.[6] And yet in the Liturgy actions are never found without words, and above all those words that express in linguistic form the Word of God itself, whether directly, as with the readings from Scripture, or indirectly, through texts composed by the Church. The gestures of the liturgical action illuminate the Word of God in both those forms, as with the various ceremonies which the Church has created to draw out the meaning of the sacraments. At the same time, and to repay the compliment, when the gestures concerned are themselves dominically instituted – as with the basic nucleus of each of the seven sacraments – the Word in verbal form comes to their assistance so that, arousing the response of faith, those signs can generate the life of the Kingdom for those who witness or receive them.

---

[4]Leonardo da Vinci, *Treatise on Painting* (E.t. Princeton 1956), nos. 248–250.
[5]M. Barasch, *Giotto and the Language of Gesture* (Cambridge 1987), p. 5.
[6]Ibid., p. 8.

In this account of the interplay of word and gesture in the rites the *Catechism* echoes, whether consciously or not, its own account of revelation in the sub-book on the Creed. In the companion volume to the present work we saw how God uses for his self-disclosure both event and language, and the two in reciprocally reinforcing fashion.

> Events interpreted by language; language finding its referent in events: these will be the means of his encounter with us.[7]

In this sense the Liturgy is salvation-history in microcosm.

This alerts us to the more than aesthetic character of the Liturgy: the *mirabilia Dei* which the sacramental rites proclaim can only be seen as 'wonderful' if our vision is assisted by the holy Trinity:

> The Spirit makes present and communicates the Father's work, fulfilled by the beloved Son.[8]

That is not to say, however, that humankind's aesthetic sensibility, our imagination, cannot be integrated into the trinitarian economy and used, like all our faculties, in the service of the faith-response. In his wise study *The Integrity of Worship,* the American Protestant theologian of Liturgy Paul Whitman Hoon remarks that

> While we must be always aware of the seduction of Liturgy into art for art's sake, it must be recognised that man engages more readily in the dialogue of worship when its forms please his sensibilities at the same time as they are appropriate to the majesty of God.[9]

One of the glories of the Catholic Church is her production, at various epochs, and in a number of diverse though interrelated styles, of a sacred art that simultaneously feeds the hunger of

---

[7]Nichols, *The Splendour of Doctrine,* p. 20.

[8]Paragraph 1155.

[9]P. W. Hoon, *The Integrity of Worship. Ecumenical and Pastoral Studies in Liturgical Theology* (Nashville and New York 1971), p. 41.

homo religiosus for meaning *and* renders in imagistic form the
content of the salvation history which the Liturgy expresses.
Cosmas the Melodist's canon for Christmas Day, Fra
Angelico's *Annunciation* at Cortona: these embody in
miniaturised form, in poetic speech and visual art respectively
the mystery of the incarnation which is the divine answer to
the human condition.

And it is, in fact, through sacred chant on the one hand,
holy images on the other, that, for the *Catechism*, the Liturgy
and the human artistic impulse meet and embrace. Hymnology
and iconography: for the health of the Liturgy, and so for our
salvation (the Latin *salus* means both), we must get these
right. No one could deny the biblical origins of liturgical
hymns, so here the *Catechism* contents itself with citing some
relevant texts from the Old and New Testaments. More
controversial will be its interpretation of a relevant section of
the Second Vatican Council's Liturgy Constitution on the
musical setting of the hymnography evolved from those
scriptural beginnings. Here the makers of the *Catechism* come
down on the side of liturgical musicians over against pastoral
liturgists, for by offering as criteria 'unanimous participation'
understood as participation in the *purpose* of the liturgical
words and actions (which can, then, include *silence*), as well as
'beauty expressive of prayer' and the 'solemn character of the
celebration', they evidently set their faces against any (further)
dismantlement of the choral patrimony of Catholicism – a
liturgically devastating development which has followed
ineluctably in many places from the misplaced insistence that
everyone present should be able to sing absolutely everything.
The answer to the consequent charge of élitism is that the
beauty of the Church's rites has an evangelical significance.
The citation to this effect from Augustine's *Confessions* is the
more powerful for the reticence whereby the authors refrain
from pointing the moral:

> How I wept, deeply moved by your hymns, songs and the
> voices that echoed through your Church!

Despite the sobriety of his approach to the Liturgy, Augustine
knew of the rich differentiation of function of precentor and

choir,[10] and in the Church's *jubilatio* he overheard, as the Dutch historian of early Church practice Frederick van der Meer noted, 'the sound of the distant heavenly music'.[11] The capacity of chant and hymns to haunt us with the sense of transcendence depends not only on the spiritual culture of the worshipper, but on the quality of music and text, on which latter the *Catechism* ends by noting the need for isomorphism with the doctrine of the Church.

For inspiration on images – that other essential adjunct of liturgical worship – the *Catechism* turns to the Eastern tradition, and notably to one dogmatic source, the *horos* or dogmatic definition of the Second Council of Nicaea,[12] and one theological, the defence of the holy images by the iconophile theologian John of Damascus. Since the Secretary of the Commission which produced the *Catechism* had himself authored a substantial book on the doctrinal foundations of the image of Christ in the iconoclast controversy,[13] the account presented here does not fail to draw attention to the privileged place of icons of the Word incarnate in the liturgical setting. The distinctive saving economy flowing from the incarnation justified a reinterpretation of the prohibitions on images of the divine in the Old Testament. But the *Catechism* goes beyond the dogmatic affirmation of Nicaea II when it offers a specifically Christological legitimation for images of the Mother of God, the saints, and the angels as well. In the lives of the saints Christ is glorified, while the activity of the angels is summed up in him. There must be, the authors are saying, a *Christological concentration* of the images in the church building, just as there is in salvation history which the Church's Liturgy represents: everything there that is other than Christ must be related to him, for it finds its goal in him.

[10]Augustine, *Enarrations on the Psalms*, 87, 1.

[11]F. van der Meer, *Augustine the Bishop. The Life and Work of a Father of the Church* (E.t. London 1961; 1978), p. 337.

[12]A. Nichols O.P., 'The Dogma of the Image at Nicaea II', in idem, *Scribe of the Kingdom. Essays on Theology and Culture* (London 1994), I, pp. 180–191.

[13]C. von Schönborn, O.P., *L'Icône du Christ. Fondements théologiques* (Fribourg 1976).

And why does all this matter? Because of the power of imagistic beauty to move us to contemplation, so that, in collaboration with the meditated Word of God of the biblical readings and the singing of liturgical hymns, the mystery of redemption itself may become imprinted in the hearts of the faithful and fruitful in their lives. As that star of the inter-war intellectual revival of Catholicism in France, Stanislas Fumet wrote in his *Procès de l'Art*, 'Beauty is goodness making a spectacle of itself so that being may be loved'.[14] As with liturgical music, we are furnished here with a *programme* for liturgical art, not a *description* of the often quite inadequate religious painting found in modern Western-rite churches today.

When is the Liturgy, thus visually and aurally contextualised, to be celebrated? Here the *Catechism* lays out its heortology, its theology of feast and fast or, more widely, its account of 'sacred time'. The Church year recalls in carefully conceived sequence the mysteries of our redemption, which the *Catechism* also calls, in this connexion, unfoldings of the (single) mystery of Christ.

The liturgical commemorations of the temporal cycle of the Lord's life, death and resurrection are no bare memorials, but entrances open to the gracious irruption of the saving power of those happenings where Jesus was, under God, the principal actor. More specifically, it is the supratemporal force of the *Passover of Christ* – in which the earlier history of his actions and words is encapsulated – which explains how his time and our time intersect in the Liturgy with saving effect. As the Irish Dominican sacramental theologian Colman O'Neill underlined: not only are the other mysteries of Christ's life efficacious for human salvation inasmuch as they were lived by him in preparation for, and in the same spirit of obedience as, his paschal mystery. Also, for Christ,

> holding in his mind his redemptive act, there is no succession from Calvary to the present day. Certainly, the external acts of Calvary, the suffering and the visible

[14]'Le beau c'est le bien qui se donne en spectacle pour faire aimer l'être.'

sacrifice, are past and the history of the Church moves forward through time, but Christ's mind moves to another rhythm as does that of God and that of the angels.[15]

The unique constitution of the God-man, and the similarly unique redemptive mission received from the Father in the Spirit, entail that the Sacrifice which renews all things abides for ever.

And this means, as the *Catechism* points out, that the heart of the liturgical year is Easter, 'the Feast of feasts', the 'Solemnity of solemnities', just as the highpoint of the liturgical week is the hebdomadal Easter – Sunday.[16] Not for nothing, but rather with profound insight into the paschal mystery, does the Irish tradition call Christ *Rí an Domhnaigh*, 'the King of the Sunday'. On the archetypal Sunday of Easter Day, in Melito of Sardis' words:

> The Law became the Word,
> the old became the new,
> the commandment became grace,
> the model became the reality,
> the lamb became the Son.[17]

Pointing out how various essential elements in the Church's life – not only Liturgy but also typological exegesis, much catechesis and theological doctrine and even some of the canonical Scriptures – appear to have taken their rise from the ancient Easter, the Franciscan liturgiologist Raniero Cantalamessa provides the key to the *Catechism*'s 'paschology' when he remarks:

> There was a time in the life of the Church when Easter was, in a way, everything [for] it commemorated the whole history of salvation from the creation to the Parousia without having to share it with any other festival ...[18]

[15]C. O'Neill, O.P., *Meeting Christ in the Sacraments* (Staten Island, NY 1964), p. 77; this is, in effect, a Thomist reinterpretation of Casel's *Mysterientheologie*. See also O'Neill's essay, 'The Mysteries of Christ and the Sacraments', *The Thomist* XXV (1962), pp. 1–53.

[16]Paragraph 1169.

[17]Melito, *On the Pasch*, 7.

[18]R. Cantalamessa, *Easter in the Early Church. An Anthology of Jewish and Early Christian Texts* (E.t. Collegeville, MN 1993), p. 1.

And indeed, the *Catechism* can speak of the festal cycle
surrounding the incarnation – from Annunciation, through
Christmas, to the Epiphany – as a preparation for the mystery
of Easter (as it unfolds through the paschal *triduum* to the
Ascension and Pentecost) and the communication of its fruits.
Congruently, it is possible that not only the feast of the
Epiphany but also those of the Annunciation and the Nativity
(despite the likely influence on the latter of the pagan festival
of the Unconquered Sun) were fundamentally arrived at by
paschal computation, based on considerations both
astronomical and symbolic, and so were fixed from an assumed
starting-point in Christ's passion.[19]

However, none of this is to the exclusion of the accompanying
sanctoral cycle which celebrates the manifestation of the
redeemed life in the Mother of God and the saints. Those
whom the Church recognises canonically as saints are human
beings in whom the Christian people have seen some
outstanding manifestation of the single Christ-life which all are
called to share. Invocation of the saints, so far from diminishing
Christ's prerogatives, 'serves to glorify his redemption'. As
found in the Liturgy, where it is always made 'through Jesus
Christ our Lord', it implies no essential increment to Christ's
mediation but rather a realisation of its potentialities as the
many 'apply' the fruits won by the One.[20]

That is true in superlative measure of holy Mary, an image
of whom is always to be found in every place set aside for the
celebration of the Liturgy. Citing the words of *Sacrosanctum
Concilium*:

> In her the Church admires and exalts the most excellent
> fruit of redemption, and joyfully contemplates, as in a
> faultless image, that which she herself desires and hopes
> wholly to be.[21]

---

[19]For the whole argument see L. Duchesne, *Christian Worship. Its Origin and
Evolution* (E.t. London and New York 1912⁴), pp. 261–265.
    [20]M. S. Driscoll, 'Saints, Cult of the', in P. E. Fink, S.J., (ed.), *The New Dictionary
of Sacramental Worship* (Dublin 1990), p. 1143.
    [21]*Sacrosanctum Concilium* 103, cited Paragraph 1172.

Finally, on the Liturgy's sanctification of time, it is not enough to hallow the rhythm of yearly time, or weekly time; the Liturgy must embrace daily time also. The 'Hours' consecrate the course of time, extending the praise and petition of the Eucharist to different hours of the diurnal round. In the wonderful words of Casel:

> As the year is an image of the life of man and of mankind and thus of sacred history, each day too, with its rising of light and life, in growth to zenith and descent to sleep, forms an image which can serve as framework and symbol of the mystery of Christ. As Christ's sacrificial death is the climax of the world's history, Mass is the climax of the day. In the Church's year the Logos explains and expands the paschal mystery; in a single day the Office clothes and comments on the Mass: the Office is the prayer which the Church puts round about the Sacrifice.[22]

Emphasising the meditative aspect of the Hours, their capacity to provide an *entrée* at a deeper level to both Liturgy and Bible, the *Catechism* does not forget the way in which they, like the Mass itself, have stimulated the *devotional* instincts of the faithful. Popular devotions, so far from being beneath the attention of the liturgically well-instructed Christian, are crystallisations of the mystical or contemplative understanding of the drama of salvation the Liturgy opens up. Rightly, pride of place here goes to the cultus of the reserved sacrament. Though in modern Anglophone Catholicism, Benediction (the most popular form of such cultus, where the Sacred Host is shown to the people in a service of hymns and prayers, and they are blessed with it) is sometimes sniffed at as a new-fangled importation by Italianate Ultramontanes, historians know better:

> Its roots lay deep in the recusant tradition ... It would, in fact, be difficult to find a more quintessentially

---

[22]Casel, *The Mystery of Christian Worship*, p. 71.

old-Catholic devotion, if one considers its distinguished pedigree from Douai to Challenor.[23]

Commenting on the long-sustained Catholic habit of calling the consecrated species the *Sanctissimum*, the 'Holy of Holies', Balthasar – the eminent Swiss interpreter of Catholic theology we have met before in these pages – asks why that phrase, so far from being restricted to the Father in heaven, is deliberately extended to the Son's Eucharist on earth. His reply is that, in the Sacrifice of the Altar,

> the two flames fall upon each other: the holiness of heaven falling down like fire on earth, devouring the earthly prayers and sacrifices, and the holiness rising up to heaven of the Man who obeys and offers himself and is devoured for the sake of all.

Not surprisingly – and here there becomes audible the *glissando* from Liturgy to devotions – the moment of actual sacramental reception is too short to take this in.

> The sacramental action [of the Mass] suggests beyond itself, and indeed contains – for primarily it is the *receiving* of God's love – an essentially contemplative challenge …I must and will think over deeply and widely 'what great things the Lord has done for me'. I must and will open up the dimension of my spirit and my existence to the impact of the material eating and drinking – for it is just these dimensions which are addressed by the Lord who gives himself to me [in the Eucharist].[24]

It remains to consider *where* all this shall happen, the Liturgy's spatial, and above all architectural setting. Though the language in which the *Catechism* was written (French), like English, makes a play on words with the term 'church' – at once

[23]M. Heimann, *Catholic Devotion in Victorian England* (Oxford 1995), p. 51. The reference is to the academy-seminary established by Elizabethan exiles in French Flanders (Douai), and the most distinguished of the 'vicars-apostolic' of the recusant period (Challenor).

[24]H. U. von Balthasar, *Elucidations* (E.T. London 1975), pp. 120, 123.

the faithful, the 'living stones' of First Peter, and the building – by no means all the tongues of Christendom follow suit. The *double entendre* can lead people to play down the significance of the church-building, as the *Catechism* itself does on immediately introducing the theme. At the same time, however, and more positively, it can invite one to see the house of bricks and mortar (or better, stone and wood) as the icon of the Church mystery.

The building must be a *sign* of the Church that celebrates there; the *Catechism* is at its best when describing the eschatological dimension of this sign-character.

> To enter the house of God, we must cross a *threshold,* which symbolizes passing from the world wounded by sin to the world of the new Life to which all men are called. The visible church is a symbol of the Father's house toward which the People of God is journeying and where the Father 'will wipe away every tear from their eyes' (Apocalypse 21:4).[25]

Given the overall aim of the *Catechism*'s project – the reconstitution of Catholic identity on the basic of an evangelical and traditional construal of the gospel – the definition of liturgical space as more specifically the space set aside symbolically for the Kingdom, over against the space of a fallen world, is congruent with the tenor of the text as a whole. Yet there are other features of church architecture – narthex and naos, door and screen, dome and tower – which also belong to the distinctively sacred and ecclesial 'vocabulary' of church or chapel.

Of the furniture which such a building houses, the *Catechism* has most to say about the altar. Also mentioned are the eucharistic tabernacle and the aumbry for the holy oils, the chair and the lectern. But despite the attempt to draw in an Oriental, as well as Western, account of the significance of the altar, these objects are somewhat functionistically described, at any rate in comparison with the rich symbolic theology of such

[25]Paragraph 1186.

earlier Latin sources as Durandus or abbot Suger, not to
mention the current understanding of these matters in the
churches of the Byzantine East.

That reference to liturgical diversity leads naturally into the
Catechism's final liturgiological discussion, the plurality of rites
and 'inculturation' within the bosom of a single mother
Church. The *Catechism* accepts that wider concept of rite which
would in effect equate the latter with the very substance of the
life of a ritual church – Latin, Byzantine, Syrian, Armenian or
whatever. In other words, a particular form of Catholic liturgy
is not to be sundered from the wider set of mind and heart –
spiritual, theological, cultural – which the living out of the
Christian mystery takes on in some portion of the Christian
oikoumenē. The complementarity of the liturgies, Eastern and
Western, witnesses to the symphony of the *Catholica*, the many
players in a single orchestra, or, as the *Catechism* itself puts it,
shows how:

> the Church is catholic, capable of integrating into her
> unity, while purifying them, all the authentic riches of
> cultures.[26]

Pastoral theories of the legitimate diversity of rites in the
service of a gospel too plenary for articulation by one
worshipping tradition alone have been, one assumes, *post
factum* explanations of *de facto* states of affairs. But, consonant
with a theme in the pastoral strategy of post-conciliar
Catholicism, the *Catechism* calls for a policy of future matching
of the celebration of the Liturgy to the 'genius and culture of
the different peoples', including, doubtless, those only in the
early stages of evangelisation. True, following a letter of Pope
John Paul II, distinction is made between invariable (because
essential) and variable (because more accidental) aspects of
the Liturgy: it is only in regard to the latter that the Church has
the power (let alone the duty) to make such culturally-calibrated
adaptation.[27] For as Cardinal Joseph Ratzinger has put it in an

---

[26]Paragraph 1202.
[27]Paragraph 1205, citing John Paul II, *Vicesimus quintus annus*, 16.

important paper, what is feasible, and even imperative, in this realm is a '*transforming* conservation', such as the Fathers practised in relation to ancient culture, but at the same time a new note of ambiguity is struck in the modern situation where, in contrast to that which the Fathers faced, a

> relativistic-rationalistic world ... has severed itself from the common sustaining basic insights of mankind.[28]

What we should look for in these matters is not the celebration of particularity or distinctiveness – whereupon we should end up worshipping culture itself – but the capacity of a cultural 'translation' to render in a new idiom both the wider human patrimony (where the anthropological basis of the Church's worship is under review) or, more importantly still, the fulness of revealed truth (where it is the Dominical givenness of the sacraments, through Scripture and Tradition, that is the question). What the *Catechism* makes of those sacraments we shall see in the trio of chapters that follow.

---

[28]J. Ratzinger, 'Beyond Inculturation', *Briefing*, 18 May 1995, p. 43.

V

---

*The Sacraments of Initiation**

The *Catechism* is now in possession of enough insights into the nature of the Liturgy, the sacraments in general, and the rôle of ritual, to embark upon an account of each of the seven sacraments: Baptism, Confirmation, Eucharist; Penance and the Anointing of the Sick; Marriage and Order. The *Catechism* disposes them not only in this sequence but in these groupings: as sacraments of initiation; sacraments of healing, and sacraments 'in the service of communion and the mission of the faithful', while fully recognising that this is not the only illuminating fashion in which to lay out the component parts of the sacramental organism as a whole.

Baptism, for the *Catechism,* is the foundation of all Christian living as it is the doorway opening onto life in the Spirit, not least through the reception of the other sacraments which it makes possible. It is indeed that fundamental sacrament which enables us to receive the Word of God not as foreign to our nature but, on the contrary as the renewal of our true nature, now assumed into the ambit of the life everlasting. The difference it makes is ontological (it renovates our being), ecclesiological (it renders us members of the Church); and missiological (it gives us our share in the mission of Christ). Taking a cue from the fourth-century Cappadocian Father, St Gregory Nazianzen, the significance of Baptism can be charted by reference to its various names: not only *baptismos,* a

---

*=Catechism, Paragraphs 1210–1419.

43

'plunging' into the waters of death in symbolic burial with Christ in his atoning sacrifice but also *lavacrum regenerationis*, the regenerative washing away of guilt by the Spirit; and *phōtismos*, the radical (and therefore embryonic, for roots are beginnings) enlightenment of mind and heart by the Word who joins himself in this rite to the soul, and so to the body likewise, for the body's passions are not irrelevant to the working of our higher powers.[1]

The *Catechism* sees this primordial rite of human remaking as unfolding via three great stages in salvation-history – that of the Old Testament, in numerous foreshadowings, from the 'breathing' of the Creator Spirit on the waters in Genesis, to the exodus crossing of the Jordan, with Israel's entry into the land flowing with milk and honey, symbol of the life everlasting; that of the 'event' of Jesus Christ, where Baptism and the baptismal command begin and close, respectively, the Lord's ministry, appropriately enough for his own Baptism is the manifestation of his *kenōsis* and (its consequent accompaniment) the Spirit's remaking of creation, while in the saving passion, which inaugurates the Kingdom of God, he 'opened to all men the fountain of Baptism', their personal entry into the life of the Kingdom; and that, finally, of the post-Pentecost New Testament Church which from the beginning celebrated holy Baptism, as numerous voices, notably from the different Pauline letters, bear witness.

The *Catechism* contextualises the Church's administration of this sacrament in the wider setting of Christian 'initiation' which, following not only the restored rites of the adult Catechumenate but also the scholarly investigations of patristic practice which preceded them, it sees as chiefly 'mystagogical' in character, a matter, namely, of the reception of sacraments *with understanding*. In the case of the Baptism of infants, the mystagogical explanation is, of course, deferred, taking the form of post-baptismal catechesis, in which, the *Catechism* ventures to hope, its own existence will be a useful aid. By taking the reader through the principal gestures of the

[1]Gregory Nazianzen, *Oration* 40, 3–4, cited Paragraph 1243.

(Western) baptismal rite, from the initial signing with the cross at the door of the church to the post-baptismal clothing with a white garment and reception of a candle lit from the Easter flame, the text rehearses in brief what such a mystagogical catechesis should contain.

Already evident, though the *Catechism* will not discuss this issue fully until it deals with the sacrament of Confirmation, is a concern to allay the anxieties of Eastern Catholics (and, doubtless more weighty, the Eastern Orthodox who stand behind them) about the disruption of the primitive unity of Baptism, Chrismation and First Holy Communion in the Western practice of initiation. Thus the yawning gap between infant Baptism and adolescent Confirmation in (most of) the Latin church is presented as filled with post-baptismal catechesis (thus rejoining what Church practice had sundered), while the hiatus separating paedo-Baptism from first reception of the Eucharist in the West is discreetly veiled by the suggestion that the custom of bringing the newly baptised child to the altar for the recitation of the Our Father 'expresses the orientation of Baptism to the Eucharist'.[2] The fuller ecclesiological explanation of this state of affairs will follow some fifty paragraphs later.

It follows from everything said so far about the doctrine of Baptism that this sacrament cannot, of its nature, be repeated, and so a cursory reference to the Latin and Oriental Codes of Canon Law on this point may suffice. But apart from the already baptised, who *can* receive Baptism? All the world, which must mean, then, adults and children, the grown and the babe. Theologically, as distinct from statistically, the adult candidate for this sacrament must be accounted typical, since, citing the Second Vatican Council's Decree on Mission

> the catechumens should be properly initiated into the mystery of salvation and the practice of the evangelical virtues, and they should be introduced into the life of faith, liturgy and charity of the People of God by successive sacred rites.[3]

[2]Paragraph 1244.
[3]*Ad Gentes* 14, cited Paragraph 1248.

This is not to say, however, that the *Catechism* betrays any *arrière-pensées* about the Church's wisdom in letting adults bring children, too, to the font. Infant Baptism reveals as nothing else can the 'sheer gratuitousness' of baptismal regeneration, and so of the entire divine economy of salvation to which it attaches individual lives. The motherly solicitude which urges the Church to recognise even catechumens before Baptism as her own leads her to encourage the earliest possible recourse to the baptismal waters for tiny babies. Why that should be will only emerge when the *Catechism* treats of the graces that flow from Baptism, but already we are alerted to the *more than psychological* nature of the transformation Baptism entails (since those in an immediately post-natal state are barely conscious). Meanwhile, the authors can point out the congruence whereby parents take this responsibility on themselves for the supernatural life of their child. Parents exercise, after all, a God-given rôle in nurturing the natural lives of their children – without asking their permission!

And yet the vicariousness of the faith brought to the baptismal liturgy in the case of children entails no dissolution of the bond between faith and that sacrament which St Thomas called *the* sacrament of faith *par excellence*. Though the faith of the Church, expressed through parents and godparents (and the *Catechism* stresses the seriousness of the obligations of the latter, for godparenting is an ecclesial office), must go proxy for that of the as yet evangelically unawakened child, all the baptised whether adults or children are in fundamentally the same position inasmuch as they stand at a threshold, a 'beginning that is called to develop', through the increment of faith, faith's growth.[4]

The liturgical celebration of Baptism, which is this sacrament's right and proper mode of administration, requires the presence of a bishop or presbyter, though in the Latin ritual church a deacon (also attached, through his Order, to the apostolic ministry) will do. However, such is the urgency, and solemnity, with which the New Testament speaks of this mystery of supernatural rebirth ('Unless one is born of water

[4]Paragraph 1254.

and the Spirit, he cannot enter the Kingdom of God', John 3:5), that, rather than let a candidate for Baptism die without contact with these life-giving waters, the Church permits any person – including those themselves unbaptised – to go proxy for her ministers where they cannot be procured. It suffices to have the will to do whatever the Catholic Church herself wills to do in baptising, and to invoke the trinitarian Name when pouring water, the bare minimum that can constitute the rite, the guarantee, therefore, of its 'validity'.

'The Church does not know of any means other than Baptism that assures entry into eternal beatitude':[5] this careful statement excludes all reductionist whittling down of the missionary imperative to bring to every rational creature both the gospel and the sacraments of salvation which give entry to the life it offers while at the same time disclaiming all would-be certitude that the divine mercy is thus limited in its ambit. And indeed, as the *Catechism* goes on to recall, the Church from earliest times has spoken of baptismal grace as surely not denied to martyrs put to death on account of faith in Christ, for their deaths were a conformation to the saving passion inscribed in their very existence, and not simply in the order of signs. By extension, she has treated as her own holy members, both on earth and in heaven, those catechumens who, desirous of Baptism and preparing to receive it, died in faith, repentance and charity towards God and neighbour. The question remains as to whether, for unbelieving adults, there be other surrogates for the baptismal celebration. The Second Vatican Council, picking up the trail of a centuries-long doctrinal development, speaks of the possibility, grounded on the biblical revelation of the divine universal saving will, that every human being may somehow, in the course of a life, partake in the paschal mystery, whose forgiving and transfiguring power Baptism applies to believers. This, however, for the Council, takes place (in those cases where it *does* take place) *modo Deo cognito*, 'in a way known [only] to God'. Those theologians who pontificate about just how this happens, and, for instance, declare the world religions,

[5]Paragraph 1257.

in politically correct fashion, to be themselves 'extraordinary' or even 'ordinary' means of salvation, go beyond the constraints furnished by Scripture and Tradition. That they be right, no one can tell. An even more pronounced reverent agnosticism afflicts the *Catechism* when it comes to speak of the destiny of unbaptised children, for in their case there would seem to be no human act which God *could* regard as an act of conversion. Rather than speak, in their connexion, of a possible *limbus puerorum*, a kind of happy attic, with restrictive prospect, in the house of heaven whose windows look out on the vision of God (an analogy, fundamentally, with the *limbus patrum*, the antechamber of that house where the just who lived before Christ awaited the advent of the Redeemer), the *Catechism* prefers more simply to entrust these babes to the mercy of God.

Since the chief symbolic valencies of the placing of others in contact with water are purification and regeneration – as a pair of dirty hands, and a parched azalea would testify – the *Catechism* speaks of the specific grace of this sacrament as both negative – the forgiveness of sins, and positive — the gift of sanctification. The simplicity of the fundamental gesture encased within the baptismal liturgy is appropriate as the communication of so simple an act as forgiving someone (simple, though costly: for the incarnate and crucified Son the baptismal waters first flowed in the bloody flux from his opened side). Not that *everything* which follows from the Fall and our personal replications thereof in actual sin can be so 'easily' obliterated, but, citing the Council of Trent, the *Catechism* considers our continuing sinful impulses to be, under grace, not only harmless, because resistible, but also the very stuff of the Christian combat, necessary if we are to develop our spiritual muscle by an ascetic and demanding discipleship and thus win our crown. In speaking of the grace of Baptism as, additionally, that of supernatural regeneration (of course these are not two discreet moments, for sin to leave us *is* for grace to come), the *Catechism*'s authors appeal to the description of the *régime* of grace found in the great Scholastics. Sanctifying grace makes possible the theological virtues whereby we tend through faith, hope and love to God himself; it enables us to

respond to him promptly and with facility through the gifts of
the Holy Spirit; and by the infused moral virtues – dispositions
to good not simply our own – lets us grow in that goodness
which mirrors God's own. Here the *Catechism* looks ahead to
the account of the moral life of Christians, at once natural and
supernatural, it will provide in its third book.

Baptism thus makes us not only sons and daughters of the
Father but children of Mother Church. Though the authors
miss the opportunity to underline the essentially maternal rôle
of the Church in our regard – something which ancient Christian
writers, inscriptions, iconography associate precisely with Baptism
– they do not for all that miss the ecclesiological significance of
the sacrament. As that curious text of the subapostolic period
The Shepherd of Hermas sees, the 'tower' which is the Church is
built on water.[6] Baptism, in other words, is ecclesiologically
foundational. Allusively, the *Catechism* brings out many facets of
this fact: Baptism integrates human beings divided by race and
gender, culture and nationality, into one new people. It gives a
share in the priesthood of Christ, expressed in the cultic activity
of believers, as well as in his prophetic and royal missions to
illuminate and dominate by peace a darkened, violent world. It
situates its recipients within a sacred sociology, the sociology of
communion, where, in acknowledgement of Christ's Lordship,
others are served, the Church's pastors obeyed and loved for
their rôles. While mentioning first the responsibilities and
duties (rather than rights) Baptism brings – and how could a
community gathered by a crucified King do other in its
catechetical charter? – the authors *also* speak of the rights of the
baptised. These they see, not in fashionably contemporary terms
as provision of a voice in Church administration – here the
model provided by synodical government in the Anglican
Communion is hardly encouraging – but in terms of the right to
share the sacramental celebrations, the right to be nourished
with the Word of God, and the right to sustenance from
whatever other spiritual helps the Church possesses. Indeed, the
right to an orthodox faith, of the kind the *Catechism* itself

---

[6]*The Shepherd of Hermas,* 'Visions' III. 3, 5.

represents, is not the least of such spiritual helps, and indicates the paradox that what liberal commentators would regard as unwarrantable interference by, for instance, the Roman doctrinal dicastery, in the spiritual democracy of the faithful at large, could be described as, in intention, a defence of the fundamental human rights distinctive of Catholic Christians as such. But Baptism joins us to all our 'even Christians', as the late mediaeval English vernacular would have it, linking us even to those who enjoy only imperfect participation in the visibility of the Church's communion.

The inevitability of the ecumenical imperative by which is sought the full integration of all Christians into the unity of the Church depends, ontologically speaking, on the sacramental character given with Baptism to each and all, so a miniature theology of the specifically baptismal character fittingly rounds off the *Catechism*'s account of this most primary of sacraments. Despite the simultaneously Christocentric and ecclesiocentric theology of character laid out in its exposition of sacramentality in general,[7] the *Catechism*'s authors allow these to fall back into a tacit dimension: the baptismal seal is, in their explicit teaching, above all *theo*centric. It engages the Christian for a godly life, animated by the Liturgy and witnessing to itself in personal holiness and practical charity, and promises him or her life with God, if they keep the seal unbroken, at the end of (both individual and cosmic) time.

The *Catechism*'s account of the sacrament of *Confirmation* opens with a resounding acclamation of the *unity* of the initiation rites of the *Catholica* – Baptism, *Chrismation* and Holy Eucharist. In this section, the authors show themselves acutely aware that the Latin ritual church – for so many observers, and poorly instructed Catholics, identical with 'Roman Catholicism' *tout court* – composes merely one lung of the mystical Body. In the Chalcedonian East (here the distinction between Orthodox and Oriental-Catholic is of no pertinence), Chrismation is *doctrinally and theologically* distinct from Baptism, for the East too, like the West, and partly under its influence, knows of *seven*

---

[7]See the comments above in Chapter III, 'The Sacraments at Large'.

sacraments and reaches this total by treating Baptism and Confirmation as a duo. There, however, Baptism and Chrismation are not *liturgically* distinct or (better) disparate, since both are conferred in the one place, at the one time. Conscious of the objections of contemporary Orthodoxy to the West in this matter, the framers of the *Catechism* will go out of their way to soothe ruffled sensibilities.

This they do in the first place by emphasising the intimacy of the theological link connecting chrismal to baptismal grace, the first 'completing' the second.[8] The text spells out what that 'perfecting' involves by reference to the relevant section of *Lumen Gentium*, the Dogmatic Constitution of the Second Vatican Council on the Church,[9] and the entailments are at once missionary and ecclesiological. Though these consequences are indeed a prolongation of Baptism, they incorporate new emphases which sacramental grace must encompass. And so Confirmation does not merely, by its ceremonies, unfold the content of Baptism. Distinguished from the gift of the Spirit in regeneration (though always to be related to it) is a special outpouring of the Spirit for the promulgation of the gospel in the Church.

Before confronting directly, however, the disparity between Western and Eastern practices, the *Catechism* locates this sacrament in the widest salvation-historical ambit. In the prophetic books of the Hebrew Bible, the Messiah is endowed for his mission by the Lord's own Spirit; in the New Testament, the conception and ministry of Jesus take place from within a giving of the Spirit unmeasured in generosity, and this same Spirit, promised by Jesus to his disciples, the nucleus of the messianic people, is poured out anew at Pentecost, the foundational moment *par excellence* of the missionary Church. Citing Pope Paul VI's Apostolic Constitution on this sacrament which sees in it 'the perpetuation of Pentecostal grace in the Church',[10] the *Catechism* alludes discreetly to a subjacent theological typology. As in the life of Christ there were two

[8]Paragraph 1285.
[9]*Lumen Gentium*, 11.
[10]Paul VI, *Divinae consortium naturae*, 659.

stages to his paschal mystery – Easter and Pentecost, so, in the life of the Church which is typically modelled on Christ's, there are likewise two stages – Baptism and Confirmation – to her initiation into that saving mystery in its evangelical and catholic form. Just as Pentecost strengthened the apostles with the power of the Spirit for their mission in the Church, so too this sacrament has been seen as an empowering: *robur ad pugnam*, strength for the fight, something associated particularly, in the twentieth century, with 'Catholic Action', the social outreach of the faithful into a world increasingly unheeding of Christian truth and values. This is what the *Catechism* has called, in its opening statement of the rationale of the sacrament, the 'stricter obligation' of the confirmed to 'spread and defend the faith by word and deed'.

Though the crucial, defining ritual gesture of Confirmation is the laying on of hands (Hebrews 6:2), the anointing with perfumed oil which has given this sacrament its Oriental name brings out the inner (and indeed outer!) significance of what is done – the conferring of a share in the mission of *the* Anointed One, the Christ. The Western family of liturgical uses, while likewise employing chrism, preferred an overall title suggestive of the ratification (sealing) of Baptism and the strengthening of baptismal grace: hence 'Confirmation'.

That suggestion of two complementary, rather than competing, perspectives on the sacrament advises the alert reader of the line the *Catechism* will take on the disparity of liturgical practice. Where the Eastern lung of the Church does the breathing the primitive unity of the sacraments of initiation is maintained; where the Western lung governs the flow of air, the Spirit is not quenched, for the insistence on the link between (even) delayed Confirmation and the person of the bishop highlights the latter's rôle as chief pastor of the local church and living bridge to the apostolic fellowship whose missionary charge this sacrament embodies for the people of God as a whole.

As with Baptism, so here: the mystagogy of the sacrament's ritual brings out its evangelical meaning. Drawing on sources both Syrian and Latin, the *Catechism*, perfectly reasonably, considers the ceremony of consecration of chrism on Holy

Thursday to be the preparation Liturgy of Confirmation. The prayers for consecrating the *myron* (chrism) in the West Syrian rite evoke the polyvalent symbolism of Confirmation as seal of the new life begun in Baptism

> anointing with gladness, clothing with light, a cloak of salvation, a spiritual gift, the sanctification of souls and bodies, imperishable happiness, the indelible seal, a buckler of faith and a fearsome helmet against all the works of the adversary

– a catalogue which corresponds well enough to the *Catechism*'s linguistically more measured description of what this 'seal' marks out: total belonging to Christ, permanent enrolment in his service, and the promise of divine protection in the 'great eschatological trial' of judgment and transfiguration.[11] And yet, as the epiclesis prayer for the sending of the Holy Spirit on confirmands in the Roman rite makes clear, Confirmation has to do not only with the beginning and end of the Christian life but with its intermediate stages also, for it is not least a sacrament of spiritual progress to which the gifts of the Holy Spirit, object of the bishop's prayer, are all-essential. Wisdom and understanding, right judgment and courage, knowledge and reverence, wonder and awe in God's presence, these we never possess in a manner that is *de trop*, nor do they become superfluous until we enjoy the vision of God. After that prayer comes the essential gesture of the rite: the laying on of hands with, at the same time, application of oil – in the Eastern churches not to forehead alone but more lavishly. The sign of peace, given at the rite's close as early as the *Apostolic Tradition* ascribed to Hippolytus, 'signifies and demonstrates', according to the *Catechism*, 'ecclesial communion with the bishop and with all the faithful'.[12] There is perhaps an additional nuance to the *osculum pacis* in this particular context, namely, the recognition of the newly confirmed person's entry upon their full dignity as members of God's *laos*, their 'ordination' to the laity.

[11]Paragraph 1296.
[12]Paragraph 1301.

After recapitulating briefly the sum total of the effects of the specifying sacramental grace of Confirmation, including the sacramental character which is, given human collaboration, a warranty of that grace's abiding power of reviviscence, the *Catechism*'s section on this subject moves briskly to its close in a flurry of practical considerations, by which is meant considerations of *spiritual*and *ministerial*practice. The authors emphasise the need for proper preparation for its reception, by suitable catechesis, the making of a good Confession, and prayer, as well as the helpfulness of a well-chosen sponsor (if possible a godparent, to bring out the unity of Confirmation with Baptism). Ministerially, for the reasons of differentiated yet complementary ecclesiology already set forth, the principal liturgist of Confirmation is, for adults seeking entry to the Church for the first time, the *presbyter*, in West as in East, but for children, the priest only in the East, the *bishop*in the West. Here the *Catechism* warns Western bishops not to exercise their canonical discretion in delegating this rôle to their presbyters too lightly, since the separation of Chrismation from Baptism in the Latin church has been effected precisely in order that the bishop might always be present.

On the *Holy Eucharist* it follows from the decision to present this solar centre of the sacramental planet system as, formally speaking, a sacrament of Christian initiation that, in the first instance, the authors can present the Church's sacrifice only as the full completion of what was begun in Baptism and Confirmation.[13] A glance ahead at the disproportionately lengthy treatment of the Eucharist when compared with the other sacraments will soon show, however, that there is far more to it than that.

The fine citation from the Constitution of the Second Vatican Council on the Liturgy which prefaces the *Catechism*'s fuller description indicates the four main motifs of eucharistic doctrine: the Eucharist as Sacrifice; the Eucharist as Communion in the Presence; the Eucharist as foundation of the Church; the Eucharist as pledge of the final Kingdom. The *Catechism*'s theology of the Mass will consist in an orchestration

[13]Paragraph 1322.

of these themes that echoes their sources in the Bible and their resonances in the Church's tradition and life, as well as the predestined outcome of these in the glory of the end. And if Baptism has prompted the devising of a number of names founded on its constituent themes, that first sacrament is completely outdone by the plethora of titles a theological imagination has bestowed on the Mass. The *Catechism* selects nineteen or twenty from this 'inexhaustible richness'. Ranging from the biblical *coena Domini*, 'Lord's Supper', with its overtones not only of the Synoptic dark night of the betrayal but of the wedding banquet of the Lamb in the Book of the Apocalypse, to the 'Holy Sacrifice', that favoured term of the Roman Liturgy itself, denoting as it does the inclusion, in the Eucharist, of the Church's self-offering in the re-presentation of the unique sacrifice of Christ, this inventory of terms does not fail to mention the favoured vocabulary of the Christian East, whether ancient (the *Synaxis* or gathering of the faithful for their most significant action) or modern (the 'Holy and Divine Liturgy', since this is Liturgy *par excellence*), nor indeed that of the simplest Catholic parlance: 'Holy Mass', so called because

> the liturgy in which the mystery of salvation is accomplished concludes with the sending forth (*missio*) of the faithful, so that they may fulfil God's will in their daily lives.[14]

Linguistic exploration is followed by a broad sweep of the salvation-historical background to the institution of the Eucharist with its multiple prefigurings in the agrarian offerings of the priest-king, Melchisedek of Salem, a 'holy pagan'; the spring sacrifice interpreted anew by the Jews in the wake of their exodus deliverance; the unexpected gift of the bread-like 'manna' on their wilderness wanderings; the cup of blessing of the Passover *seder*, the developed 'order of service' of the time of Jesus – as well as the Lord's own actions in the (Synoptic) multiplication of the loaves and the (Johannine) transformation of water into wine at Cana. All this is familiar enough in

[14]Paragraph 1332.

Christian typology and catechesis: where the *Catechism* breaks new ground is in its perceptive alignment of passion and Eucharist as the twin 'stumbling blocks' of faith for the disciples, and their contemporaries. Pointing out the peculiar difficulties Jesus created for himself in his anticipatory references to these two things, the authors find a clue to their inner identity. The Mass and the cross are the *same mystery*.

It was Passover-tide – the 'time of Passover', as the *Catechism* formulates carefully, conscious as no doubt its framers were of the slight discrepancy here between the first three Gospels and the fourth – when Jesus chose to carry out the promise made at Capernaum to give the disciples his own body and blood, his own being in self-donation. The apostles, and, by implication, their successors until the final Parousia, are liturgically to memorialise Christ's sacrifice, and his ongoing intercession in the presence of his Father. '*Do* this!' and, the *Catechism* comments, with mild understatement, 'from the beginning the Church has been faithful to the Lord's command'.[15] Rather could one exclaim in amazement with Dom Gregory Dix, Was *ever* a command thus faithfully obeyed?

> Was ever another command so obeyed? For century after century, spreading slowly to every continent and country and among every race on earth, this action has been done, in every conceivable human circumstance, for every conceivable human need from infancy and before it to extreme old age and after it, from the pinnacles of earthly greatness to the refuge of fugitives in the caves and dens of the earth. Men have found no better thing than this to do for kings at their crowning and for criminals going to the scaffold; for armies in triumph or for a bride and bridegroom in a little country church; for the proclamation of a dogma or for a good crop of wheat; for the wisdom of the Parliament of a mighty nation or for a sick old woman afraid to die; for a schoolboy sitting an examination or for Columbus setting out to discover America; for the famine of whole provinces or for the soul of a dead lover; in

---

[15]Paragraph 1342.

thankfulness because my father did not die of pneumonia; for a village headman much tempted to return to fetich because the yams had failed; because the Turk was at the gates of Vienna; for the repentance of Margaret; for the settlement of a strike; for a son for a barren woman; for Captain so-and-so, wounded and prisoner of war; while the lions roared in the nearby amphitheatre; on the beach at Dunkirk; while the hiss of scythes in the thick June grass came faintly through the windows of the church; tremulously, by an old monk on the fiftieth anniversary of his vows; furtively, by an exiled bishop who had hewn timber all day in a prison camp near Murmansk; gorgeously, for the canonisation of S. Joan of Arc – one could fill many pages with the reasons why men have done this, and not tell a hundredth part of them. And best of all, week by week and month by month, on a hundred thousand successive Sundays, faithfully, unfailingly, across all the parishes of christendom, the pastors have done this just to *make* the *plebs sancta Dei* – the holy common people of God.[16]

In turning now to describe the 'Mass of all ages', the *Catechism* makes much use of Justin Martyr's celebrated account of the primitive Liturgy in his *First Apology* by way of setting out the basic structure or, better, *movement* of the eucharistic action. Though Justin's version was written, optimistically, for the pagan Roman emperor Antoninus Pius, and possibly adapts a more hieratic vocabulary to unevangelised ears (as with the description of the celebrant as the 'president' of the rite), his presentation faithfully reflects that binary pattern of a Liturgy of the Word followed by a Liturgy of the Eucharist proper that all subsequent rites, Western and Eastern, repeat after their own style. The Second Vatican Council spoke of the twinned tables in the refectory of the incarnate Logos, one for his Word, the other for his Flesh and, ingeniously, the *Catechism*'s authors find this already suggested in the Lucan resurrection appearance

---

[16]G. Dix, *The Shape of the Liturgy* (London 1945²), p. 744.

on the way to Emmaus, where Christ's exegesis of the ancient Scriptures was followed by his breaking of the bread.[17]

So as to prescind from the rich particularity of the various eucharistic liturgies of Catholic Christendom, from the Mozarabic at Toledo to the Syro-Malankarese at Trivandrum (India), the *Catechism* must perforce give a merely schematic outline of the 'shape of the Liturgy'. Still, the main stages are indicated – the gathering under the bishop or presbyter who stands for Christ, the Church's Head; the readings; the presentation of the gifts (and here the *Catechism* ignores the scruples of purists in keeping, at any rate in parenthesis, the centuries-old name of 'the Offertory'); the collection (a kind of pecuniary option for the poor, though one should not forget here the other principal aim of such alms – to sustain the Liturgy itself); the Eucharistic Prayer strictly so called, with – prior to the consecration, its constituent moments of 'preface' (a thanksgiving for creation, redemption or sanctification, or all of these together), epiclesis (a prayer for the Spirit's descent on the *oblata*),[18] and institution narrative where, as Fr Robert Sokolowski has written:

> in a sacramentally and grammatically perceptible way, Christ becomes the speaker of the words of institution and the doer of the gestures associated with them. Through quotation, the words and gestures of institution become those of Christ, as the 'we' of the community, the Body of Christ, becomes the 'I' of Christ the Head of his Body, the Church. In this assumption of the words and gestures of the priest, Christ becomes not only the one offered, but also the one who offers the sacrifice of the Mass.[19]

In the *anamnēsis* that follows, the Church not only calls to mind the saving Christological events, up to Ascension or Parousia,

---

[17]Luke 24:13–35; cf. *Dei Verbum* 21, both referred to in the notes of Paragraphs 1346–1347.

[18]As the text notes (Paragraph 1353), the epiclesis may be post-consecratory also (or instead).

[19]R. Sokolowski, 'Steps into the Eucharist. The Phenomenology of the Mass', *Crisis* (September 1994), p. 18, summarising a crucial stage in the argument of his *Eucharistic Presence. A Study in the Theology of Disclosure* (Washington 1994).

but also presents to the Father the reconciling offering of the Son, while by means of the intercessions, she prays for all sorts and conditions of men (and women, and children!) in union with the Church here and hereafter, throughout soteriologically defined space and time. Finally, in the communion, prepared for by the fraction of the Host, the faithful receive the Lamb who was slain in his broken body and outpoured blood.

To spell out what all this entails the *Catechism* devotes an ample half-century of paragraphs to eucharistic *doctrine*. It treats in succession of the Real Sacrifice; the latter's necessary corollary in the Real Presence and its outcome, Holy Communion; and lastly, after so much realised eschatology, by way of complement, the Eucharist as pledge of the Kingdom that is still to come in fullness. The remaining member of the quartet of themes suggested by the Mass, the Eucharist as that which makes the Church, is not missing; rather, its part in the score is written into the section on Communion since, as we shall see, communion in the Presence can have not only a mystical (personal) but also an ecclesiological (corporate) rationale.

The *Catechism*'s discussion of eucharistic Sacrifice and its corollary must count among its most highly wrought passages since the three submotifs it identifies: thanksgiving, memorial, presence are worked out triadologically in relation to, respectively, Father, Son, Spirit. *Paterologically*, the Mass is (literally) Eucharist, that is, thanksgiving for all the Father has done for human beings by way of creation, redemption, sanctification. At the same time, the *Catechism* does not fail to draw in the cosmic dimension whereby through Christ the Church 'sings the glory of God in the name of all creation'.[20] *Christologically*, the Mass is the commemorative sacrifice which makes present and offers in sacramental sign the unique Passover the Son accomplished on Calvary's tree. And here the authors could hardly do better than make their own the splendid statement of Trent as to the rationale of 'the Church's sacrifice'. Because the priesthood exercised for humankind's

---

[20]Paragraph 1361.

everlasting redemption on the altar of the cross was not to expire with the death of Christ, he willed to leave to his Church-Spouse a visible sacrifice – of the sort, then, that the nature of a ritual-using animal demands – so that the sacrifice made in blood once for all might not only be memorially perpetuated until the world's end but have its saving power applied to sinners' daily needs. Once the mystery of the Atonement was achieved, in history and beyond, the power and providence of God could (and did!) furnish it with an effective rite owing all its value to that mystery but passing onto us its fruits. With the Mass's expression of the intercessory offering of Christ the whole Church is united – not only the pope, as 'sign and servant of the unity of the universal Church', and the bishop as his analogue for the local church, but also the faithful departed, dying in Christ yet not fully purified, and those too who are already in the glory of heaven, with the Blessed Virgin at their heart.

> In the Eucharist, the Church is as it were at the foot of the Cross with Mary, united with the offering and intercession of Christ.[21]

Or, as a Catholic bishop of the Byzantine rite has put it:

> In our strict tradition of iconography, there is a great icon of the holy Theotokos in the apse of the altar, directly behind and above the holy Table, showing the blessed Mother of God, in whom all creation rejoices, with her hands raised up in prayer to her divine Son, accompanying our offering with her prayer and intercession.[22]

Pneumatologically, the Mass is the Real Presence of Christ, not only in his Word but by the Holy Spirit. Although the mainly Latin sources appealed to, in exposition of the Church's faith about the Real Presence – itself constituted by the eucharistic conversion 'fittingly and properly called transubstantiation' – do not highlight the rôle of the Spirit, the authors of the *Catechism* decided judiciously in situating the *Sanctissimum*, the

---

[21]Paragraph 1370.
[22]B. H. Losten, *Holy Things for the Holy* (Stamford, CT 1995), p. 24.

eucharistic Presence, at least formally and structurally, within a pneumatological framework. Only the Holy Spirit, whose economy consists in bringing the end of the ages to bear upon the world in the sacramental living of the Church, can account for the accessibility here and now of the glorified Lamb of the heavenly assembly, on our altars, in our tabernacles. Consequently:

> In his Eucharistic presence he remains mysteriously in our midst as the one who loved us and gave himself up for us, and he remains under signs that express and communicate this love.[23]

The *Catechism* catches authentically enough, however, the accents of the Catholic tradition on the sheer *isness* of that Presence. In the Holy Eucharist *is* our Lord Jesus Christ himself, living and adorable as at his Father's right hand, given to us in a sign of self-emptying to be our food – 'self-emptying' befitting the sacrificial purpose for which this rite exists, 'food' making possible the sacramental communion by which the sacrifice is completed.

But before turning to Communion itself, the 'Paschal Banquet', the *Catechism* lingers over the many ways of entrance to the eucharistic Presence open to the faithful. The author of the *Ancrene Riwle* (c. 1200) encouraged Christians to greet the Host at its elevation with the words

> Hail, principle of our creation,
> Hail, price of our redemption,
> Hail, food for our pilgrimage,
> Hail, reward of our expectation.

Soon after that date, the 1222 Council of the Province of Canterbury meeting at Oxford reminded the faithful that, when the Lord's body was carried out – presumably in the little box called a pyx for the communication of the housebound ill – they should kneel 'as to their Creator and Redeemer, and with hands joined humbly pray until he has gone past'.

---

[23]Paragraph 1380.

Highpoint of such moments, as, citing Pope Paul VI's letter on
the Holy Eucharist *Mysterium Fidei*, the *Catechism* recalls, is the
solemn procession of the Host associated especially with
Corpus Christi, a feast which is the obverse of Maundy Thursday,
in that it celebrates the institution of Eucharist not, as in Holy
Week, in sorrow but rather in joy. And finally, as the abiding
locus of the Presence, there are the reserved elements in the
tabernacle, on which, conscious no doubt of a tendency to
marginalise both physical location and spiritual significance,
the *Catechism* warns that it

> should be located in an especially worthy place in the
> church, and ... constructed in such a way that it emphasizes
> and manifests the truth of the real presence of Christ in
> the Blessed Sacrament.[24]

The eucharistic Presence is for our *contemplative consumption*,
and the time has come to insist on the force of the second of
these terms – the real eating (and drinking) which, however,
need this wider context of adoring devotion if they are not to
be approached materialistically, trivially, with a confidence in
the mere happenstance of frequent reception that is (as the
Catechism's comments on the sacraments as sacraments *of faith*
has already suggested to us) sadly misplaced.

Emphasis on the 'required dispositions' – cool language for
an ardent subject – typifies the *Catechism*'s approach to the act
of Communion. Due preparation, the observance of the
eucharistic fast (unfortunately now reduced to a bare
minimum in the Latin Code), the examination of conscience
with, when appropriate, recourse to the sacrament of
Confession, precede; a suitable bodily demeanour in gestures
and clothing accompanies; and, the text might have added,
thanksgiving follows. Above all, humility and faith are needful,
and both are perfectly expressed in the confession before
Communion in the Byzantine Liturgy:

> Of thy mystical Supper, O Son of God,
>   accept me this day as a partaker: for

---

[24]Paragraph 1379.

> I will not speak of the Mystery to thine
> enemies, nor will I give thee a kiss
> like Judas, but like the thief I will
> acknowledge thee: Remember me, O Lord,
> in thy kingdom.

Less sublime comments about the obligation to assist at the Liturgy on Sundays and the great feasts, and the manner of administering Communion (in the West, under the sign of bread remains, legitimately, the more common form, though in the East the symbolic fulness of the twofold sign is usual) provide, however, practically useful information.

What, though, is Holy Communion *for*? The *Catechism*, in accord with theological tradition, knows of two principal rationales: the first is personal union with Christ, which superlatively positive charge has also its negative force in sundering us from sin; the second is an intensifying manifestation of the unity of the Church – and not least as she exists in her poorest members.

Lastly, on this sacrament of sacraments, the Eucharist has an eschatological dimension. As the present author has written elsewhere:

> If the Eucharist is the real presence of Christ – *autobasileia*, 'the Kingdom in person', as Origen of Alexandria called him – and if, also, its offering is one with that heavenly Sacrifice which, for St John in his Apocalypse, is the central reality of the New Jerusalem, the City of the End; and if, finally, its celebration lies at the foundation of the Church, herself the 'sacrament of the Kingdom', as the Second Vatican Council puts it, then how can the Holy Eucharist *not* be the icon, and the foretaste, of the feast of the Kingdom, when we shall be, in full reality, God's people, and he, in truth, our God.[25]

[25] A. Nichols, O.P., *The Holy Eucharist. From the New Testament to Pope John Paul II* (Dublin 1991), p. 8.

VI

The Sacraments of Healing*

Here the *Catechism* brackets together Penance and the Anointing of the Sick, for, in its own explanation, the Saviour as physician of both souls and bodies, not only forgave the sins of the paralysed man at Capernaum, according to the Gospel of St Mark, but also, famously, restored him to health of body so that all 'were amazed and glorified God' (Mark 2:12). The Christ-life can be weakened, and even lost, by sin; it can also be occluded by suffering, illness and death.

Jesus Christ as the God-man is the reconciler between God and human beings. He brings to their true home in God those who have wandered far away from him – and the furthest such estrangement is by sin. Of these two sacraments, then, that of 'Penance and Reconciliation' must be treated first. The twofold name used in the *Catechism*'s section heading betrays the fact that, while the post-conciliar reform of the rite of Confession in the Latin church introduced the title 'the Sacrament of Reconciliation', with a view to highlighting the positive significance of the act of Confession in the life of grace, the older name of 'Sacrament of Penance' is too deeply engraven on the Catholic mind to be thus lightly expunged. These are by no means, however, the only names this sacrament has borne in Christian history, and following its usual method, the *Catechism* pauses to list, with explanatory comment, a wider selection.

---

*=*Catechism*, Paragraphs 1420–1532.

The authors begin with the name given this sacrament by the Greeks: *to mystērion tēs metanoias*, the 'Sacrament of Conversion'. The *Catechism* will eventually make clear that owing to the primacy of the call to conversion in the preaching of the Kingdom, this must be accounted Confession's primal name. For those who are already disciples – for the baptised – Confession is the sacramental re-presentation of the Son's converting address, and for this reason it is a sacrament of return to the Father.

Secondly, we are dealing here with a sacrament of *Penance*. Now, prior to being a sacrament, Penance must count as an abiding and constituent dimension of the Christian life. It is a state of mind and heart (and even body) which, by turning into reality the death to sin promised in Baptism, shares in the passion of Christ. Thanks to the detachment from sin that Penance brings about, it progressively (though no doubt with many setbacks) assimilates the Christian to Christ, conforms her to him. But Penance as a Christian virtue, a permanent disposition to practise repentance of heart, is confirmed and brought to completion by a sacramental act, the sacrament of Penance itself. Only in union with the Church, Christ's mystical Body, can the sinner find again peace and the Holy Spirit. Christian Penance is only fully effective when united with the Church.

But then thirdly, this is a Sacrament of *Confession*, and that not simply, as the *Catechism* points out, in the sense of entailing the auricular confession of sins, but also in that of doxology, the worshipful acknowledgement of the divine holiness and mercy. These two are indeed internally connected, since the confession of our sins in the expectation of their absolution at the Church's tribunal of mercy allows us to apprehend the long-suffering divine goodness, while conversely our confession of faith in the biblical Lord whose attributes these are gives us confidence to admit our own sinfulness and approach the sacrament of the Church.

Fourthly, therefore, this is a sacrament, *par excellence*, of forgiveness, which, in the words of the modern Latin formula of absolution, procures for us the grace of pardon and peace. In his *Autobiography*, G. K. Chesterton gave this sacrament as the 'first essential answer' to the question why, in July 1922, he had entered the Catholic Church. When a Catholic comes from confession:

> he does truly, by definition step out again into that dawn of his own beginning and look with new eyes across the world to a Crystal Palace that is really of crystal. He believes that in that dim corner, and in that brief ritual, God has really re-made him in his own image ... The accumulations of time can no longer terrify. He may be grey and gouty; but he is only five minutes old.[1]

Finally, this is a sacrament of reconciliation, of reconciled friends. Not simply a divine fiat, which would be cheap grace, the movement of the divine generosity requires and elicits a corresponding, and sometimes costly, movement from the side of man. Reconciliation, as the Neo-Orthodox Protestant dogmatician Karl Barth saw, presupposes not only the divine beneficence and pardon, but also our own engagement to live by gratitude, which is the proper response to grace.[2] This is how God's reconciling act *vis-à-vis* the sinful human member of the Church comes, like some great stone entering the waters of a sluggish pool, to create ripples which may free blockages in the stream of social living, with benefit to others. As the *Catechism* puts it, less imagistically:

> He who lives by God's merciful love is ready to respond to the Lord's call: 'Go; first be reconciled to your brother.'[3]

As with all theological ethics *noblesse*, the supernatural nobility of the redeemed creature, obliges.

And yet since the primary application of God's transforming righteousness, in its reconciliation of the world in Christ to itself, must be, for the individual person, the grace of

---

[1] G. K. Chesterton, *Autobiography* (London 1936), pp. 329–330.

[2] K. Barth, *Church Dogmatics* IV/1 (E.t. Edinburgh 1956), sections 39–43. Barth has in mind the foundational divine reconciling act which is the mission of the Son, but his comments are eminently applicable to this sacrament in which the explicitly reconciling aspect of Christ's work retains its visibility in the Church.

[3] Paragraph 1442, citing Matthew 5:24.

justification, which has its ecclesial expression in the sacrament of Baptism, the question naturally arises, What need is there for a *further* sacrament of reconciliation in the Church? The answer is that while the mysteries of Baptism clothe the newborn members of the Church in immaculate garments, few keep them unstained thereafter. Such is the frailty of human nature when, foolishly, we leave it to its own devices, and so potent the continuing force of concupiscence (the temptation, left us as a relict of the Fall, to thwart the good) that the crown of sanctification is unlikely to be won without sustaining not merely scratches but, on occasion, serious flesh-wounds. Here the *Catechism* must walk a tightrope between, on the one hand, lack of psychological realism and, on the other, giving the misleading impression that for those regenerate through holy Baptism, sin is inevitable. The same difficulty was already registered by the New Testament, most notably in the *Prima Joannis*.[4]

The *Catechism*'s solution is couched in terms of an aural metaphor: the call to conversion, which brought about our faith and Baptism in the beginning, like any cry launched on the air *continues to resound*. And this continuing resonance elicits a process of 'second conversion' – subsequent ('second') both chronologically and ontologically or, abstracting for the moment from grace, psycho-genetically. And while the Church, conscious of the weakness of her members and therefore that her common life is *semper reformanda*, 'always to be reformed', acts as Christ's surrogate in making this call sound out, in a more fundamental sense ongoing conversion is a response to divine grace itself, which never ceases to draw human wills to the good. Beautifully, the *Catechism* recalls Ambrose's words on this subject in a letter: the Church knows two conversions: that of water, for pagans coming to Baptism, and that of tears of repentance, for the already baptised.

---

[4] Cf. I John 1:8, 'If we say we have no sin, we deceive ourselves, and the truth is not in us', cited by the *Catechism* at Paragraph 1425, is counterpointed by the same letter, at 4:18: 'We know that any one born of God does not sin.'

Weeping is, in different respects, both a symptom and a catalyst of emotional change. Fittingly, then, the *Catechism* pauses at this point to reflect on the dialectic of interiority and exteriority in the conversion of Penance, 'second conversion'. The call of Christ aims above all at interior conversion, which the *Catechism* glosses as a 'radical reorientation of our whole life': *negatively* a 'turning away from evil, with repugnance toward the evil actions we have committed', *positively* 'the desire and resolution to change one's life, with hope in God's mercy and trust in the help of his grace'. Drawing on the ascetic tradition, we can speak here of a 'salutary pain and sadness' at what we have been, done and are. Guilt and depression are not only, as our contemporaries seem to think, dysfunctional: they can also be *eu*functional, in which case they are termed 'compunction' and 'affliction of spirit'.[5]

Supremely, the means of conversion is the image of the crucified. As the authors remark:

> It is in discovering the greatness of God's love that our heart is shaken by the horror and weight of sin and begins to fear offending God by sin and being separated from him.[6]

The countless devotional prayers of Catholicism that focus on the passion of Christ find their rationale here. This eleventh-century prayer by Peter Damian of Ravenna, hermit and cardinal, may stand proxy for them all:

> Like that bunch of grapes from the land flowing with milk and honey, thou art crushed in the winepress of the Cross, to suffer us the cup of eternal salvation and to bedew our dried up hearts with the outpouring of the Holy Spirit ... By thy continued grace, keep this heritage of thine, which thou hast purchased with thy Blood.[7]

[5]Paragraph 1431.
[6]Paragraph 1432.
[7]*The Manual of Catholic Prayer for all Days and Seasons and every Circumstance of Christian Life. Compiled from the Holy Scriptures, the Liturgical Books of the Latin Rite, other Catholic Liturgies and the Writings of Saintly Men and Women* (London 1962), p. 373.

Peter Damian's text, in referring in (literally!) crucial fashion
to the Holy Spirit also concurs with the *Catechism* in making the
Spirit the 'Consoler who gives the human heart grace for
repentance and conversion'.[8]

But such interior movements, whether of the soul, or of God
in his 'premotion' in the soul by grace, are not without their
proper exterior expression. Visible signs of penance are the
natural fruit of the inward change; moreover, they so act as to
'accomplish' conversion in everyday life. The three great
Lenten works, for instance, of fasting, prayer and almsgiving
can be seen as manifestations of conversion in relation,
respectively, to self, God and neighbour. Patristic and
hagiological tradition know many more such effective gestures,
from efforts at reconciliation with one's fellows and concern
for their salvation to the acceptance of fraternal correction,
of suffering, and of persecution for righteousness' sake. The
penitential seasons of the Church's year, pilgrimages and
liturgies which take penance as their theme, and voluntary acts
of self-denial of numberless kinds, highlight the importance of
continuing conversion in the Christian life. The meaning of
these is best seen in the Lucan parable of the Prodigal Son, at
whose centre, as the *Catechism* rightly says, stands no son, but
the 'merciful father'.

Without this wider spiritual *culture* of penance, the *sacrament*
of Penance stands excessively isolated and alone, and while the
habit of examination of conscience withers from disuse, the
seeing of our life in the light of Christ's passion comes to
exceed the practiced ability of the moral imagination.

The sacrament is divine absolution by way of human mediation:
through the Church, and above all, through her *priesthood*. The
Catechism reiterates a distinctive Catholic conviction when it
maintains that Christ not only willed that the entire Church, by
her life of prayer and action, should be a sign and instrument
of reconciliation, but entrusted a specialised apostolic ministry
with the exercise of a power to absolve from sin, making the
latter, in Paul's words in Second Corinthians (5:18) a 'ministry
of reconciliation' in the strongest sense. It follows from what

[8]Paragraph 1433.

the *Catechism* has said earlier about how the 'power of Christ and his Spirit act in and through [a sacrament], independently of the personal holiness of the minister',[9] that, in Robert Hugh Benson's words:

> [this] system which is denounced as usurping Christ's prerogative is a great deal more than a system ... it is in fact, in one sense, actually Jesus Christ himself, doing that work exteriorly and authoritatively which cannot be done with any certain success in the interior life – subject as that is to a thousand delusions and misunderstandings and complications for which there is no other remedy.

The promises of Christ to 'guide those who *corporately* seek him', in the common body whose life the apostolic ministry guards, are 'indefinitely more emphatic than any pledge he expressly gives to any single soul'.[10]

The *Catechism* presents the history of the sacrament of Penance as a matter of theme and variations. As the patristic reception of biblical revelation took definite shape, this sacrament began to take on clear form not, however, without attendant uncertainties. To the authors of fourth-century texts on this subject, such reconciliation with the Church is essentially an effective sign of peace with God, the Holy Spirit restoring to the penitent the graces given with baptismal regeneration. But soon a division appeared over just how rigorously rationed the celebration of such 'canonical' Penance should be. According to some, it was only to be permitted once for fear of encouraging laxity. And even this one-off experience of 'second Baptism' (as Penance was sometimes called) was placed beyond the reach of clerics who, it was thought, should be more exigent with themselves; and also of a married person in the event of their spouse withholding consent. Perhaps owing to the influence exerted by rigorists, resort to 'unofficial' forms of Penance became more common. Among such monastic

[9]Cf. Paragraph 1128.
[10]R. H. Benson, *The Friendship of Christ* (London 1912), p. 58, citing such passages as Matthew 16:19, 18:18, 28:19–20; Luke 10:16; John 20:21.

founders as Pachomius, Basil, Cassian and Benedict we find
'private' confession highlighted as a means of spiritual direction
and of growth in Christian perfection. The bringing together
of the two – the canonical public Penance and the alternative
more private kind – provided the sacrament of Penance with
its eventual, enduring form. As the authors of the *Catechism*
point out, by, on the one hand, opening the way to 'regular
frequenting' of the sacrament and, on the other, integrating
both grave and venial sins within the unity of a single celebration
of pardon, this became 'the form of Penance the Church has
practised down to our day'.[11]

Persisting through all such changes are two principal
elements: Christian conversion (with its three internal
'moments' of contrition, confession and 'satisfaction', on
which more anon), and the divine, ecclesially mediated action,
which simultaneously heals the rupture between God and the
individual person and re-establishes the latter in the
communion of the Church.

It follows from everything the *Catechism* has said about the
process of conversion as the true locus of the sacrament of
Penance that *contrition* has to count as its most significant
constituent factor from the human side. That is now discussed
with the care which the Roman genius has traditionally brought
to issues on the interface of sacramentology and moral theology.
Sorrow for sin of an aesthetic or prudential kind (based on
respectively, perception of the ugliness of sinful behaviour and
fear of its possible consequences) cannot of itself draw down
the divine forgiveness of grave sins, but it is eminently useful
for disposing one towards such forgiveness through the
sacrament of Penance. By contrast with such 'imperfect'
contrition, a sorrow for sins that issues from the sheer love of
God alone ('perfect' contrition) involves the immediate divine
cassation of our guiltiness, though always (for the *ecclesial*
dimension of conversion and therefore Penance is never
superfluous) on the understanding that the penitent will
approach this sacrament as soon as possible. There is no
resurrection of grace without confession to the brother, just as

---

[11]Paragraph 1147.

there was no Easter without the Good Friday when the Lord Jesus Christ made the good confession of the world's sin before his brethren.

Confession, then, is also necessary: as the *Catechism* cites Jerome of Bethlehem, how can the doctor heal a wound the patient is ashamed to reveal? Neither shame nor pride is to inhibit the recital of one's sin, for, as in a Gaelic prayer from the Scottish islands, we are to condemn ourselves at the chair of confession lest we be condemned at the chair of judgment. This is not, however, a wallowing in self-hatred, for, in a good confession, such candour is married not only to asking forgiveness for the past but also to seeking strength for the future. Conscious, no doubt, of the decline of frequent confession in much of the Latin church, the *Catechism* goes out of its way to explain the rationale of the confession of everyday sins (mostly, perhaps, peccadilloes) in terms of that wider concept of post-baptismal conversion. Such confession

> helps to form our conscience, fight against evil tendencies, let ourselves be healed by Christ and progress in the life of the Spirit. By receiving more frequently through this sacrament the gift of the Father's mercy, we are spurred to be merciful as he is merciful.[12]

Satisfaction is more difficult to grasp if, that is, we fail to bear in mind the wider context of the sacrament in what was called above a 'spiritual culture' of penance. Initially, the satisfaction imposed on the penitent, prior to absolution, remitted the ancient canonical penance, itself originally performed on a protracted basis (perhaps involving enrolment in an 'order of penitents') before a person could be restored to eucharistic fellowship. By the twentieth century, the penances people are invited to perform are usually token in character, gestures that do not pretend to complete the healing suffering which Penance entails. Though the *Catechism* enjoins on confessors the setting of penances that 'correspond as far as possible with the gravity and nature of the sins committed',[13] practical limits

[12]Paragraph 1458.
[13]Paragraph 1460.

on such possibility generally mean that post-baptismal sinners in the contemporary period express their sense of sharing in Christ's liberating passion by works of self-denial and supererogation *at other times*. Evidently, all of this lies above and beyond the obligation imposed by natural justice to restore what has been stolen by our actions: stolen goods, stolen reputations.

The *Catechism* sets a very high standard for the minister of this sacrament, the priest (or bishop), so much so that one begins to understand why in the Greek church only a minority of priests (it seems) are licensed to hear confessions. The *Catechism*'s feeling for the high office of a priest-confessor emerges in part by tacit indirection, from its typological account of the minister's rôle: he is to fulfil the ministry of the Good Shepherd seeking out the lost sheep, of the Good Samaritan binding up wounds with the application of unguent, of the Father not only awaiting the prodigal but embracing him at his return home, of the just judge, who manages to be at once just *and* merciful. In part its demands are expressed more explicitly, in a weighty list of *desiderata*. The priest:

> should have a proven knowledge of Christian behaviour, experience of human affairs, respect and sensitivity towards the one who has fallen; he must love the truth, be faithful to the Magisterium of the Church, and lead the penitent with patience toward healing and full maturity. He must pray and do penance for his penitent entrusting him to the Lord's mercy.[14]

What the *Catechism* has to say about the *effects* of sacramental absolution will be crucial for taking the measure of its lengthy excursus on the vexed topic of *indulgences*. *Vis-à-vis* God, the celebration of this sacrament brings about 'spiritual resurrection', the content of which the *Catechism* unfolds as 'restoration of the dignity and blessings of the life of the children of God', among which, it goes on to add, the divine friendship itself is the most precious gift. *Vis-à-vis* other human beings in the Church, absolution intensifies the

---

[14]Paragraph 1466.

exchange of spiritual goods among all the living members of the Body of Christ, whether still on pilgrimage or already in heavenly homeland.[15]

These citations make clear that the grace of the sacrament of Penance augments that coinherence which holds good among the redeemed, the circumincession of spiritual life and relationship they give and receive. And this in turn explains why indulgences are inseparable from Penance: recourse to the communion of saints, with Christ – the 'only Holy One', as the *Gloria* calls him – at their centre enables the contrite sinner to be the more promptly and effectively purified of the punishment due to sin. For it is part of the 'humanity' of God's redemptive plan that in our dignity as forgiven sinners we should be allowed to make some repair ourselves to the torn fabric of the right order of the world. But it follows from the principle of coinherence activated by this sacrament that we do not do so alone. We can draw on a common spiritual purse: the 'Church's treasury', the spiritual goods of the *sanctorum communio.*

The *Catechism* has left to the end the fact that the sacrament of Penance is celebrated by a liturgical act, however elementary this may seem to be. The communal celebration of Penance in special 'Penance services' makes possible a richer deployment of texts and gestures, though the Byzantine form of private confession is itself already powerful, especially in the Slavonic use. In the latter, the priest brings the penitent before a desk positioned, commonly, before the 'royal doors' of the iconostasis. On the desk has been placed the book of the Gospels, and an icon of the crucified Saviour. Standing at the side he admonishes him:

> See, my child, Christ is standing here invisibly and receiving your confession; so do not be ashamed or afraid and conceal nothing from me. But tell me without hesitation all things you have done; and so you shall have pardon from our Lord Jesus Christ. See, his holy image is before us; and I am only a witness, bearing testimony before him of all the

[15]Paragraph 1469.

things you have to say to me, But if you conceal anything
from me, you will have the greater sin, so take heed lest,
having come to a physician, you depart unhealed –

an address which, though not cited by the *Catechism*, echoes the
text of St Jerome on deliberately mutilated confessions which
it quoted earlier. After absolution is given, 'deprecatively' (in
a prayer form) in the Greek use, with its accumulation of
biblical references to such great penitents as David, Peter, the
woman taken in adultery, the publican and the prodigal of
Jesus' parables; deprecatively and 'declaratively' (in the form
of an assertion) in the Slavonic, the rite ends with a reference
to the communion of saints in which both priest and penitent
are, thanks to the character of the philanthropic Lord of the
Church incorporated.

> May Christ our true God through the prayers of his most
> holy Mother and all of the saints, have mercy upon us and
> save us, for he is gracious and loves mankind.

The Latin formula of absolution is also, in the post-conciliar
liturgical reform, at once declarative and deprecative, and, as
in the past, ends with a similar invocation of the saints to its
Byzantine equivalent.

In the eleventh century we hear of some bemusement over
'general absolution', pronounced by pope or bishop over a
multitude of people at the same time, without opportunity for
the concrete confession of personal sins. Contemporary
theologians regarded this either as a *prayer* for absolution or as
a remission of the *satisfaction* the penitent was otherwise obliged
to make. In the modern Roman rite, such absolution is foreseen
for those who cannot make individual confession owing to
their great numbers, and the relative paucity of confessors or
time. The *Catechism*, as other authoritative sources, regards it
as dependent for its sacramental actuality on the willingness to
make a personal confession when circumstances at last permit.

And so to the second of the sacraments of healing, the
Anointing of the Sick. For the *Catechism*, illness is anthropologically
ambiguous. In terms of *disclosure*, sickness reveals human
finitude, man's being towards death. And since this can both
depress and inspire, in terms of *agency* sickness may prompt

either self-absorption or the identification of what is really essential; it can lead away from God, or towards him.

Against its background in the Elder Covenant, the reconciling work of Christ can also be regarded as a healing work. The *Catechism*, so far from denying the thaumaturgical character of Christ's healing activity, resoundingly affirms it as a 'resplendent sign' that 'God has visited his people'.[16] At the same time, however, Jesus' healing miracles also have a parabolic significance, pointing to that greater healing whereby the Church acclaims Jesus as Saviour – Bestower of *sōtēria*, at once 'health' and 'salvation' – for the whole human race. In terms of this more radical healing – the recovery from sin and death through the passion and resurrection of the Lord – the inherent anthropological ambiguity of illness is not so much ended as changed.

Illness retains an ambivalence within the Christian dispensation. It is a sign of the mission of the risen Lord and his Spirit in the Church that the sick recover. And yet the suffering to which Christ gave new meaning by his redemptive passion does not exclude illness. The Christian may need, like St Paul, to learn that God's grace must suffice him or her, since God's power is 'made perfect in weakness'.[17] Not only apostolic sufferings – those inflicted on bearers of the gospel *comme tels* – but biological sufferings too may fall within the purview of the Letter to Colossae when its writer *rejoices* that

> in my flesh I complete what is lacking in Christ's afflictions for the sake of his Body, that is, the Church (1:24).

This tension helps to explain the *Catechism*'s manner of introducing the fifth of the sacraments with which it deals.

> The Church believes and confesses that among the seven sacraments there is one especially intended to strengthen those who are being tried by illness …[18]

---

[16]Paragraph 1503, citing Luke 7:16.
[17]II Corinthians 12:9, cited Paragraph 1508.
[18]Paragraph 1511.

This sacrament aims at raising up the sick, but this can mean, in accordance with that basic ambiguity, either to heal them or to strengthen them in spirit.

The *Catechism* refers much more briefly to the historical background than was the case with the sacrament of Penance. In the age of the Fathers, Christians saw anointing as, in Caesarius of Arles' phrase, 'the Church's physic'. But soon the sense developed that this physical healing was ordered to, and therefore *sub*ordinate to, spiritual well-being. That shift of emphasis can be documented, for example, in the Roman church's prayers for the blessing of the oil of the sick on Holy Thursday. A more holistic sense of what Christian healing might be was gaining ground, but never to the complete exclusion of the idea that actual physical recovery was a possible effect of this sacrament.

If, in recent centuries, the Anointing of the Sick has been too restrictively reserved for those in grave danger of dying, the pendulum of the capricious clock of human reaction has now swung towards an excessively latitudinarian, and thus in the last analysis trivialising, interpretation of when this sacrament is needful. The Dogmatic Constitution of the Second Vatican Council on the Liturgy was prescient, therefore, in remarking both that the holy anointing is not simply for those on the point of death *and* that it is

> as soon as anyone of the faithful begins to be in danger of death from sickness or old age [that] the fitting time for him to receive this sacrament has certainly arrived.[19]

The Letter of James declares the proper ministers of this sacrament to be 'the presbyters of the Church', in the plural, just as, in and around the basilicas at Lourdes, that shrine of the sick, gaggles of priests go round applying oil to the infirm. Bishops also anoint, since the Church has not forgotten that once the bishop was the presiding presbyter in the corona of elders before the apostolic ministry in its fulness passed into his hands. This does not mean, however, as the *Catechism* points out, that the community of the faithful should not also attend

---

[19] *Sacrosanctum Concilium* 73, cited Paragraph 1514.

the sick in their own persons. Many lay confraternities have taken on the task of sustaining the sick and dying; many saints have made it their way to holiness.

After reminding its readers that the Anointing of the Sick is always a liturgical act, even when it takes place at home or in hospital, the *Catechism* comes to the heart of the matter: the 'effects of the celebration of this sacrament'. It speaks, of a threefold sacramental grace, the three aspects of which it refers discreetly, but unmistakably, to the trinitarian Persons each in turn. Pneumatologically, the gift anointing brings is

> strengthening, peace and courage to overcome the difficulties that go with the condition of serious illness or the frailty of old age.[20]

Its finality is always healing of the soul, and sometimes that of the body too. Here the *Catechism* shows itself attuned to the teaching of both St Thomas and the Fathers of Trent. In his commentary on the *Sentences* of Peter Lombard, Thomas considers that this sacrament was instituted to provide for spiritual enfeeblement, itself provoked by sin (both original and personal) and aggravated by the demoralising effects of illness. Such enfeeblement is evangelically perilous, for it hinders the sick person from carrying out those acts of faith, hope and charity that bring about in us the life of grace and glory. The Fathers of Trent distinguished between the habitual, and the merely occasional, effects of anointing. The first consists in the grace of the Holy Spirit relieving and strengthening spiritually the sick person. The second entails pardon and healing where, that is, a person needs to come to spiritual health by way of either forgiveness or physical healing (or both of these together).

Christologically, the effect of anointing for the *Catechism*, is a being consecrated to 'bear fruit by configuration to the Saviour's redemptive Passion'.[21] Since the Christian is called to live and die creatively and sacrificially, this sacrament welcomes the sick member of the Church into the mystery

[20]Paragraph 1520.
[21]Paragraph 1521.

manifested in Christ's own person as the Priest who is also Victim.

Paterologically, anointing is celebrated as Extreme Unction, the last application of that oil which has as one of its symbolic valencies the oil of paradise of Jewish tradition, the restoration to life of the elect at the final judgment. In the *Catechism*'s words, it

> completes our conformity to the death and Resurrection
> of Christ, just as Baptism began it.[22]

Such anointing – the *sacramentum exeuntium,* or sacrament for those departing – is indeed linked to the resurrection of the body. Just as at Bethany Jesus' body was anointed for the destiny the Father had in mind for it: to die and be buried, so as to overcome death and be raised to share his glory, so the holy anointing passes into the giving of *viaticum,* the eucharistic 'travellers' food', and the commendation of the dying.

[22]Paragraph 1523.

VII

---

*The Sacraments that Serve Communion**

It remains for the *Catechism* to consider two sacraments which confer special missions on certain members of the royal and universal priesthood: Order and Marriage. The latter are not simply 'social' sacraments, just as the five whose description has preceded theirs cannot be regarded as purely concerned with personal spirituality.

> In the Church the 'personal' is lived in the mysterious communion of the Body of Christ, and the 'social' has no truly Christian dimension if it does not maintain a deep and radical relationship with grace and holiness, in view of the ultimate personal vocation of the human being, which is glory.[1]

Order is that sacrament whereby, through incorporation in the original ministry of the apostles, the Church's Lord endows certain Christians who already live out the royal and universal priesthood of all the baptised, entered by Baptism, Confirmation and first Eucharist, with another, 'ministerial', or 'serving' priesthood which aims to equip the members of the Church with the graces which flow from Christ as Head upon his Body, his people. Although those who share in Order are properly called bishops, presbyters and deacons, the office of the first two groups (assisted by the third) is known not only, therefore,

---

*=*Catechism*, Paragraphs 1533–1666.
[1]J. Medina Estévez, 'Reflections on the *Catechism of the Catholic Church* – 10', *Osservatore Romano* (English edition), 5 May 1993, p. 10.

as the 'apostolic ministry' but also as 'the priesthood'. How does the *Catechism of the Catholic Church* approach this topic?

Within the seven-starred constellation of the sacramental universe, Order finds its place, with Matrimony, as a 'sacrament in the service of communion'.[2] The term 'communion' is, we may note, crucial for the *Catechism*'s treatment of the mission, structure and life of the Church at large. It is true that its initial defining statement of the Church's mystery makes no use of the word. Faithful to sound etymology, its authors speak, rather, of the Church as the divine *convocation* of human beings into God's presence.[3] Yet they soon find themselves obliged to appeal to an ecclesiology of communion, not however, for anthropological (much less sociological!) reasons, by way of stressing human solidarity, though this is not excluded, but in order to refer to the trinitarian origin of this 'convoking', to evoke its Christological means of execution, and, most importantly, to explain its purpose, its end. This Church, to express whose mystery many imagistic symbols and a variety of concepts must be brought into play, takes its origin from the trinitarian communion, is realised through the pentecostal resumption of communion between the crucified and exalted Christ and his disciples, and has as its aim the communion of human beings with God and thereby with one another.[4] In the high doctrine the *Catechism* has made its own:

> Christians of the first centuries said, 'The world was created for the sake of the Church'. God created the world for the sake of communion with his divine life, a communion brought about by the 'convocation' of men in Christ, and this 'convocation' is the Church. The Church is the goal of all things ...[5]

The question arises, then, in what sense does the sacrament of Order subserve this transcendent goal?

---

[2] Book II, Chapter 3, Title.
[3] Paragraph 751. Cf. Nichols, *The Splendour of Doctrine*, p. 112.
[4] Paragraphs 737; 787–788; 775, citing *Lumen Gentium* 1.
[5] Paragraph 760, with an internal citation of *The Shepherd of Hermas*, 'Visions', 2, 4.

That enquiry cannot be satisfied, as the *Catechism* itself points out,[6] by exclusive attention to its peculiar theology, straitly conceived. For Order is the sacramental *means* whereby the mission of the apostles within and to the wider Church is continuously re-created after their demise. Order tells us that the apostolic ministry perdures in the Church as a special sacrament; it does not, of itself, tell us that ministry's rationale. That we discover when we focus on the third of the 'notes' or tell-tale signs of the true Church listed in the Creed: 'credo in *apostolicam* Ecclesiam'. In the *Catechism*'s comments on the Church's apostolicity it emerges that the Church could hardly abide in the 'salutary words she has heard from the apostles' unless she simultaneously continues to be 'taught, sanctified and guided by the apostles until Christ's return, through their successors in pastoral office'.[7] For the saving word of Christ, prolonging as it does his own being and mission as the divine Word from the Father, finds expression in doctrinal teaching, becomes incarnate in the sacramental rites of the Church, and preserves its reconciling efficacy in the construction of the Church's own theocentric common life. The magisterial teaching, sacramental sanctifying and ecclesial governance which Christ's 'salutary words' entail are committed to the shepherding care ('pastoral office') of the bishops, with the pope as their divinely instituted head, assisted – so the *Catechism* notes, following the Second Vatican Council's Decree *Ad Gentes* on the missionary activity of the Church – by *presbyters*. For the evolution of the episcopate, as that office in which the continuing apostolic ministry was chiefly invested (exclusively so for the universal Church, and primarily so for the local church) cannot overthrow the fact that the presbyterate, from among whose presidents the bishops appeared, is chronologically first among the Church's ministries. It is that ministry to which the apostles delegated, for the local communities of the dispersed New Israel, a share in their own dominical authority in the service of the Word.[8] Notice however

[6]Paragraph 1536, attached parenthesis.

[7]Paragraph 857.

[8]See on this my *Holy Order. The Apostolic Ministry from the New Testament to the Second Vatican Council* (Dublin 1990), pp. 18–47.

that the *Catechism* is silent on deacons in its remarks on
ministerial apostolicity as crucial to the persistence in the later
Church of her Christ-given apostolic foundation.

The issue which the *Catechism* addresses when it reverts to
this topic under the heading of the sacraments is, Does the
apostolic ministry itself take sacramental form? Or rather the
Catechism both presumes and resumes (sums up) the answer
given to that question in the Catholic tradition, tacitly from the
beginning but with increasing explicitness, in the doctrinal
articulation of tradition, from the Middle Ages onwards.
Although the language of Order (*ordo*) derives from the Latin
Liturgy of the patristic age, conscious as its makers were that
the Church, like the secular society of their (and presumably
any) time was a *structured* people, it is in the mediaeval period
that transmission of the apostolic ministry receives its enduring
official title: Order with an 'O' majuscule. Although different
mediaeval divines accentuate it variously, the general tenor is
the same: the apostolic ministry, in structuring the faith,
worship and government of the Church, reflects the *orderly*
fashion in which God expresses his own perfections in creation
and redemption. But if this specifically ecclesial version of the
wider ordering principle so functions as to convey to the
members of the Church the sources of grace, it is only fitting
that it be itself sacramental – equipped, through the faithful
performance of a solemn rite, with the graces which those
exercising so onerous (and privileged) an office require.[9] And
this is the point from which the *Catechism*'s explicitly
sacramentological account of the 'ordained ministry' (as we
significantly say, telescoping the theology and history I have
summarised) sets forth.

The *Catechism*'s most fundamental statement about Order is
that it is the *sacrament of the apostolic ministry*. As such, it is not
confined to bishops and presbyters but embraces also those
auxiliaries of bishops called deacons. Although the threefold
apostolic-ministerial office of teaching, sanctifying and
governing is not invested in their persons, nevertheless deacons
are sufficiently important in their service of the bishop to be

[9]Ibid., pp. 74–75.

included within the sacramental graciousness with which that office has been surrounded since earliest times. We, like the *Catechism*, shall return to them in a moment, but only briefly. The reason for the comparatively cursory character of this theology of the diaconate in the *Catechism* lies in its authors' decision to centre their account of the sacramental significance of the ordering principle found in the apostolic ministry on the *munus sacerdotale*, the way the ordained (which must mean here bishops and presbyters) share in a distinctive way in the mission of Christ as high priest. All theologies of Order must take a decision on how to arrange their materials about the threefold office of teaching, sanctifying and governing and whether, tacitly or *expressis verbis*, to prioritise one by interpreting the others in its terms. The creators of the *Catechism* have made a clear option: following Catholic parlance generally, the episcopate and presbyterate are for them first and foremost the *priesthood*.

And since the most properly and specifically priestly dimension of this office is its liturgical aspect, it is in terms of the mystery of Christian worship that the *Catechism* primarily presents the life of the bishop or presbyter – the *priest*. It should be said at once that this choice is not intended to obscure the other complementary offices of teaching and pastoring but to present them in a particular light, as incapable of being understood aright until they are seen in relation to the sacred Liturgy which is the priest's principal defining task. This, after all, is how the reformed Pontifical of the Latin Church, successor to the ancient *ordines romani*, the Roman bishop's own service-book, sees the matter – as its consecratory prayers with their copious references to the Aaronic and Levitical priesthood of Old Testament times, makes clear. Nor does the *Catechism* fail to quote them in this context.[10]

The high priesthood of Jesus Christ is, as the Letter to the Hebrews shows, essentially a function of the sacrifice of Calvary, and if that sacrifice has its sacramental renewal in the Church then the ordained ministers who, by virtue of their centrally liturgical priesthood, celebrate that sacramentalised sacrifice

[10]Paragraphs 1541–1543.

for the sake of all, will necessarily do so themselves as sacramental renewals of the high priestly office of Christ in their own persons. And here of course *tout est grâce*, 'Everything is grace', or it would be blasphemy. As the seventeenth-century French theologian of priesthood M. Olier puts it: 'Jesus Christ alone can do in the priest what the priest does every day in the Church.'[11] The *Catechism* itself prefers to cite an earlier authority, St Thomas, who insists that 'only Christ is the true Priest, the others being only his ministers', which makes the same point in (we might think) a less positive way.[12]

Being oriented as it is to the upbuilding of the Church in its entirety (which is why, incidentally, there can be such a thing as an ordained hermit, for the Church is not only the Church of sociologists, but the Church in the heart of Christ), the ministerial priesthood is at the service of the universal and royal priesthood of all the faithful – from which of course, at the most fundamental level, priests are never subtracted. I am, Augustine wrote, a bishop for you, a Christian with you. The *Catechism* addresses something of an ambiguity in much Catholic writing on this subject when it proposes to deal with the way the ministerial priesthood at once stands over against the common priesthood, by acting in the person of Christ, to whom the whole Church is responsive, sponsal, as Bride, and yet also acts in the name of the common priesthood, which must have its accredited representatives when presenting itself liturgically before God. Its solution is that only because the priest is a minister of Christ can he also be the representative of the Church: in other words, when the ministerial priest prays in the name of the Church-body, he does not do so as representative of that body *over against* its Head but of the body as *inseparably conjoined to* that Head. As representative, then, of the 'whole Christ', members-with-their-Head, in the Augustinian (and wider patristic and indeed New Testament) sense recovered for us this century by the researches of the Belgian Jesuit historian of doctrine, Père Emile Mersch. Otherwise, addressing

---

[11]J. -J. Olier, *Traité des saints Ordres*, III. 2.
[12]Thomas Aquinas, *In Epistolam beati Pauli ad Hebraeos*, 8, 4; cited Paragraph 1546.

a modern controversy which the *Catechism* barely touches on, one might suppose that the liturgical representative of *Mother* Church should be exclusively female!

The *Catechism*, however, does not make that point, but considers rather the implications for its high doctrine of the priesthood of ministerial frailty – the human, all-too-human, reality of priests. While rehearsing the principle that as a God-given sacramental sign the priesthood retains its fundamental valency even in gross human imperfection (cf. Graham Greene's *The Power and the Glory*), the authors give greater emphasis to the harm priestly aberrations do to the 'apostolic fruitfulness of the Church'.[13] The time of combined Church crisis and media scrutiny we live in is certainly one when Catholics can no longer afford to be breezy about *ex opere operato* in this area.

If the ordained ministry is triune (threefold) in its exercise of the *munus triplex* of Christ as Shepherd, Priest and Teacher, it is also in a second sense – as composed of bishops, presbyters and deacons. By placing at the head of its comments on the 'three degrees of the sacrament of Order' an excerpt from Ignatius of Antioch's letter to the church at Tralles which includes the words 'Let everyone revere the deacons as Jesus Christ' and ends, 'Without them [i.e. deacons, bishop and presbyters] one cannot speak of the Church', the *Catechism* fills in the lacuna of its silence on diaconate heretofore. Actually, what the *Catechism* offers here is no more than a mosaic of passages on bishop, presbyter and deacon from the relevant documents of the Second Vatican Council which, firstly, dogmatically defined the episcopate to be a sacramentally distinct Order from the presbyterate, and as such, the 'fulness' of whatever Order brings to the Church; secondly, provided a synthesis of the deliverancies of Catholic tradition on the presbyterate in the much underrated text devoted to ordinary priests, and third, retrieved the permanent diaconate, and so a fuller profile for this degree of ministry, in the Latin church. Though recording the essential point that the deacon typifies the *servant* Christ an opportunity was missed here to bring out the significance of Ignatius' strong statement. When the pope

[13]Paragraph 1550.

on Holy Thursday removes those garments of Christian authority, the pallium and chasuble, he reveals a deacon's dalmatic – the suitable vestment for washing the feet of others.[14]

The *Catechism*'s presentation of this sacrament ends, fittingly enough, with an account of its initiation rite and the consequences thereof. After the rationale, the realisation. The sacrament is confected by the laying on of hands and prayer – the crucial elements in its making identified as such since the work of the Oratorian Jean Morin in the early seventeenth century. Self-evidently, and modern attempts to insinuate a notion of congregational or 'community' ordination, wholly foreign to Scripture and Tradition, notwithstanding, the bishop is the crucial minister in the creation of the ordained: if Order is the sacrament of the apostolic ministry, only one in whom that ministry in invested in plenary fashion can appropriately be its celebrant.[15] In repeating the constant asseveration of the tradition that only those human beings who share the gender in which the Word became incarnate can typify him at the Eucharistic altar, the *Catechism* moves naturally, if unself-consciously, to a statement of the obvious. There can be no 'right' of individual or community to receive this sacrament, or imperatively to require its reception. Persons have rights *vis-à-vis* the State which is ontologically secondary in their regard; *Christifideles* – persons *in Christ* – do not have rights *vis-à-vis* the Church, which is ontologically prior to them, their Mother. (They only have blessings, and on the basis of blessings, duties.) As is well-known, this particular debate is not unconnected with the point to which the *Catechism* moves in concluding its account of the recipients of this sacrament – for bishops, in East and West, for presbyters in the West, *celibacy,* as the evangelical lifestyle of the apostolic group in *logia* of Jesus too persistently present in the Gospels for dismissal, is intimately connected with priesthood. The presbyterate of the Oriental churches has other excellencies, but here it lacks a certain

[14]T. Galligan and B. Harbert, 'Diaconus alter Christus', *Clergy Review* 66 (1981), pp. 355–360.
[15]Paragraph 1576.

consonance with its modelling on the apostles (my words, not those of the *Catechism!*). Nonetheless, the Eastern example provides a basis for the 'economic' dispensation from this rule, the permitting of occasional married priests, in the West also.

And what follows? Why, character – the permanent consecration of a Christian man in his heart of hearts, and the grace of state to express that character in all the duties of his office. Here the *Catechism* is at its most eloquent, assisted by a judicious selection of texts from the East: the Byzantine liturgy, and the Cappadocian doctor Gregory Nazianzen, and from the West: the Roman liturgy and the Curé d'Ars.

If we really understood the priest on earth we would die not of fright, but of love.[16]

Marriage, by contrast with Order, is a sacramental transfiguration of a relation between human beings that pre-exists the gospel in the divine creative plan. Seen theologically, marriage is an institution arising from human origins which, after many perplexities, was renewed 'in the Lord' thanks to the new covenant of Christ with his Church. As such it joins together the aeons. Not for nothing, as the *Catechism* points out, does Scripture open with a man and a woman in a garden and end with a wedding-feast, the nuptials of the Lamb.

For the *Catechism*, as for the faith of the Church at large, marriage is 'not a *purely* human institution'.[17] The Book of Genesis presents marriage as given in the very moment when God created male and female in his own likeness. It images, then, something of God himself. As the revelation contained in Scripture unfolds, it transpires that this 'something' is in fact the capacity for love in interpersonal relationship and its fruitfulness. 'Some sense of the greatness of the matrimonial union', comments the *Catechism*, 'exists in all culture',[18] there appealing not so much to the Bible as to a biblically enlightened sense of natural law, a scripturally clarified perception of the moral meaning of human life as essence becomes existence, nature history.

[16]Recorded saying of St John Vianny, cited Paragraph 1589.
[17]Paragraph 1603. Italics added.
[18]Ibid.

But marriage, like all human things, was soon distorted. With the Fall – that primordial going astray at the beginnings of our race – marriage too fell. Even within Israel, the chosen people, emerge such practices as polygamy and divorce. Yet, as the Old Testament presents matters, marriage never lost the blessing of God. It remains a vehicle of relationship with him. More, though a natural reality, the prophets spoke of it as a lived metaphor – the Bride Israel and her Bridegroom – for God's seeking out his people. In other words, it tended towards the sacramental order, the order of friendship with God.

> The nuptial covenant between God and his people Israel had prepared the way for the new and everlasting covenant in which the Son of God, by becoming incarnate and giving his life, has united to himself in a certain way, all mankind saved by him ...[19]

The Redeemer of marriage, as of all other constitutive dimensions of human life, is Jesus Christ. With the incarnation the union begins of 'things in heaven and things on earth' (Colossians 1:20). Already at Cana of Galilee Christ adorned and beautified this estate with his presence and the first miracle that he wrought. This the *Catechism* sees as not only the 'confirmation of the goodness of marriage' but also the 'proclamation that henceforth marriage will be an efficacious sign of Christ's presence',[20] an example of Scripture achieving its 'plenary sense' in Tradition.

In his preaching Jesus reveals the new kind of marriage to be practised among his people, an indissoluble marriage based on the gracious origins of mankind, a restoring of the original creation. But here as elsewhere 'ought' implies 'can', and the strength to live out such fidelity one's whole life long comes from the royal power attained by the exalted Saviour on the cross. Lord of all, he draws those of the baptised who marry into the sphere of his own marriage-covenant, enabling them to experience the nuptial meaning of their own bodies as sacraments of his sacrificial love for his Bride, the Church.

[19]Paragraph 1612.
[20]Paragraph 1613.

Thus the writer to the Ephesians cannot think of the marriage made on the cross without simultaneously thinking of Christian marriage (and vice versa): this 'great mystery' (5:32) is a bipolar ellipse. The grace of the sacrament of Marriage corresponds perfectly, in fact, to that profile of all authentic sacramentality sketched by St Thomas: a genuine sacrament must bear some relation to the passion of Christ, and here in the life-giving faithfulness of those married 'in the Lord' we taste the fruit of the cross.

It may seem strange that the *Catechism* interrupts its account of Marriage to speak of the meaning, in the Church, of a virginity maintained for reasons of devotion. Its authors are not thinking of those saints who, on their wedding-night, decided for the love of God not to consummate their marriage (Edward the Confessor is the best known of these in English-speaking lands.) Their example is, in general, more to be admired than followed. What is at stake is, rather, the reciprocally illuminating complementarity of two distinct ways of life in the Church: marriage and celibacy. The married layperson, it can be suggested, typifies Christ's mystical Body, the fruitfulness of whose inner relationships is vital if the Father's will is to be made effective in the world. The consecrated virgin, by contrast, typifies the Spirit who rests on Christ, bringing a foretaste of the spiritual fruits of the age to come where life will be wholly centred on God, in communion with others but without giving or being given in marriage. The *Catechism* does not furnish a particular theological typology of its own to explain the mutuality of the figures of virgin and married man or woman, but, not least with the help of a text of Chrysostom's, it opens a space where such typologies can flourish.

> Whoever denigrates marriage also diminishes the glory of virginity. Whoever praises it makes marriage more admirable and resplendent.[21]

As always the rites whereby a sacrament is celebrated throw the most light on its meaning. The Western custom of making the marriage vows within a 'Nuptial Mass' brings home the

---

[21]John Chrysostom, *On Virginity*, 10, 1; cited Paragraph 1620.

inner connexion between the kind of love that is characteristic
of marriage (sacrificial and generative) and the saving charity
of the cross. It also makes clear that the 'one body' man and
woman are to become is not an *egoisme à deux* but a cell of the
eucharistic Church constructed on the Body of the Lord. In
the Eastern liturgies, the couple are crowned with wreaths of
flowers or actual crowns of metal and stones. The East Syrian
Liturgy brings out the significance of this when it prays:

> O Christ, adorned Spouse, whose betrothal has
> given us a type,
> complete the foundation and the building and
> their [the couple's] laudable work;
> sanctify their marriage and their bed;
> and dismiss their sins and offences;
> and make them a temple for you and bestow on their
> marriage chamber your light;
> and may their odour be as a roseshoot in paradise,
> and as a garden full of scents,
> and as a myrtle tree may be for your praise.
> May they be a bastion for our orthodox band and a
> house of refuge.

Though the *Catechism* does not say so, a similar symbolism was
once in vigour in the West as well, when during the Nuptial
Blessing the bridal pair were placed beneath a canopy, as in the
Sarum rite, or had a veil draped round their shoulders, as at
Milan: both symbols of the Shekinah, or divine presence. In
the East, the bishop or priest is deemed to be the minister of
marriage; in the West, the more common theological opinion
is that the couple themselves mediate the sacrament to each
other. And, as the *Catechism* points out, all the liturgies, whatever
their provenance, abound in epicletic prayers of blessing: the
'seal' of sacramental marriage – itself a vocational mission
undertaken within the wider commitment of Baptism and
Confirmation to give the latter more concrete form – can only
be that of Christian initiation itself, the Holy Spirit.

Because sacramental marriage takes up and transforms a
natural reality, we cannot always be at this exalted level of
soteriological doctrine. Such earthy matters as the basic

conditions of validity for a marriage compact are also highly
germane. The *Catechism* will say more about these when it
addresses the question of the 'goods and requirements of
conjugal love', but in the immediate aftermath of its treatment
of the Liturgy of Marriage, it confines itself to singling out a
fundamental one suggested in unmistakable fashion by the
rites themselves. Since marriage is the self-donation of two
finite freedoms to each other, the consent which those about
to be married give to their new covenant in Christ must itself
be (internally and externally) *free*. Were some inner compulsion
or outer coercion to displace the act of responsible self-gift
then the marital consent would be in a state of contradiction
with itself. Moreover, such freedom must be exercised in a
public and ecclesial setting if it is to be the instrument of a
specifically Christian marriage, which is not a private
arrangement but an entry upon duties and rights,
responsibilities and privileges of a Church-defined nature. For
this reason, the couple must seek preparation for their new
state from those mandated by the Church, and marry before a
priest or some other person delegated (or permitted) to
receive their vows by the bishop. The *Catechism* is chary about
'mixed marriages' whether these be of the 'inter-Church'
variety or between a Catholic Christian and an adherent of
some other, non-Christian, faith, or non-faith. While admitting
there are positive possibilities here, its accent falls on the less
encouraging probabilities when marriage and parenthood
lack spiritual concord at this level.

What, then, are the *effects* of the sacrament of Marriage? In
a phrase, they amount to *gracious bondage*. The Spirit and the
Son join the couple whose marriage is *concluded* in the union
of minds and wills in the exchange of vows and consummated
in the union of bodies in the marriage act by a divine bond
which cannot be broken. The Church 'does not have the power
to contravene this disposition of divine wisdom'.[22] At the same
time, however, the couple are strengthened by a grace
conditioned to their new state, helping them to make the love

[22]Paragraph 1640.

of Christ, crucified and risen, a present reality, sanctifying one
another in the suffering and joy of daily life.

As the *Catechism* presents things, within the 'totality' of
conjugal love, a concept borrowed from Pope John Paul's II's
'Apostolic Exhortation on Marriage and Family', *Familiaris
consortio*, lie three distinct 'goods'. Sacramental moralists have
been analysing their character at least since the age of
Augustine. The good of *indissolubility* has its deepest basis in
the fact that the union between God and humankind cannot
be broken: Christ cannot separate from his Church. The good
of *faithfulness* is most fully seen when we realise that treating the
indissoluble union as non-exclusive falsifies the 'one flesh' by
(in the context) simulated self-giving. The pattern of marriage
is now the nuptials of the ever-faithful Lamb to the Bride he
renders immaculate by his union with her. The good of
offspring, or openness to fertility, manifests the essentially
fruitful nature of the faithful, indissoluble love specific to the
marriage bond – in accordance with its Christological and
ultimately trinitarian archetype on the cross and in the
processions of Son and Spirit which their redemptive mission
embodies. Such fruitfulness – which in the words of *Gaudium
et Spes*, constitutes the 'supreme gift of marriage',[23] that is, the
purpose that essentially determines the specific character of
this union as distinct from all other forms of loving communion
– is not of course exhausted in the simple procreation of
children, but includes their education in moral, spiritual and
supernatural life. At the same time, the authors of the *Catechism*
take note of the situation of couples who remain, for no fault
of their own, childless. They find an analogue to children, in
such cases, in a 'fruitfulness of charity, of hospitality, and of
sacrifice'.[24]

And if that last trio of terms define the ethos of a common
life open to others, the *Catechism* in fact concludes its account
of the sacrament of marriage by a sketch of the *ecclesia domestica*,
the Church in the form of a household, a home. Here should
be the first school of Christian living, where parents and, it may

[23] *Gaudium et Spes*, 50, 1.
[24] Paragraph 1654.

be, other relatives and familiars, minister to children and incomers within a common peace. Though accepting that home may be the last haven of a Christian civilisation, the *Catechism* is not content with sprinkling holy water on the four walls. The doors of homes must be thrown open, especially to those who lack a family of their own. Some words of an English Dominican writer constitute a pertinent commentary of their own:

> The smallest of local church, the Christian married couple, has the task of the *Catholica* itself to go constantly beyond itself. This church in miniature must be the dynamic nucleus of a new society, the exemplary unit which actively draws disordered elements into its own pattern of faith, hope and love. It is not enough for a couple to be a mutual admiration society, with closed doors and interior comfort together, an 'égotisme à deux'. Certainly, some safeguards are necessary: the nucleus must have its own existence in friendship and affection and warmth. Aelred of Rievaulx remarks, in a bold adaptation of words of St John, that 'Where friendship is, there is God'. But the measure of the Christian genuineness of this relationship is the measure in which others are drawn into its affection and warmth. Any cell of the Church is actively missionary in this sense or it is nothing.[25]

---

[25]G. Preston, O.P., *God's Way to be Man. Meditations on Following Christ through Scripture and Sacrament* (London 1978), p. 70.

VIII

---

*Sacramentals, and the Sense of an Ending**

Sacramentals are lesser signs which surround those concretisations of the divine *philanthrōpia*, as it seeks to save and transfigure humankind in the midst of creation, which are the seven sacraments themselves. *Sacrosanctum Concilium*, cited by the *Catechism* in its opening statement of this topic, ascribes to sacramentals a certain 'affinity' to the sacraments, since both are, in the largest sense, mediations of the sacred in the order of signs. Expressed in more distinctively Christian terms, what sacramentals signify are effects brought about by the Church's intercession (not, then, by the signs themselves, as with the sacraments). And if this serves to distinguish sacramentals from sacraments, here we have a case of *distinguer pour unir*, since the Conciliar Constitution goes on to say that by the sacramentals the Church's members are the better disposed to receive the grace of the sacraments themselves. To which is added by way of indicating the life of the *ecclesia domestica* created by the sacraments, that through the sacramentals 'various occasions in life are rendered holy'.[1]

In different respects, then, disposing us towards or flowing from the sacraments, sacramentals enrich the life in Christ that the septet of mysteries performs – in the strong sense of *enacts* – in the Church. They are, as a contemporary liturgical theologian has put it:

---

*= *Catechism*, Paragraphs 1667–1690.
[1] *Sacrosanctum Concilium* 60, cited Paragraph 1667.

'occasions' for the gracing process of the sacraments to take hold of us and for the Christ-life to deepen in us.[2]

Thus, for instance, the sacramentals of blessed catechumenal oil and the blessing of water for the purpose of lustration whether ceremonial (the Asperges) or domestic are, respectively, ordered to and derived from the sacrament of Baptism, while the rites of religious profession and the consecration of virgins are sacramentals that display the baptismal life in particularly 'pure' form. The consecration of chrism, the ritual blessing of abbots and abbesses, the sacring of kings and queens, the dedication of places of cult and the objects used liturgically therein have been treated as bound up with the sacraments of Confirmation and holy Order, since all these testify in various ways to the holiness of the royal and universal priestly people of God in its two most fundamental *ordines*, that of laity (entered by Confirmation) and of the apostolic ministry (conferred through Order). Again, blessed ashes are linked to the sacrament of Penance; the sacrament of Marriage generates its own sacramentals in the rites of espousal, the blessing of the ring and the nuptial blessing, as well as those of the home and expectant and delivered mothers; the blessing of the oil of the infirm is connected with the Anointing of the Sick, and the commendation of the dying and burial of the Christian dead with the most final of all ecclesial uses of oil, Extreme Unction. Directly or indirectly each and every one of these sacramentals relates in some wise to the Holy Eucharist, since the grace of the eucharistic Sacrifice sums up in unity the diversified grace of the seven dominical signs.[3] Sacramentals are constituted by a prayer (generally, a blessing) and some special sign, or piece of signifying activity. They are frequently formed by custom, but always sanctioned by the hierarchical authority to which the care of everything touching the worshipping life of the people of God falls.

---

[2]P. Bishop, S.J., 'Sacramentals', in Fink, *The New Dictionary of Sacramental Worship*, pp. 1114–1115.

[3]Cf. J. H. Miller, C.S.C., *Fundamentals of the Liturgy* (Notre Dame, IN 1959), p. 431.

It follows from all that has been said about the connexion of sacramentals with sacraments, what an older theology termed their 'imitation' of sacramental reality, its allotropic rendition, that sacramentals bear some relation to the source of all sacramental grace, the death and resurrection of Christ.[4] This leaps to the eye with, for instance, the striking of the new fire from flint on Easter Eve, with its symbolism of the Spirit of Christ bringing light from the sepulchre stone (or, possibly, the Rock which is Christ giving warmth and life from out of dead silence). The same is true of the paschal candle which originally

> represents the God-hallowed material world, and by extension the whole of creation, which as a result of the Incarnation and the advent of end-time following the Resurrection, has now become potentially redeemable ... For the wax, produced parthenogenetically by bees – so it was believed – symbolised Jesus' birth from a pure virgin; the papyrus, which served as a wick in the Candle, grew in river-water, the element hallowed by Jesus through his own Baptism; and the silent flame recalled the Burning Bush with its foliage still intact.[5]

Later, in the high Middle Ages, the candle came to stand for the visible presence of the risen Lord (hence its extinguishing on Ascension Day or thereabouts), and by extension, the new teaching and life made available to believers as sharers in Christ's radiance. The five grains of incense, inserted into the incised cross on the waxen 'flesh' of the Easter candle, further symbolised the glorified wounds of Jesus, transfigured yet not healed, as the Seer of the Apocalypse saw them.

Though such Paschaltide sacramentals are unmistakably related to the Source of our redemption, the same is hardly less true of – in receding order of chronological, but not symbolic, closeness to the passion and resurrection – the blessed palms of Palm Sunday, harbingers of the victorious tree; the ashes of

[4]Paragraph 1670.

[5]A. J. MacGregor, *Light and Fire in the Western Triduum. Their Use at Tenebrae and at the Paschal Vigil* (Collegeville, MN 1992), pp. 302–303.

the first feria of Lent, commemorating Christ's entry into the desert, painfully to prepare for his final ordeal; 'holy water', a reminder of Christ's baptism, itself already a 'death and resurrection' *in parvo* and the archetype of our own sharing in his redeeming mystery.

The sign of the cross is itself the principal instrument of blessing in other sacramentals, the range of which is simply enormous since, as the *Catechism* reminds its readers, sacramentals are instituted not only for the 'sanctification of certain ministries of the Church [and] certain states of life', but also for the hallowing of 'a great variety of circumstances in Christian life, and the use of many things helpful to man'.[6] From the blessing of an abbess to the profession of a friar; from the dedication of an altar to the blessing of a church bell or chalice or cope; from grace over meals to a parent's blessing of children going on a journey: all can be brought into spiritual contact, through the Church's prayer, with the life-giving cross whose virtue the sign of the cross recalls and invokes.

In the canonical tradition, at any rate, there are also what may be called 'negative sacramentals', as the *Catechism* now goes on to maintain. There it has been customary to distinguish between 'constitutive' blessings, making someone or something sacred to God in an abiding way; 'invocative' blessings, calling down upon the recipient the favour of God; and then, more darkly, those apotropaic blessings known as *exorcisms* whose aim is to shield, by the divine power, the subject of the sacramental from the influence of evil. Simple exorcisms, praying for the augmenting of good, the diminution of evil, occur in the course of celebrating many sacraments and sacramentals. But the solemn exorcism, a sacramental provided by the Church, in the name of and following the example of Christ, for the deliverance of a possessed person from the predominating influence of an evil angelic intelligence, is a different matter. Hedged around with procedural restraints, and requiring the express permission of a bishop, it is rarely resorted to, but remains nonetheless a proper and inalienable part of the Church's repertoire of benedictions.

[6]Paragraph 1668.

Also needing prudential judgment and the discernment of spirits are the various forms of popular piety which the *Catechism* now proceeds to discuss. Though here and there, at times and seasons, that piety may need some pruning back, or, to change the metaphor from gardening to seamanship, a guiding hand on the tiller, *au fond* it represents the 'religious sense of the Christian people'.[7] More readily recognised by social anthropologists and Church historians than by theologians themselves, the contribution of popular piety to the creation and sustenance of sacral community is indispensable. One thinks, for example of the rôle of pilgrimages, a lived metaphor as these are of the whole of life as a journey towards God's Kingdom, offering graces of renunciation and discipline, as well as the spontaneous release of fellow feeling that befits the Church's *koinōnia*. Then there is the veneration of relics of the saints, which brings home to us that the divine plan is to save us not atomistically – individually, nor merely mentalistically – in disavowal of our bodies, but as whole persons in relation with others in the mystical Body of Christ, by incorporation into a redeemed community which embraces both this life (and place) and that age to come into whose distinct temporality (and, with the general resurrection, spatiality) the saints are drawn forward. A Dominican commentator on *The Catechism of the Catholic Church* should not fail to mention (as indeed the *Catechism* itself does not) the rosary of the Blessed Virgin Mary, that 'compendium of the Gospel' where we look at (contemplate) the events that founded our religion, and changed the direction of the world's history, through the eyes of the Mother of the Church. The rosary is, in the mystical domain, the people's charter: a prayer that can be said in different ways by the least sophisticated and the most sophisticated, all of whom can find their prayer life in the best sense of the word *simplified* so that it comes to consist in just looking at God, what the spiritual tradition calls the 'prayer of simple regard'. We begin to see, perhaps, why the bishops of Latin America, gathered at Puebla de los Angeles (Mexico) in 1979 called popular piety the creative combination of

[7]Paragraph 1674.

the divine and human, Christ and Mary, spirit and body, communion and institution, person and community, faith and homeland, intelligence and emotion.[8]

There remains the 'sense of an ending', and the *Catechism* concludes its sub-book on the Christian Liturgy by capturing the essence of the final ritual service the Church can do her members, which is also, as it happens, a symbolic performance of the meaning of the last article of the Creed. Everything that the *Catechism* has had to say about Christian worship, and the commentary found thereon in this short study, must be seen in the light of the account of divine revelation, and the altered perception of the human situation before God that follows from it, in that earlier book. Summarising, then, both the Liturgy of the dead and the concluding affirmation of the Creed of Nicaea-Constantinople, the *Catechism* introduces this most final of all subjects with the words:

> All the sacraments, and principally those of Christian initiation, have as their goal the last Passover of the child of God which, through death, leads him into the life of the Kingdom. Then what he confessed in faith and hope will be fulfilled: 'I look for the resurrection of the dead, and the life of the world to come'.[9]

The *Catechism*'s thanatology – its theology of death – consists of a three paragraph commentary on this affirmation, a commentary which succeeds in rehearsing, in pithy form, the principal themes of its entire liturgical sub-book. And these are: the paschal mystery as the central event, to eternal, ever-renewed effect, of the Christian dispensation; the sacramental life as the heart of liturgical existence; the (always dependent) collaboration of the Church with the grace-giving of the divine Being in human sanctification.

Thus the Christian significance of death appears only in the light of the Easter events; the *dies natalis*, when the Christian enters on his true life, with God, is the proper outcome of what began in sacramental initiation:

[8]Cited Paragraph 1676.
[9]Paragraph 1680.

the fulfilment of his new birth begun at Baptism, the definitive 'conformity' to 'the image of the Son', conferred by the anointing of the Holy Spirit, and participation at the feast of the Kingdom ... anticipated in the Eucharist ...[10]

though the *Catechism* warns, against a certain modern tendency in Western Catholicism peremptorily to canonise the departed, however average their Christian lives, on the day of their funeral, that 'final purifications' – a discreet reference to the doctrine of Purgatory – may well still be necessary before the soul had its first glimpse of the nuptial garment of transfiguration. Lastly, and here the *Catechism* makes good its own omission in not rehearsing this theme during its discussion of Baptism, the Church as Mother – *Ecclesia Mater* that loving turn of phrase that came so easily to, in particular, the lips of North African Christians of the patristic age – must accompany to the end the child she bore in the womb of the font.

> She offers to the Father, in Christ, the child of his grace, and she commits to the earth, in hope, the seed of the body that will rise in Glory.[11]

The funeral Liturgy itself consists of rites of translation of the body from the home, or place of death, to the church (for Abbot Fernand Cabrol, this was probably the earliest instance of a liturgical *procession*[12]); the Mass of Requiem (perhaps preceded by some Hour of the Office of the dead); then the last journey to the cemetery ('God's acre') and the final committal of the body. Though the funeral rites are patent of accommodation to the 'situations and traditions of each region', what the *Catechism* has to say about the spirit in which the eucharistic Sacrifice is offered on this occasion – petition for the purification of the deceased from his sins, and a plea for his admittance to the table of the Kingdom – seems a far cry

---

[10]Paragraph 1682.
[11]Paragraph 1683.
[12]F. Cabrol, O.S.B., *Liturgical Prayer. Its History and Spirit* (E.t. London 1925), p. 229.

from the 'sanitised' tone that some have detected in, for instance, the *Order of Christian Funerals* sanctioned in 1991 by the Latin bishops in England and Wales.[13]

Interestingly, nothing is said in the *Catechism* about the possible replacement of inhumation by cremation, the latter in the past forbidden to Catholics because of its association with eschatologies contradictory to those of the Church, then permitted in restrictive terms, and subsequently more widely. As is well-known, this indulgence is not found among hierarchs of the Eastern-rite Catholic churches. It is especially appropriate, then, that in recalling the Byzantine custom of planting a final kiss on the beloved dead before burial, the *Catechism* should draw its sub-book to a close with a text from a Greek author of the period when schism was fomenting. In his *The Order of Burial*, Symeon of Thessalonica wrote of how that greeting signifies not only departure from this life and so separation but also communion and therefore reunion.

> For even dead, we are not at all separated from one another, because we all run the same course and we will find one another again in the same place. We shall never be separated, for we live for Christ, and now we are united with Christ as we go toward him ... We shall all be together in Christ.[14]

[13]See for sharp criticism, E. Duffy, 'An Apology for Grief, Fear and Anger', *Priests and People* 5, 11 (1991), pp. 397–401.

[14]Symeon of Thessalonica, *On the Order of Burial*, 336, cited *Catechism*, Paragraph 1690. Archbishop Estanislao Esteban Karlic of Paranà (Argentina) has pertinently noted: 'In an effort to express the catholicity of the faith, special care had to be taken during the drafting of the Catechism to assure that the Eastern tradition and that of the West were both kept in mind to an equal degree; in this way the text was enriched with the doctrine, piety and beauty of both. This purpose characterized the whole Catechism, but its influence is especially felt in the exposition of the sacramental economy. It is important to note the ecumenical value contained in this attitude with respect to our Orthodox brothers and sisters, who will find in the Catechism new proof of the respect and great love that Catholics have for every authentic Christian tradition.' In: 'Reflections on the *Catechism of the Catholic Church* – 9', *Osservatore Romano* (English edition), 28 April 1993, p. 9.

PART TWO

THE SPRINGS OF GOODNESS

ETHICS

Lord God, source of all good,
hear our prayer:
inspire us with good intentions,
and help us to fulfil them.

Oratio **of the Roman rite for**
the Tenth Sunday of the Year

IX

A Word in Preamble

In Jane Austen's *Mansfield Park*, Mary Crawford expresses her irritation at the discovery that her new friend, Edmund Bertram, will take Holy Orders by describing a cleric as, in the world of real agency, a zero quantity – 'nothing'. To which is returned the brisk reply:

> I cannot call that situation nothing, which has the charge of all that is of the first importance to mankind, individually or collectively considered, temporally and eternally – which has the guardianship of religion and morals, and consequently of the manners which result from their influence.

But the age of the Enlightenment, like our own, found in the disparity between the moral teaching of the priesthood and the moral achievement of its members a handy implement for hauling down from their thrones the traditional arbiters of morals. In distinguishing between the office and its exercise, Bertram makes the necessary response:

> No one here can call the *office* nothing. If the man who holds it is so, it is by the neglect of his duty, by foregoing its just importance, and stepping out of his place to appear what he ought not to appear.

Bertram speaks of 'religion and morals': theologically informed Catholics would say, rather, 'faith and morals', and the sense, either way, is clear enough. But what does Bertram mean by 'manners'? It was a word whose sense was shifting from an ancient meaning to a modern. He has to clear away the (largely irrelevant) contemporary associations so as to expose a root meaning stretching back into antiquity.

> ... with regard to their influencing public manners, Miss Crawford must not misunderstand me, or suppose I mean to call them the arbiters of good breeding, the regulators of refinement and courtesy, the masters of the ceremonies of life. The *manners* I speak of might rather be called *conduct*, perhaps, the result of good principles; the effect, in short, of those doctrines which it is their duty to teach and recommend ...

The teaching is not intended to be theoretical only, but to shape the ethos of the people.

Bertram does not let the topic drop, finally, without the concession that, in any case, teaching by itself is not enough; example must follow.

> It will, I believe, be everywhere found, that as the clergy are, or are not, what they ought to be, so are the rest of the nation.[1]

Jane Austen's character sets out perfectly the rôle that the Catholic Church ascribes to the ministerial priesthood – one of presenting, but also representing, the ethical convictions of the wider constituency of her faithful members. The *Catechism of the Catholic Church* is an authoritative instrument for ascertaining that life which can truly be called good. It needs, however, the complement of innumerable persuasive examples – both clerical and lay – if those seeking moral direction are to apprehend the intrinsic 'authority of goodness'. That is why this commentary on the *Catechism*, beginning in a previous volume with the doctrinal vision of the Catholic Church – her account of the truth of the human person, in his relation to the source and goal of the world, the holy Trinity[2], and proceeding via a study of what the *Catechism* has to say about the sacramental liturgy, where the redemptive action of the triune God is

---

[1] J. Austen, *Mansfield Park*, chapter XI.
[2] Nichols, *The Splendour of Doctrine* (Edinburgh 1995).

applied to our souls and bodies – cannot end (as, then, a truncated trio, merely) with the topic of theological ethics. The music must play on until we have considered what the *Catechism* has to say about spirituality, the making of saints. The goal of catechesis is transfiguration.

X

Foundations *

The *Catechism* entitles its sub-book on ethics 'Life in Christ'. This tells us straightaway that we shall be offered no purely natural morality, backed up with reasons of a generally accessible philosophical nature. However, since Christ is the Saviour not only of human persons but of human *nature*, the formula 'life in Christ' also may (and does!) imply that natural morals and their rational justification will not be denied but, rather, taken up into a wider synthesis of a soteriological sort.

Christian dignity

The cue comes in the words from Pope St Leo's sermon on the Lord's Nativity with which the *Catechism*'s entire treatment of ethics opens. It is to the nobility of the redeemed creature – on the principle of *noblesse oblige* – that the *Catechism* appeals in order to waken its readers to the exigencies of Christian ethics. Though the language of 'deification' is sometimes (wrongly) regarded as alien to the West, an exclusively Oriental affair, Pope Leo defined this nobility first and foremost in terms of the share the baptised are privileged to enjoy in the divine nature – a reference to the biblical charter of a doctrine of deifying grace in the Second Letter of Peter (1:4). Christians are not to revert to their 'former base nature' by sinning. They are not, so to speak, to abandon the transformed life of a true

---

*=*Catechism*, Paragraphs 1691–1698.

civilisation in order to return to a miserable existence scratched out in the bush. The civilisation in question is one founded on Jesus Christ, who is the Head of the Body of which the Christian is a member – that medical language of the organism was commonly employed in Late Antiquity as a way of speaking about society. The citizenship Christians can boast of is that of the Kingdom of God into whose light they have been ushered, delivered as they are from 'the power of darkness' – an echo of Paul's paean to grace in the Letter to the Colossians (1:13), itself part of that epistle's opening prayer that Christ's faithful at Colossae will

> lead a life worthy of the Lord, fully pleasing to him, bearing fruit in every good work and increasing in the knowledge of God (1:10).

Speaking in their own name, rather than via that fifth-century Roman bishop, the makers of the *Catechism* point out that such a *theological* ethics requires the totality of their two previous 'sub-books' – on Christian believing (the Creed) and Christian worship (the sacramental Liturgy) – as its necessary presupposition.

> The Symbol of the faith confesses the greatness of God's gifts to man in his work of creation, and even more in redemption and sanctification. What faith confesses, the sacraments communicate ...[1]

The (credal) dogmas and the (sacramental) mysteries are, then, *ethically enabling*: the first provide a vision of man's worth as ennobled by the Father, and this constitutes the true standard of ethical aspiration ('a life worthy of the gospel', Philippians 1:27); the second, as vehicles of the grace of the Son and the gifts of the Holy Spirit offer resources of supernatural energy which fuel our pursuit of this vision, and counteract any tendency to give up on it. So little or nothing I have said in commenting the two previous sub-books of the *Catechism* is irrelevant now.

[1] Paragraph 1692.

From the Father

And just as the authors of the *Catechism*, when laying the foundations for its whole enterprise in their exposition of doctrine, created a tripartite structure based on the being and work of Father, Son and Holy Spirit,[2] so here too, in their brief preamble to the sub-book on morals, the good life as the Church sees it is presented in trinitarian terms. As in all theism, the divine perfection is the ultimate source and goal of moral effort. Whereas, however, the Hebrew Bible grounds the categorised imperatives of its 'Holiness Code' on the all-sustaining injunction to replicate the holy character of the divinity at large ('You shall be holy, for I the Lord your God am holy', Leviticus 19:1), the New Testament couches this transcendent foundation of morals in specifically paterological terms: 'You must be perfect, as your heavenly Father is perfect' (Matthew 5:48). But the unique glory of *Christian* theism is that the Father, the invisible source of all that is good, whether created (in the world) or uncreated (his Word and Spirit), does not remain in every sense unseen, the remote archetype, through his originating possession of the divine perfections, for everything worthwhile about ourselves. Instead, he is visually presented to us through his incarnate Image, Jesus Christ. The *Catechism* has two ways of speaking of how the Son made flesh presents the fontal goodness of the Father. Jesus, in the words of the Fourth Gospel, always did what was pleasing to the Father (cf. John 8:29); moreover – and here the *Catechism* cites no single New Testament theology, but decants the sense of the whole – he ever lived in 'perfect communion with him'.[3] It is on the twofold basis of the unerring consonance, then, of Jesus' action with the Father's will (itself the true Form of the Good sought by the philosophers), and the unbroken communion of life between the Father and the humanised Son which made that coincidence of willing perfectly possible, that the *Catechism* can portray Jesus Christ as the way to the Father's perfection.

[2]Paragraphs 26–1065.
[3]Paragraph 1693.

Through the Son

In the first place, however, and here the emphasis shifts from
Father to Son, this is a question not so much of imitating Christ
as of incorporation into him. In this sense the 'life in Christ'
which figures as the overall title to the *Catechism*'s ethics is
sacramental living within the eucharistic fellowship of the
Church, within which Christian ethics must be situated. Only as
those immersed in the Lord's paschal mystery by their baptismal
participation in his death to sin and resurrection to newness of
life, can the Church's members hope to have the 'mind' of
Christ – his characteristic mind-set and disposition – and to
follow his example. The late mediaeval spiritual writer who
penned *The Imitation of Christ* was not barking up the wrong tree.
Yet the mimetic representation of Christ's own behaviour in the
different medium of our lives belongs within the wider reality of
discipleship and union, based on our incorporation in him
through the sacraments of faith. Outside of these, 'imitation'
loses that context in which alone the creative, yet faithful,
replication of his example in the indefinitely varied circumstances
of a myriad lives becomes a possible venture.

In the Holy Spirit

But the foundation of Christian ethics is not only paterological
and Christological; it is also *pneumatological*. Through the
adoptive sonship of Baptism, those who apprehend the
Father's gift of righteousness in the Son are justified and
sanctified, thereby becoming temples of the Holy Spirit. The
Spirit of the Son, who, as the *Catechism*'s final section will
explain, teaches them to pray '*Abba*, Father', also renders them
ethically fruitful through active charity. The Holy Spirit
becomes a new principle of action, rectifying the disturbed
pattern of our motives so that we can embrace 'all that is good
and right and true' – a compendious phrase from the Letter to
the Ephesians (5:8, 9) which usefully reminds the reader that
the trinitarian foundation of ethics embraces natural as well as
supernatural morality.

For, in the language of an ancient Christian text, which may
be contemporary with the New Testament itself, there are,

morally speaking, *two ways*, only one of which, whose blazon is 'Do good, avoid evil', leads to life, while the other journeys to death and destruction. That fundamental statement of the *Didache* has its parallels, not only in the Gospels, but in the Old Testament, the literature of other religions, and the writings of philosophers ever since ancient times.

A programme

Before beginning its exposition of fundamental morals, the *Catechism* lists nine signposts to the way that leads to life, of which the last occupies an altogether special position. It proposes to set forth a catechesis of the good life which will (1) be inspired by the Holy Spirit in whose strength the moral odyssey takes place; (2) depend on grace without which salvation, and therefore any *permanently* abiding fruits of our activity, is impossible; (3) find itself summed up in the Beatitudes, the high point of the Sermon on the Mount, itself the charter of the life of the Kingdom of God; (4) take into account sin and forgiveness, for without a grasp of human wickedness effective progress towards the good cannot be made, while a knowledge of our negative moral capacity without the concomitant apprehension of the divine forgiveness can only subvert; (5) display the good as manifested in a whole range of virtues which stud human life with starlight and attract us by their beauty; (6) go beyond the natural virtues to take in, as a distinctively *Christian* ethic, those of faith, hope and charity whereby people become not just exemplary human beings but also saints; (7) not for all that forget the fundamental commandments of the Law of Christ – to love God and one's neighbour, and the ramifications of these through a variety of precepts which specify the good in different areas of life; (8) be lived nowhere save in the communion of saints, embodied visibly in the Church, where an ecology of grace links us, by multiple relations of receiving and giving, to all those in whom God is active, which means everyone except the damned. Finally (9), the alpha and omega of the *Catechism*'s ethical teaching – as of the catechesis it wants to see everywhere expounded to others – will be Jesus Christ himself, 'the way, the truth and the life' (John 14:6), the furnace of love at the centre of creation, as revelation shows him to be.

These preliminaries completed, the *Catechism* can settle down to its first major task – the setting out of a teaching on *fundamental morals*: the basic structure of the moral life, and the dynamics, both natural and supernatural, which fill that structure with purposive movement.

XI

---

*Consider your Call**

Any philosophy, any religion, must consider whether in the last analysis it thinks that persons exist for the sake of society or for some wider whole, however defined, or whether, by contrast, the rationale of society – or, more generally, the order of things – is meant to serve the flourishing of those who are the bearers of understanding and love since they are equipped with intellect and will. Although the *Catechism*'s account of the human vocation by no means neglects the communitarian dimension of humankind, to which it will quite explicitly devote over seventy paragraphs,[1] it makes the (correct) option to give the primacy to persons, who alone are capable of beatitude, able to enjoy a conscious sharing in the ceaseless exchange of the divine life.

To his image and likeness

The *Catechism*'s lengthy disquisition on the basis of morals – over three hundred and fifty paragraphs, i.e. over a third of its ethical sub-book as a whole[2] – opens by situating the dignity of the human person within a theology of the *imago Dei*, the image of God in man. In the crowded room of the Church Fathers, we can pick up, if we attend, the nuances of a conversation: there

---

*=*Catechism*, Paragraphs 1699–1876.
[1]Paragraphs 1877–1948. See above, Chapter III.
[2]Paragraphs 1699–2051, cf. the total span of the book on morals, which runs from Paragraph 1691 to Paragraph 2557.

are different ways of presenting what it is about man in history which displays, or ought to, the divine image. All have in common, however, the revelation-derived belief that the human capacity to be the icon of God in the temple of the world was founded on our creation, disabled by our fall, and restored by salvation in Jesus Christ, through the power of his Spirit. The Second Vatican Council highlighted – at any rate in one crucial text, cited by the *Catechism* – that theme in the patristic discussion whereby, in an interpretation especially associated with Irenaeus of Lyons, the image in whose likeness man was created is, and always has been, that of the *incarnate* Word of God, Jesus Christ.

> Christ, ... in the very revelation of the mystery of the Father and of his love, makes man fully manifest to himself and brings to light his exalted vocation.[3]

To say that no conciliar text has been more often cited than this by Pope John Paul II,[4] is simultaneously to assert that the pope of the *Catechism* aimed to implant as deeply as possible that Christocentric anthropology and soteriology – and therefore theological ethics – for which the Council of 1962–1965 cleared the ground. The choice of the title *Redemptor hominis*, 'The Redeemer of Man', for his first encyclical bears him witness.

> It is in Christ, Redeemer and Saviour, that the divine image, disfigured in man by the first sin, has been restored to its original beauty and ennobled by the grace of God.[5]

This is not to say, however, that the *Catechism* would depart from the earlier tradition by maintaining an *imago Christi* in the human animal *over against* an *imago Dei*. True, Christ is not only God, for he is also man; nor is he alone God, for that the Father

---

[3] *Gaudium et Spes* 22, cited at Paragraph 1701. It should be noted that this text stands in a certain tension with *Gaudium et Spes* 12, where the Christological dimension of the image is not (yet) mentioned.

[4] J. Saward, *Christ is the Answer. The Christ-Centred Teaching of Pope John Paul II* (Edinburgh 1995), p. 75.

[5] Paragraph 1701.

and the Spirit are likewise. Yet his possession of the divine nature, and the indwelling of the hypostases of Father and Spirit in the hypostasis of the Son, as his in theirs, by circumincession, mean that where the image of the pre-existent Word is inscribed in the creation there the divine Substance and the wondrous interplay of the trinitarian persons who possess it find reflection in the world. The divine image is present, accordingly, in every human being made to the Word's likeness, and, moreover,

> shines forth in the communion of persons, in the likeness
> of the union of the divine persons among themselves.[6]

In these words, the *Catechism* reminds its readers that the iconic character of man is not invested in his spirituality in an atomistically individual fashion, but is displayed in those relations with others where our powers of understanding and will are both tutored and set to work. Man is made not only in the image of Christ but also in the image of God and indeed in the image of the holy Trinity.

The Fathers of the Church frequently distinguished between the divine *image* in man – an inalienable gift, persisting as long as the person himself subsists, and therefore 'stative' (a word to be preferred in this context to 'static'), an *abiding condition* – and the divine *likeness* in him, a call which may or may not be heard and answered, to develop the potentialities of the image by progressive, and therefore dynamic, assimilation to God, and so a *process*. As the Jesuit patrologist Father George Maloney has written:

> By his creation according to God's image, man contains
> in his intellect and will the faculties of hearing God's
> invitation ... to answer God's Word within him in order to
> put on the life of Christ. Thus God does not impose
> himself as a task, but freely gives man, as a gift, the
> opportunity, the responsibility to return to God the love
> that he has first had for man. God has constituted man
> a total entity distinct from himself, an *I* that will be

---

[6]Paragraph 1702.

complete only in relation through loving submission to a greater *Thou.*[7]

Beatitude

The primary 'mood' of God's creative work is therefore not so much the imperative of a command as the indicative of a description, pointing out God's goodness: 'Thou art mine, if thou wishest'.[8] The *Catechism* too privileges this aspect by speaking first of man's vocation to beatitude, his call to share God's own life, entailing as this does not only a supernatural participation in the light and life of the Spirit of God but also the natural apprehension of the moral order of the world, since without the right use of our free will we cannot move towards our true Good. Only subsequently does the *Catechism* turn its attention to human freedom as already, and indeed continuously, a manifestation of the divine image, and so consider the imperative laid on us by the moral law: to do good and avoid evil.

The determination of the *Catechism*'s authors to avoid a merely naturalistic ethics, dusted with just the lightest sugaring of the supernatural, or an ethics divided into two self-contained parts, one natural, the other supernatural, externally juxtaposed, is shown in the way that, prior to their developed account of human freedom, they alert the reader to its contrasting phases in salvation history. The resources and conditions of freedom change dramatically when our focus shifts from man's original creation to his Fall, from his post-lapsarian state to his redemption by Christ's passion, from his redemption – which merited for him life in the Holy Spirit – to his actual transfiguration by incipient sanctification here and blessedness hereafter:

> In union with his Saviour, the disciple attains the perfection of charity which is holiness. Having matured

---

[7]G. A. Moloney, S.J., *Man, the Divine Icon. The Patristic Doctrine of Man Made according to the Image of God* (Pecos, New Mexico, 1973), pp. 8–9.
[8]Ibid., p. 9.

in grace, the moral life blossoms into eternal life in the glory of heaven.[9]

The *Catechism* opens its account of beatitude by reminding the reader of the importance of the 'macarisms' in the Sermon on the Mount, those sayings which we call precisely the 'Beatitudes'. If the *Sermo Domini* is, as Augustine believed, the charter of the morality proper to the Kingdom in the preaching of Jesus, then the Beatitudes are that Sermon's heart. They are so not only by listing the virtues distinctive of an evangelical ethics but by their promise of blessedness with God in the age to come. In a superb passage of concentrated insight into these riddling but all important words:

> The Beatitudes depict the countenance of Jesus Christ and portray his charity. They express the vocation of the faithful associated with the glory of his Passion and Resurrection; they shed light on the actions and attitudes characteristic of the Christian life; they are the paradoxical promises that sustain hope in the midst of tribulations; they proclaim the blessings and rewards already secured, however dimly, for Christ's disciples; they have begun in the lives of the Virgin Mary and all the saints.[10]

Here the *Catechism* looks back towards the Christocentric soteriology typical of its opening section, on Christian believing, and forward to the programme of conversion and sanctification laid out in its concluding section, on Christian spirituality. At the same time, by insisting that the Beatitudes illuminate 'actions and attitudes', it draws attention to their properly ethical character.

That character is ordered to the goal the Beatitudes promise – what the *Catechism* terms specifically 'Christian Beatitude' – and yet it also answers to the natural desire for happiness set by God, as suitable texts from Augustine and Aquinas explain, within man's very being. Drawing on the *philosophia perennis*,

[9]Paragraph 1709.
[10]Paragraph 1717.

the best of ancient philosophy, purified and extended by exposure to the truths of revelation, the *Catechism* embraces a eudaimonistic ethic, centred on happiness, while giving this ethic, in company with the Fathers and the mediaeval doctors, the theistic twist which makes happiness altogether dependent on openness to divine reality. Citing St Thomas, Josef Pieper wrote:

> 'To seek happiness is nothing but to seek the satiation of the will' – *ut voluntas satietur*. Thus, the entire energy of human nature is considered a hunger which demands satiation, a thirst that requires quenching. And the quenching of this thirst is happiness ... It is inherent in the concepts of hunger and thirst that their gratification is expected from 'elsewhere', and that no one can requite with himself and by himself alone. If the thirster were himself the drink, or if he possessed it – how could he thirst?[11]

No, nothing less than the *bonum universale* can completely quench the craving of man for happiness, and as Thomas, again, remarks:

> The whole good cannot be found anywhere in the realm of created things; it is encountered in God alone.[12]

That satiation by the infinite good bears the name of happiness – and of all those other names which sacred Scripture has found for God as our ultimate fulfilment: eternal life and light and glory, or, in those preferred by the *Catechism* itself for our entering upon that fulfilment – the coming of the Kingdom, the vision of God, the joy of the Lord, God's rest.

This fundamental claim – at once both theological, an interpretation of the message of Old and New Testaments in their interconnected entirety, and philosophical – a statement about finite spirit's essential relation to the whole of reality,

[11] J. Pieper, *Happiness and Contemplation* (E.t. London 1958), pp. 33–34, with an internal citation of *Summa Theologiae* Ia., IIae., q. 5, a. 8, c.
[12] *Summa Theologiae*, Ia., IIae., q. 2, a. 8.

and so to the totality of being, of truth, and of the good, enables the *Catechism*'s authors to draw a quartet of important conclusions. First, it licenses their restatement of what is to English Catholics of a certain vintage the best remembered of the questions and answers of the 'Penny Catechism': 'Why did God make you':

> God made me to know him, love him, and serve him in this world, and to be happy with him for ever in the next.[13]

To this the *Catechism of the Catholic Church* barely adds an iota.

> God put us in the world to know, to love, and to serve him, and so to come to paradise.[14]

Secondly, the identification of happiness as our creaturely participation in the infinite and uncreated richness of God means that ultimate fulfilment can be further described by reference to the biblical revelation of how the divine fulness is communicated and deployed. Our happiness will be a sharing in Christ's glory, and the joy native to the life of communion of the trinitarian Persons. Thirdly, such happiness, though necessarily – if it to be truly immanent within us, with effects working inwards – our very own action, must also be the pure gift of God. In no other way than gratuitously, by the sheerest generosity, could the Holy One allow us to possess him in knowing him as he is. God *might* have created man without divine grace and a supernatural destiny, but he did not. Instead, he planted the desire to see the supreme Good deep within man's being, proposing to meet, and more than meet, that desire by the manifestation to his human creature of his uncreated glory. Fourthly, the beatitude promised us also makes demands upon us. Specifically, it requires us so to order our loves – our moral choices in this world – as not to lose the *Delectabilissimum*, the cause of supreme rejoicing, in the next. Augustine wrote in the *Tractates* on the Johannine Epistles:

> Let not Satan steal a way into your heart, saying as he is wont, 'Enjoy God's creature: why did he make it but for

[13]*A Catechism of Christian Doctrine* (Ditchling 1931), No. 2.
[14]Paragraph 1721.

your enjoyment?' ... God forbids not the love of these things, but only the finding of our happiness in the love of them: we are to make the love of their Creator the end of our esteem for them. Suppose, brethren, a man should make a ring for his betrothed, and she should love the ring given her more than her betrothed who made it for her, would not her heart be convicted of infidelity in respect of the very gift of her betrothed, though what she loved were what he gave? Certainly let her love his gift; but if she should say, 'The ring is enough, I do not wish to see his face again', what should we say of her? ... The pledge is given by the betrothed just that in his pledge he himself may be loved. God, then, has given you all these things; love him who made them.[15]

The order of love requires that all other loves be ordered to the love of God – and this is true of proper self-love as well. In another text from the North African doctor:

the true and highest interest of the self is served when God is loved more than the self, so that a man chooses to be God's rather than his own.[16]

And so the neighbour, the beloved fellow human being, is not to be loved by way of alternative to God (for 'not even the Lord [Jesus] himself, in so far as he deigned to be for us the Way, would keep us holden, but willed that we should pass through'),[17] but so that he or she may love God with a perfect love themselves:

You do not love [the neighbour] as yourself, unless you do all you can to bring them to that good which is your own.[18]

---

[15] *Tractates* on the Letters of John, 2, 11. Augustine subtly contrasts the more general verb to love, *amare*, with *diligere*, to love with conscious election, in a way impossible to capture in English. The translation is John Burnaby's in *Amor Dei. A Study of the Religion of Saint Augustine* (London 1938), p. 115.

[16] Augustine, *De diversis quaestionibus* LXXXIII, 36.

[17] Idem, *De doctrina christiana* I, 37.

[18] Idem, *De moribus Ecclesiae Catholicae*, 26.

Beatitude, to return to the *Catechism*'s own words, is

> not found ... in any creature, but in God alone, the source
> of every good and of all love.[19]

There will be more to say on this subject when the *Catechism*'s architect's plan of the structure of the moral life reaches *charity*. For that is, as the Thomists put it, the 'form', or supernaturally animating principle, of all the virtues.

Freedom

Meanwhile, however, we must turn our attention to that necessary, if often humdrum, precondition of growth in likeness to God – the responsible *freedom* which distinguishes man, made in the image of God, from the rest of the animal creation. The existence of free will is sometimes disputed by philosophers. The *Catechism* spends no time on its defence, thus implicitly maintaining with the eighteenth-century English *savant* Samuel Johnson, 'Sir, we know the will is free; and there's an end on't'.[20] Since not all the decisions we make by the use of free will have moral significance (for example, to select pistachio rather than loganberry from a range of ice-creams), free will is sometimes distinguished from moral freedom as the enabling context in which the latter, for good or ill, carries out its work. Certainly, the *Catechism* knows of the difference between what might be termed 'negative' freedom, namely, the absence of coercion, whether exterior or interior, and 'positive' freedom, whereby we are not merely exempt from restraint but so act as to realise or fulfil our nature, man as he was meant to be. For on the one hand it describes freedom in terms which are morally neutral save that they imply the personal engagement of the self as agent:

---

[19]Paragraph 1723.

[20]Cited in I. Murdoch, *Metaphysics as a Guide to Morals* (London 1992), p. 55. Miss Murdoch does not distance herself here from one she calls this 'excellent philosopher'.

the power, rooted in reason and will, to act or not to act,
to do this or that, and so to perform deliberate actions on
one's own responsibility ...[21]

and this is negative freedom. And on the other hand, the
Catechism speaks of liberty as

a force for growth and maturity in truth and goodness;
[which] attains its perfection when directed toward God,
our beatitude[22]

and that is positive freedom *in excelsis.*

The latter, clearly enough, is unintelligible without the
invocation of the concepts of good and evil. An *evil* choice
would not be an example of positive freedom no matter how
complete the agent's mastery of his or her own act; indeed, the
greater the self-possession, and so self-investment, of the subject
in their ill decision, the more at the antipodes from positive
freedom their action would be. The conviction of the *Catechism*'s
authors that evil choices frustrate the development of the very
nature of the creature whose choices they are – making them,
to that degree, a *wicked* person – tells us *eo ipso* that these writers
are working on a thoroughly objective account of the good and
its contrary, the evil. Since in contemporary Western culture
such a view sometimes seems minoritarian – good and evil, we
hear, are functions of what is considered so in one society or at
one historical epoch, or even by one individual – it seems
worth insisting on this implication of our text. In J. R. R.
Tolkien's epic *The Lord of the Rings*, Eómer, disturbed by the
turbulent shifts of the crisis-time on Middle-Earth, asks Aragorn,
'How shall a man judge what to do in such times?'

'As he has ever judged,' said Aragorn. 'Good and ill have
not changed since yester-year, nor are they one thing
among Elves and the Dwarves and another among Men.
It is a man's part to discern them, as much in the Golden
Wood as in his own house.[23]

[21]Paragraph 1731.
[22]Ibid.
[23]J. R. R. Tolkien, *The Lord of the Rings* (London 1954; 1966²; 1995), pp. 427–428.

But if, as Kant put it, we are not so much gentleman volunteers as conscripts in the army of the moral law, the *Catechism* points out how, for once, such enrolment really is good for us:

> The more one does what is good, the freer one becomes. There is no true freedom except in the service of what is good and just.[24]

The *Catechism* mentions numerous factors which diminish or even take away entirely our responsibility for our actions. These include ignorance, inadvertence, duress, fear, habit, and 'inordinate attachments' – though it should be noted that each of these may be itself culpable in its *own* genesis! Also named, if more vaguely, are 'other psychological or social factors'; prudently, the writers follow up this somewhat untidy reference by the cleaner statement that every act that is directly willed must be regarded as imputable to its author. For, despite Rousseau, Nietzsche, Freud and other subverters of a classical view of the human heart, not all the seas and continents of motive are off the map which the moral and ascetical tradition has handed down. It is the entertaining of such motives – destructive aggression, fear, sloth, greed, lust, pride – which debilitates the good will and generates a viciousness only unconscious of itself because its subject deliberately avoids thinking about it through their own responsible (and therefore guilty) act.

If the world is a vale of soul-making then it is important nonetheless to leave people the opportunity to make or mar themselves by the exercise of freedom, especially, the *Catechism* notes, in matters moral and religious. This is not to say, however, that they should be deliberately started off on a 'level playing field'. It is the task of educators to ensure that moral and religious truth are so offered to young minds and hearts that they can be efficaciously appropriated, turned into the will's own good. Civil society too, though it may not coerce consciences, has the duty to see to it that the diffusion of moral and religious error is not rampant for this is what 'the common good and public order' in at least a predominantly Christian civil society require.

[24]Paragraph 1733.

Prior to investigating the elements comprised in the moral act, the *Catechism* recapitulates its teaching on the relation of freedom and the good by placing it in the specifically theological context of grace, sin and salvation. We have already seen *that* freedom's register changes dramatically through the principal phases of salvation history. Now we are shown in rather more detail *how* this is so. The self-estrangement of the Fall, itself a catastrophic exercise of freedom, gave rise to a host of other alienations from man's true good.

> By deviating from the moral law, man violates his own freedom, becomes imprisoned within himself, disrupts neighbourly fellowship, and rebels against divine truth.[25]

Hence while disregard for the economic, social, political and cultural conditions of the proper exercise of freedom impair the moral life, notably by stimulating both 'strong' and 'weak' to sin against charity (by contempt in the one case, tumult in the other), what needs to be redeemed is not in the first place the structural setting of freedom but rather *freedom itself.* Here the *Catechism* has learned from the analysis of liberation theology made by the Holy See in the course of two major documents, one negative, the other positive, in the 1980s.[26] If freedom itself is unfree – not that after the Fall, the will simply loses all power of self-determination, yet free will can no longer be the space where positive freedom breaks through to its own true end – then no *human* effort can save it. Seeking 'liberation' through total autonomy man becomes in fact so fettered that release can only come from *God.* The economies of the Son and the Holy Spirit, in this perspective, have as their aim the reconstitution of the power of liberty as positive freedom, by communion, as the *Catechism* puts it, citing the Gospel of St John (8:32), with 'the truth that makes us free', through the gift, described in Paul's Second Letter to Corinth (3:17) of the Spirit whose presence *means* transfigured liberty: 'Where the Spirit of the Lord is, there is freedom'. The transformation of

---

[25]Paragraph 1740.

[26]See on this my 'The Rise and Fall of Liberation Theology?', reprinted in *Scribe of the Kingdom* II, pp. 101–123.

sin into repentance, existential failure into fulness of life, is made possible through the assumption of our tainted nature by the hypostasis of the divine Son, who in his atoning work realigns it with its divine archetype, and whose Spirit reproduces in Christ's brethren the glorious harmony of that crucified and risen humanity with God. The wider humane task of Christians will lie, then, in making the world fit for redeemed freedom to live in.

> The grace of Christ is not in the slightest way a rival of our freedom when this freedom accords with the sense of the true and the good that God has put in the human heart. On the contrary, ... By the working of grace the Holy Spirit educates us in spiritual freedom in order to make us free collaborators in his work in the Church and in the world.[27]

Good and evil action

Having thus considered our beatitude, and the freedom which is essential if we are to attain it – for, in Augustine's words, the God who made us without us will not save us without us – the *Catechism* now turns to an analysis of the factors involved in the moral act. The most basic of these are its object, which identifies the *kind* of action it is, and its intended end, the purpose for which it is carried out. Important ancillary considerations are the circumstances of the action, under which heading the *Catechism* also includes its consequences. It will readily be seen that the pride of place given to the object of moral agency fits perfectly with the *Catechism*'s emphasis – along with Catholic Christianity at large – on the objectivity of the norms of the moral life which, as it now points out, 'express the rational order of good and evil, attested to by conscience'.[28] Intention cannot render good an evil object, and yet a good object may be chosen by some species of pseudo-virtue. The more modest position occupied by consequences is explained

[27]Paragraph 1742.
[28]Paragraph 1751.

by the conviction of Catholic moralists that the felicific calculus is a useless tool when it comes to assessing the fundamental rightness or wrongness of an act. As Professor John Finnis has put it, on the 'consequentialist' view of things:

> one stands ready to do and become anything, for the sake of becoming a mere conduit through which history will work greater amounts of good or lesser amounts of bad.[29]

But circumstances *can* augment or diminish the objective goodness (or evil) of an action, and increase or lessen likewise the subjective participation of its agent therein. The plasticity of human experience, whose ever-changing contours it is the genius of novelists to describe, leaves untouched, however, the peculiar status of certain *types* of action 'gravely illicit' (in the *Catechism*'s words) 'by virtue of their object'. Here its own examples are blasphemy and perjury, murder and adultery. As Chesterton's Father Brown remarks to the arch-criminal Flambeau:

> Reason and justice grip the remotest and the loneliest star. Look at those stars. Don't they look as if they were single diamonds and sapphires? Well, you can imagine any mad botany or geology you please. Think of forests of adamant with leaves of brilliants. Think the moon is a blue moon, a single elephantine sapphire. But don't fancy that all that frantic astronomy would make the smallest difference to the reason and justice of conduct. On plains of opal, cut out of pearl, you would still find a notice-board, 'Thou shalt not steal'...[30]

I cite there an example forced on Chesterton by his plot, that is not necessarily the gravest instance of a 'negative exceptionless norm' he could have named.

Human beings are not, however, pure intellects who make their choices by 'just registering values calmly and changing course accordingly', but 'emotional creatures, which can act

---

[29] J. Finnis, *Moral Absolutes. Tradition, Revision, and Truth* (Washington 1991), pp. 20–21.

[30] G. K. Chesterton, 'The Blue Cross', in idem, *The Penguin Complete Father Brown* (Harmondsworth 1981), p. 20.

only when [they] are moved'.[31] The *Catechism* cannot avoid the subject of the 'morality of the passions', which means, in this context, not the erotic haze beloved of Hollywood but

> emotions or movements of the sensitive appetite that incline us to act or not to act in regard to something felt or imagined to be good or evil.[32]

In less scholastic, more imagistic language, they are the 'passage-way' which ensures intercommunication between the life of the senses and the life of the mind.[33] Love and hatred, desire and fear, joy, sadness, anger: all may contribute powerfully to both good and evil action, and so the moral life is not confined to the working of rational will, sun-lit and transparent even when wrong, but reaches down to the obscure springs of action, sited far from intellectual day. Emotions and feelings 'can be taken up into the virtues, or perverted by the vices' (topics with which the *Catechism* will shortly deal *expressis verbis*). Indeed, without well-tempered passions which, where relevant, means strong ones, no one could be perfect. The incarnate Word could not have shown forth the divine perfection in human terms therefore, had he not mustered both negative and positive affect in the service of his mission. Here as elsewhere, the economy of the Spirit extends to those who are agents 'in Christ' aspects of the vocation of the Son.

> In the Christian life, the Holy Spirit himself accomplishes his work by mobilizing the whole being, with all its sorrows, fears and sadness, as is visible in the Lord's agony and passion. In Christ human feelings are able to reach their consummation in charity and divine beatitude.[34]

Conscience

And if on these points the *Catechism* is tributary to the baptised humanism of a Thomistically transformed Aristotelianism, on

---

[31]M. Midgley, *Wickedness. A Philosophical Essay* (London 1984), p. 81.
[32]Paragraph 1763.
[33]Paragraph 1764.
[34]Paragraph 1769.

its next topic, that of conscience, it has to confront a question more prominent in ethics after Kant. Essentially, the authors of the *Catechism* had to walk a tightrope between on the one hand a hyper-inflated 'oracular' view of conscience, tantamount to treating it as virtually the personal revelation of God (a 'revelation', however, remarkably careless of the law of contradiction, when one thinks of the many opposing things people claim conscience 'tells' them to do); and, on the other hand, a grossly deflated theory of conscience which would make of it just a synonym for the moral judgment and so of no particular authority whatever. They proceed by integrating elements of both of these accounts, one of which sins by excess and the other by defect, into a picture more adequate than either of them.

Conscience is authority-bearing for the moral life; but it also stands in need of sound formation. The Munich philosopher Robert Spaemann explains each in turn. First, conscience is

> the focal point of an absolute perspective in a finite being, the means by which this perspective is anchored in that being's emotional structure. It is because of this presence of the universal, the objective, the absolute, in the individual person that we talk of human dignity; there is no other reason. So if it is through conscience that man, individual man, attains to a universal status and becomes what one might call a meaningful whole, then it must follow that it is impossible for man to perceive anything as good, or as having any sense or justification, unless what is actually right and good can be revealed to him as being such by his conscience.[35]

The wider principles of morality; their instantiation in the objective good aimed at by some intelligible choice, and judgment on the concrete act whereby our will would make that good its own: all these fall, as the *Catechism* tells us, within conscience's domain.[36] And yet, as Spaemann continues:

[35]R. Spaemann, *Basic Moral Concepts* (E.t. London and New York 1989), p. 59.
[36]Paragraph 1780.

Our conscience is not always right. We cannot rely on our conscience any more than we can rely on our five senses always to lead us in the right direction, or on our reason always to preserve us from error. Conscience is a human faculty for recognising good and evil; it is not an oracle. It shows us the way, it causes us to look beyond our egoistic perspectives towards the universal and towards that which is right in itself. But reaching this viewpoint requires reflection, expertise and, if I may say so, moral expertise. This involves a correct sense of the structure of the hierarchy of values, which is not distorted by ideologies.[37]

The *Catechism* too knows of an ill-formed conscience, the unfortunate perpetrator of erroneous judgments. The two poles of conscience, the metaphysically clamant and the fallibly fragile, are not, however, implausibly disjoined, for conscience is, of its essence, *educable*.

There is no such thing as a conscience which is not prepared to submit itself to further education ...[38]

for the refusal to learn would mean only the suppression of conscience, 'bad faith'.

The *Catechism*'s own account of the lifelong task of educating conscience is, very properly, indebted to *revealed* truth which entered this world, in the form of the Logos incarnate and the Spirit of truth, the Counsellor, in order to disencumber conscience of the burdens of error and sin.

In the formation of conscience the Word of God is the light for our path (cf. Psalm 119:105); we must assimilate it in faith and prayer, and put it into practice. We must also examine our conscience before the Lord's Cross. We are assisted by the gifts of the Holy Spirit, aided by the witness or advice of others, and guided by the authoritative teaching of the Church.[39]

---

[37]Spaemann, *Basic Moral Concepts*, pp. 64–65.
[38]Ibid., p. 59.
[39]Paragraph 1785.

Although an erroneous conscience must be followed, and
inculpable ignorance on the part of such a conscience fully
exculpates, the malformation of conscience may itself be the
agent's own fault, and so, after all, return to haunt him. Not
only the bad example of others, but also factors internal to the
self can cripple the Christian conscience and invalidate its
deliverances:

> Ignorance of Christ and his Gospel, ... enslavement to
> one's passions, assertion of a mistaken notion of
> autonomy of conscience, rejection of the Church's
> authority and her teaching, lack of conversion and of
> charity: these can be at the source of errors of judgment
> on moral conduct.[40]

The virtues

It is a relief to turn from such distortions of truth and life to the
more honourable topic of the *virtues*, as the *Catechism* now
proceeds to do; though even here we should note that just
because we are capable of virtues, we are also capable of vices,
which are the defects of our qualities. The *Catechism* declares,
compendiously:

> Human virtues are firm attitudes, stable dispositions,
> habitual perfections of intellect and will that govern our
> actions, order our passions and guide our conduct
> according to reason and faith. They make possible ease,
> self-mastery and joy in leading a morally good life ...[41]

while Professor Peter Geach writes, aphoristically: 'Men need
virtues to effect whatever men are for.'[42]

In St Thomas' perspective, that a thing should reach its
proper perfection is both God's will for it and its own way of
reaching God. But the instinct for God which carries a human
being, via a certain self-transcendence, towards the supreme
Good (the 'natural desire for God') is not by itself enough to

[40]Paragraph 1792.
[41]Paragraph 1804.
[42]P. Geach, *The Virtues* (Cambridge 1977), p. 13.

teach man what his end is, much less to lead him to pursue it. Our responsibility lies in acting so as to attain the end once it is seen. While some dispositions may be innate, for some people are better temperamentally endowed in this or that respect than others, most dispositions are, by contrast, the result of the agent's own activity. When we reflect, our reasoning affects the faculty of desire, generating dispositions in the will and the sensory appetite. For Plato, accordingly, virtue comes upon us as a kind of reward for our exercise of morally disciplined attention. Virtuous habits can never be compulsive or impulse-ridden inclinations; they are, rather, the tendency to perform right acts where moral reason would call for them. Thanks to the virtues – as the *Catechism* points out with its refreshingly anti-Puritan emphasis on how *facile*, in the best sense of that word, the moral life ought ideally to be – we can have such things as virtuous passions. Even at the level of physiological engagement, we – that is, our bodies – can be the subject of virtues.

Virtues cardinal

The *Catechism* singles out a quartet of natural virtues known to the pagans, and a trio of supernatural ones which structure specifically Christian morality. And first the quartet. Prudence, justice, fortitude and temperance are the virtues which the Catholic moral tradition calls 'cardinal' or 'hinge-like', since so much of the good life turns on them.

   Prudence is practical wisdom, Aristotle's *phronēsis*; in terms native to the Jewish-Christian revelation, it can be considered as the human image of divine providence, for it inclines us in the choice of right means of action to our proper end. Without it, no other moral virtue could truly be exercised. For example, the virtue of mercy bids us help the needy, but only prudence tells us how and when to do so. Likening it, in a metaphor drawn from the ancient world, to a charioteer steering his vehicle and horses, the *Catechism* describes prudence as guiding the virtuous life by 'setting rule and measure'.[43]

---

[43]Paragraph 1806.

Justice moves us to give others their due – what is *debitum*, 'owed' to them, on whatever ground. The just person sanctions another in his or her very separateness (which is why there can be no formal justice between those who love, precisely because the loved one is not in every sense 'someone else'). In its brief account, the *Catechism* singles out the duty of justice towards the Creator God, exercised as the virtue of religion whereby we give God the worship that rightly belongs to him, and also towards other men, whether as unique persons or as composing a common life with its own good. Here the text looks ahead to huge swathes of intellectual and moral territory which its remaining sections on fundamental morals as well as several of those devoted to the Ten Words will have occasion to survey.

Fortitude is the virtue that urges us to action where we would otherwise – and unreasonably – be apt to shrink from action because of difficulties foreseen. In C. S. Lewis' *Screwtape Letters* a senior devil regrets the infernal campaign's comparative lack of success in pillorying courage, since the Enemy so made the world that its very afflictions point up courage's splendour. However, the virtue of fortitude is not present where affliction is endured, or danger faced, for the sake of a cause worthless or vicious. As the *Catechism* maintains, the laying down of one's life is the supreme instance of fortitude, but this must be for a *just* cause (or, one can add, a *true* belief).

Temperance rounds off the foursome. Of all the cardinal virtues, temperance is the only one whose practice is restricted to rational creatures that are simultaneously animals with bodily needs and appetites, and it belongs to the man who in such matters follows a golden mean. The temperate person directs his sensory appetites towards what is good, explains the *Catechism*, for temperance 'keeps desires within the limits of what is honourable'.[44] And if temperance seems a somewhat unexciting virtue (few will be tempted to an intemperate enthusiasm for its exercise), Pieper sounds a useful warning-note against its underestimation when he writes:

> The very powers of the human being which most readily appear as the essential powers of self-preservation,

[44] Paragraph 1809.

self-assertion and self-fulfilment are at the same time the first to work the opposite: the self-destruction of the moral person.[45]

As St Thomas explains, the most natural of all our activities are those which preserve the individual (eating, drinking) and the species (mating). Since pleasure follows from congenial activity, the more spontaneous our desires the stronger the pleasure they afford. All our pleasures, however, if they are to befit our human nature, should be instinct with rationality; not in the sense that, rather than enjoy things properly we simply think about them instead, but in the sense that to enjoy things in a human way is to enjoy them in that mode, quantity and degree which befits what we are and what they are, given the objective condition of man in the world before God. Both the *Catechism,* and the text from Augustine's *On the Customs of the Catholic Church* which it cites, link the old pagan decency which is *temperantia* with the biblical concept of discretion, much developed by the Fathers under the heading 'the discernment of spirits'.

It is, in fact, a general feature of the *Catechism*'s treatment of the cardinal virtues to suggest, albeit allusively, the transformation they undergo when brought into the ambit of revealed religion. These dispositions acquired by practice when put in contact with the theological virtues of faith, hope and charity (the *Catechism*'s next subject) are touched by grace: there can be an aspect of them which is not so much acquired as *infused.* 'Actual' grace – a helping hand from God – is in any case needful, in our debilitated post-lapsarian state, for the persevering practice of even the basic decencies, and so the *Catechism* rightly reminds its readers that the context of the good life is prayer and sacramental reception, thus showing Neo-Pelagianism to the door.

Virtues theological

It is the distinctive feature of the theological virtues that, as their name suggests, they connect us directly with God. In the *Catechism*'s words:

[45]J. Pieper, *Fortitude and Temperance* (E.t. London 1955), p. 56.

They dispose Christians to live in a relationship with the Holy Trinity. They have the One and Triune God for their origin, motive and object.[46]

Faith, hope and charity have already taken their bow on the *Catechism*'s stage. The sub-book on the Creed could hardly have got under way without reference to faith, which, the authors point out, cannot attain full growth without the charity through which it works, and the hope in which it abounds.[47] Again, the sub-book on the sacraments spoke of Baptism, the sacrament of faith, as the covenanted occasion when, for the 'normal' case *anno Domini*, in the era of our redemption, the theological virtues are first engrafted onto the root-stock of a life.[48] But if faith has already received a rich treatment, at once epistemological, anthropological, soteriological and eschatological,[49] its figure must be recalled by a few deft brushstrokes and set beside its sister virtues, hope and love. Believing as very truth all the declarations God had made known to us in revelation, we also believe *in* him, since those declarations include promises for our everlasting weal, our salvation, and, thus believing, we seek to do his will, such that faith apart from works, in the words of St James (2:26) is but a cadaver. Shorn of hope and love, faith does not render the believer a *living* member of Christ's Body, and hence unites her to him only in imperfect fashion. This is not to say, however, that the *Catechism* in any way plays down those human acts in which faith comes directly into play, rather than indirectly, by way of related forms of goodness. The confident profession of faith is requisite, and failure to acknowledge Christ before men deprives of the Father's salvation (cf. Matthew 10:32–33). And if it seems strange to give the act of faith a constitutive place in morals, it has to be remembered that the *telos* – the end or goal – of human life is the loving knowledge of almighty God. Will, whereby we tend to our

[46]Paragraph 1812.
[47]Paragraph 162.
[48]Paragraph 1266.
[49]See my *The Splendour of Doctrine*, pp. 27–31.

goal, is a rational appetite which cannot be redirected – as in a world like our own that lies in wickedness must be the case – without some fresh light in the understanding.

The *Catechism* offers a fuller account of hope and love in the moral context; or rather, in the English-language version, hope and *charity*, for the Australian translators have made a valiant attempt to return to currency that word for the distinctively New Testament love of God and neighbour which dared to speak its name only on the basis of the missions of the Son and Spirit. Hope, as described commodiously by the *Catechism*'s authors, is:

> the theological virtue by which we desire the Kingdom of heaven and eternal life as our own happiness, placing our trust in Christ's promises and relying not on our own strength, but on the help of the grace of the Holy Spirit.[50]

It apprehends a good end, accordingly, after the fashion of those outside an earthly story, not those within it. As Professor Peter Geach has written:

> There can barely be a hope for an individual to attain his end, except after this life in a new life; and there is not the least ground for hoping for such a new life except for God's promise of new life in the Kingdom that is to come. This or nothing.

And Geach goes on, not merely inserting the knife in the wound of secularism but twisting it:

> There is no hope for men corporately either, except the promise of the Kingdom. Men in power are not to be trusted; man is a wild animal and cannot tame himself. This is the lesson of Original Sin, taught over and over again by experience in spite of all wishful thinking ... Of what Scripture calls the kingdom of men there is no hope. In contrast to this, Scripture tells us, there was and shall again be the Kingdom of God.[51]

---

[50]Paragraph 1817.
[51]Geach, *The Virtues*, pp. 64–65.

But if what the virtue of hope disposes us to strive for without wavering cannot itself be rationally demonstrated (for the call of Abraham and the consequent election of Israel, the purification of the messianic hope in the promises of the Beatitudes, and their proleptic realisation in the exaltation of the crucified Messiah at Easter lie beyond reason, in the sheer uncalculating love of God), the fruits of theological hope in human lives can be registered nonetheless. Such hope for heaven is no pale velleity. Rather, in the strength of its divine source, which has power to fit human faculties for their destiny of sharing in the divine nature, the virtue of hope

> keeps man from discouragement; it sustains him during times of abandonment; it opens up his heart in expectation of eternal beatitude. Buoyed up by hope, he is preserved from selfishness and led to the happiness that flows from charity.[52]

Charity indeed is pre-eminent in the threesome of the theological virtues: thus the apostle to the church at Corinth (I Corinthians 13:13). By charity, through a mimetic participation in the sacrificial love shown by Jesus Christ, we are called to love God above all things and our neighbour as ourselves for God's sake. The *Catechism* opens by defining charity in Johannine terms: it is an *abiding* in the love received by the Son from the Father and passed on by him to his disciples. Taking up this cue, St Thomas will call charity-love a kind of friendship based on the communication by grace of a share in the divine blessedness. This friendship is first of all with God, and then by extension with all those to whom God would distribute his blessedness, since, for the sake of a friend, we

> love those belonging to him, be they children, servants or anyone connected with him at all, even if they hurt or hate us, so much do we love him.[53]

As the 'fruit of the Spirit' and 'fullness of the Law', charity conforms itself spontaneously to the precepts of Christ which

[52]Paragraph 1818.
[53]*Summa Theologiae*, IIa., IIae., q. 23, a. 1, ad ii.

transpose the calibre of the divine love into human terms. Here Jesus singled out for the disciples' attention the enemy, the weak (the child), and the poor – surely because the inaptitude of members of these categories to reciprocate the good done from charity underlines the latter's unenvious divinity. The *Catechism* gives no comfort to a degenerate modern tendency in preaching and spiritual writing whereby charity is reduced to general benevolence, or, worse still, a tender but inefficacious affective glow. The object of charity is exclusively God and our neighbour 'that he or she may be in God' *ut in Deo sit*, as Aquinas puts it. In other words, by charity, our lives become theocentric, and an internal aspect of this is that we necessarily want other people's lives to be theocentric too, and treat them accordingly. (Animals cannot in this sense be christianly loved, since the friendship of charity cannot meaningfully be extended to them. However, God loves them with the love of charity, since he has no other love to offer, and we by charity can want them to be kept in being for God's glory, as well as for the service of man.)

The appeal to Thomas here by way of explicating the *Catechism*'s theology of love is by no means misplaced, since in speaking of charity as the *form* of the virtues, it makes a distinctively Thomist thesis its own. Though each virtue retains its proper character, charity actively interrelates the virtues in their best order and orientates them to their final end.

Charity fructifies in joy, peace and mercy: joy, because of the lover's awareness of the unchangeableness of God's goodness; peace, because the concord of those united in charity harmonises their desires and appetites in the good; and mercy because, as Thomas explains:

> to one who loves, a friend is but another self, and so he counts his friend's misfortunes as his own and grieves over them in the same way.[54]

Subterranean reference to Aquinas leads the *Catechism* to say of charity that it 'demands beneficence and fraternal correction', an apparently ill-assorted pair.

[54] STh., IIa. IIae., q. 30, q. 2, c.

Since in this moral section of its text the *Catechism* is at
its most Thomistic, it may be appropriate to draw out from
Thomas the sense of these words. Under the heading of
eleemosynia (literally 'alms-giving' but here translated
'beneficence'), Thomas would place the entire Christian
life considered as a life lived for others. For him the word
englobes the seven corporal and seven spiritual works of
mercy, the gamut of which range from, at the one end, feeding
the hungry and burying the dead, to, at the other, instructing
people in the faith and counselling them in the moral life, as
well as (Thomas realistically remarks), putting up with them,
which, he says, means not only enduring those whose disordered
conduct makes them irksome to us but also helping them with
their own burdens, whatever these may be. Although generally
speaking, the spiritual needs of our neighbour are the more
important, the corporal works of mercy may take precedence
before them in particular situations. Thus a man dying of a
thirst needs to be given water, not instructed. And in any case,
the corporal works, when looked at in their *cause* – the love of
God and our neighbour – can also be said to produce spiritual
fruit.

All this is beautifully laid out in (literally) panoramic form
in the late sixteenth-century Jesuit treatise *Icones operum
misericordiae,* a multi-media product of Counter-Reformation
ingenuity to be pondered by anyone who thinks the Church of
the Council of Trent ignorant of the 'social gospel'.[55] Though
the 'Penny Catechism' presents the *opera misercordiae*
immediately after announcing the twofold law of charity,[56] the
Catechism of the Catholic Church delays its treatment of them till
its exposition reaches the seventh commandment, where they
are set forth under the heading 'love of the poor', since all
concern coming to the aid of our neighbour in one or another
of his or her needs.[57]

As for 'fraternal correction', this is surely mentioned distinctly
because Thomas does so. Though he might well have discussed

[55] *Icones operum misericordiae, cum Julii Roscii Hortini sententiis et explicationibus*
(Rome 1585).
[56] *A Catechism of Christian Doctrine*, Nos. 321–322.
[57] Paragraph 2447.

it under the heading of 'reproving' (a spiritual work of mercy), his sources – and notably the *Rule of St Augustine* which, as a Dominican friar, he followed – made him think it too important simply to be tucked in with something else.

The *Catechism* ends its account of the virtues by referring to the pneumatic gifts and fruits which the Spirit, in the case of the gifts, pours forth so as to render our practice of virtues not only complete but delightful to us, and, in that of the fruits, draws forth so as to form in us the first-fruits of our eternal glory. It will readily be seen that gifts and fruits, taken together, compose nothing less than a portrait of sanctity. The person endowed with wisdom, understanding, counsel, fortitude, knowledge, piety, fear of the Lord, and generative of charity, joy, peace, patience, kindness, goodness, generosity, gentleness, faithfulness, modesty, self-control, chastity: this is an identikit of the saint.

Sin

The *Catechism* concludes its account of the individual person's call to goodness, grace and glory by turning, as is unfortunately necessary, to the ugly reverse of the virtues – vice, or to give wrong-doing its proper theological title, *sin*. But so as not to evict morals from their home in the dogmatic heartlands of Christian believing, it does not begin to speak about sin until it has called to mind the quality of mercy – the divine pity which pursues the sinner with a doggedness reminiscent of the hound of heaven in Francis Thompson's poem. 'Fear wist not to evade, as Love wist to pursue.'[58] But if in the words of Paul in the Letter to the Romans (5:20), 'where sin increased, grace abounded all the more', sin must declare itself for grace to be made known.

> To do its work grace must uncover sin so as to convert our hearts and bestow on us 'righteousness to eternal life through Jesus Christ our Lord' ... Like a physician who

---

[58] *Selected Poems of Francis Thompson, with a Biographical Note by Wilfrid Meynell* (London 1908; 1925), pp. 51, 52.

probes the wound before treating it, God by his Word and by his Spirit, casts a living light on sin ...[59]

with results evoked by the poet:

> Strange, piteous, futile thing
> Wherefore should any set thee love apart?
> Seeing none but I makes much of naught?[60]

It is because sin is not simply an 'offence against reason, truth and right conscience',[61] wounding human nature and injuring human solidarity, but is an offence against the God who could not truly love the good unless he shunned and hated evil, that only in theological perspective can it be seen aright. As in Thompson's ode, the *Catechism* refuses, nonetheless, to write a hamartiology, a theology of sin, that is not counterpointed by soteriology, the theology of grace. The interweaving of the two is at its most palpable in the passion of Christ, which is also the crucial resolution of the threnody of sin.

> It is precisely in the Passion, when the mercy of Christ is about to vanquish it, that sin most clearly manifests its violence and its many forms ... However, at the very hour of darkness, the hour of the prince of this world, the sacrifice of Christ secretly becomes the source from which the forgiveness of our sins will pour forth inexhaustibly.[62]

There are, so the *Catechism* points out, various ways of analysing sin, just as sins themselves are irreducibly plural in form. Moral evil has its 'natural history', a 'set of given ways in which it tends to occur in a given species'.[63] Sins are not only, however, distinct in their unlovely objects; they also differ through subverting diverse virtues, or thwarting various commands of the moral law. They may damage the honour of God, or diminish our neighbour's good, or our own. They can be spiritual or carnal; and divide into sins of commission and

[59]Paragraph 1848, with an internal citation of Romans 5:21.
[60]*Selected Poems of Francis Thompson*, p. 56.
[61]Paragraph 1849.
[62]Paragraph 1851.
[63]Midgley, *Wickedness*, p. 12.

omission; be performed, or fail to be performed, in thought or word, or deed, for they may be in the heart alone, at the root of the person, or in its manifestations, its foetid flowers. The *Catechism* following a long tradition of reflection in the Church for which it claims a beginning, indeed, as primitive as the Johannine Epistles, concentrates on the distinction between sins that weaken charity – 'venial' sins – and those that destroy it altogether – 'mortal' sins.[64]

Mortal sins cannot come to pass without the meeting of three conditions that Catholic moralists identify as gravity of matter, full knowledge (or sufficient reflection), and deliberate consent. The 'matter' of some sins is too trifling or inconsequential to count as a total rupture in the life of charity, though a corrupt civil law may decide otherwise in its determination of penalties, as when, in the opening chapter of *A Tale of Two Cities* the hangman scarcely distinguishes between

> today, taking the life of an atrocious murderer, and tomorrow, of a wretched pilferer who had robbed a farmer's boy of sixpence.[65]

However, it should be noted that some sins are serious for reasons unavailable to common or garden reflection, since their matter is grave only by way of incompatibility, brought to light by revelation, with aspects of the life of faith.[66] This is why the *Catechism* speaks of grave matter as 'specified by the Ten Commandments' where divine law embraces natural law in a broader pattern.[67] Its discussion of *full knowledge* is subtle. Sin cannot be spiritually death-dealing unless one is aware of the opposedness of what one is doing to the law of God. Yet ignorance can be feigned, as when we choose not to think about the nature of some action, and in any case no one can be deemed ignorant of the foundational principles of the moral law, which are written on the heart. Here St Thomas would

---

[64]Paragraph 1854, with an appeal to the self-evidence of this tradition in I John 5:16–17.

[65]C. Dickens, *A Tale of Two Cities*, Chapter I.

[66]G. Grisez, *The Way of the Lord Jesus.* I: *Christian Moral Principles* (Chicago 1983), pp. 391–410.

[67]Paragraph 1858.

think not only of the primordial directive of natural law, to pursue and do good, and avoid evil, which constitutes our most basic knowledge of how to form and order choices, the equivalent in the practical order to a predemonstrative knowing about how to form and order judgments in the theoretical, but also of the directives which issue from this and enjoin us to live in society, avoid ignorance and know God.[68] And the question of *complete consent* lands us in the same boat. There can be no sin – *a fortiori*, no mortal sin – that is not personally chosen (original sin, in Catholic theology, is termed such by way of analogy). Such subjective factors as the promptings of passion, or pathological disorders, which are no less objective than their counterparts in external pressures in the public world, may diminish our responsibility. Yet a person who freely adopts an immoral way of life and becomes so hardened therein that the characteristic evil acts he produces are second nature, is not thereby excused. As Professor Joseph Boyle of Toronto has noted:

> If the Church's working understanding of the responsibility needed for mortal sin is set too permissively high, then people will not be properly directed towards reforming their lives, will continue in sinful behaviour, which is harmful to the life of faith even if not culpable, and will have to hand ready rationalizations when their sinful behaviour is culpable.

Such laxism is no true remedy for a 'repugnant rigorism'.[69]

In fact, so far from being a rare comet, bursting as a nine days' wonder across the moral heavens, mortal sin is, as the *Catechism* puts it, 'a radical possibility of human freedom, as is love itself'.[70] An echo perhaps of the placard which Dante placed over the entrance to his *inferno*: 'Divine power made me and supreme wisdom, and primal love.'[71]

---

[68]P. A. Redpath, *The Moral Wisdom of Saint Thomas. An Introduction* (Lanham, MD 1983), pp. 126–127.

[69]J. Boyle, 'The Personal Responsibility required for Mortal Sin', in L. Gormally (ed.), *Moral Truth and Moral Tradition. Essays in Honour of Peter Geach and Elizabeth Anscombe* (Dublin 1994), p. 150.

[70]Paragraph 1861.

[71]*Inferno*, Canto III, lines 5–6.

Venial sin, by contrast, is, rather, a slackening in the
momentum of the Christian life, a nibbling away at the edges
of charity, not its frank negation. And yet, as the authors of the
Catechism have the pastoral wisdom to add, 'deliberate and
unrepented', it gradually inclines us in the direction of mortal
sin.[72] Take care of the venials, one might say, and the mortals
will take care of themselves.

The direst sin, in evangelical perspective, has yet to be
mentioned. 'Blasphemy against the Holy Spirit', that terrible
phrase of Jesus' in the Synoptic tradition, the *Catechism* identifies
with the deliberate refusal to accept the divine mercy. It sets the
hardened in heart on the road to eternal loss Just so, in Hans
Urs von Balthasar's theology of damnation, the dead Christ of
Holy Saturday beholds in his soul the essence of hell when he
envisages, in the Limbo of the Fathers, what contemptuous
rejection of the selfless, reckless, kenotic love of God that
descended to the depths for sinners' sakes would mean.[73]

It is an unfortunate fact, noted by the ascetic tradition, that
sinful acts create by repetition the negative counterpart of
virtuous habits. Moreover, the vices have the uncanny trick of
constituting their own kind of unity where the capital sins – the
seven deadly sins of pride, avarice, envy, wrath, lust, gluttony
and sloth – play the same sort of pivotal rôle in moral evil as the
cardinal virtues enjoy *vis-à-vis* moral good. The *Catechism* turns
from the ascetic masters to an earlier generation of catechists
when it remarks that, from the pit to which this slippery slope
leads, certain sins 'cry to heaven': murder, oppression,
defrauding the labourer, perversion of sexual powers.

In all of which things we find as sinners ready accomplices
in our fellow men and women, sons of Adam, daughters of Eve.
The world's evil can take on, as Augustine saw, a social
organisation and counterpose an anti-city, a city of the world,
impelled by cupidity and the love of domination, to the charity-
cemented City of God. It is to this social aspect of the moral life
that the *Catechism* will now attend.

[72]Paragraph 1863.
[73]See J. Saward, *The Mysteries of March. Hans Urs von Balthasar on the Incarnation
and Easter* (London 1990), pp. 105–133.

XII

*The Corporate Context**

The human vocation to be reformed into the image and likeness of God's only Son comes home to us first and foremost as a personal call, but that is not to say that it lacks pertinence for the human community at large. Of the great Latin doctor of *reformatio* it has been written:

> Just because ideally the City of God and the Church are identical and because Church reform is personal reform, St Augustine also fervently desired that at least some of the Christians comprised by the terrestrial Church live in a Christian society on earth which, though 'on pilgrimage', would correspond as closely as possible to the eternal *Civitas Dei*, to the Church in her essence ...

And Gerhard Ladner puts the question which haunts all the Church's social prophets when he asks:

> Would Augustine find on earth those *perfecti*, those *sancti*, of whose life in a *vita socialis*, in communion with the saints and angels in heaven, he speaks of in *De civitate Dei*? If there ever had been such a society, how could it be restored? Through St Augustine's whole life there runs the search for a perfect communal or societal way of Christian life.[1]

---

*=*Catechism*, Paragraphs 1877–2046.

[1] G. B. Ladner, *The Idea of Reform. Its Impact on Christian Thought and Action in the Age of the Fathers* (Cambridge, MA 1959), pp. 281–283.

The idea of a Christian society

The *Catechism* inaugurates its theology of society by implicitly declaring the holy Trinity to be its social programme:

> There is a certain resemblance between the union of the divine persons and the fraternity that men are to establish among themselves in truth and love.[2]

Speaking more philosophically, the authors go on to describe society as natural to man. It should not, then, be opposed, except relatively, to our personhood, for the latter personalises nothing other than our nature. The social should not be considered as a distraction from the personal (though only the last can be the subject of beatitude) since it is through a process of co-exchange, by social *commercium*, that the individual responds to his or her vocation, at any rate, in part. Though the *Catechism* makes the clear option to treat persons as the true ends of social organisation (rather than subjecting them to the primacy of the social whole), it does not draw the conclusion that the social nexus adds nothing to what individuals possess already. Drawing on the vocabulary of organism found useful for the philosophical definition of society in the ancient world, the Middle Ages and (especially) the Romantic conservative reaction to mechanistic or contractual theories of a characteristically Enlightenment stamp, it defines the social group as one where people are organically bonded by a unitive principle and constituted as a generation-transcending assembly, simultaneously visible and spiritual. The English (or Irish) reader can hardly fail to be reminded of the Anglo-Irish philosopher of the civic order Edmund Burke when the *Catechism* describes society as gathering up the past and preparing the future. By calling the social assembly not only visible but also spiritual, the 'heirship' and identity-enriching 'talents' which it goes on to ascribe to every child born into a particular society are, evidently, not intended as a reference to inherited property alone, but to the cultural, and so moral and intellectual goods passed down in such a society's history to

[2]Paragraph 1878.

everyone who breathes its atmosphere. That is not to say, however, that access to the shared cultural patrimony should not be facilitated by human art; though the appeal of the *Catechism* at this point to the Lucan parable of the talents places the emphasis less on the notion of the 'right' to such access and more on the 'duty' of making good use of it.

By switching from the singular 'society' to the plural 'communities' in the course of its opening section on the 'communal character of the human vocation', the *Catechism* alerts us to the fact that is not speaking exclusively, or even particularly, of the State. The person owes 'loyalty' to more than one community, and 'respect' to the authority encharged with the oversight of the common good in each. Of such communities, only two are absolutely necessary – the family, and the State – but a host of others are, we hear, eminently desirable. Without the multifarious associations economic, social, cultural, recreational, charitable, that make up civil society, the individual, despite the community of the family, and of the State, has too few opportunities to practise initiative and responsibility. In more sinister language, the *Catechism* adds that these intermediate communities of civil society help to guarantee his or her 'rights', since, as the example of Central-Eastern Europe in the Communist era suggests, the family, faced with a partisan State which has deliberately golloped down civil society into either its *étatiste* stomach or its Party maw, will be too weak to defend the individual on its own. (Evidently, even an association of families for the defence of the family institution is itself an instance of specifically civil-social community.)

The principle of 'subsidiarity', much appealed to in Catholic social teaching, states that, in the words of Pope John Paul II:

> a community of a higher order should not interfere in the internal life of a community of a lower order, depriving the latter of its functions, but rather should support it in case of need and help to co-ordinate its activity with the activities of the rest of society, always with a view to the common good.[3]

---

[3] *Centesimus Annus* 48, 4, cited Paragraph 1883.

By grounding this desideratum in an evocation of the style of God's government of the world, which likewise entrusts to every creature those functions it can by nature perfectly well perform, the *Catechism* intends to ensure that the protest of the Catholic social tradition against *both* collectivism *and* anarchism will be treated as a doctrinally serious obligation on the part of both rulers and ruled.

For the *Catechism*, echoing here the teaching of another twentieth-century Roman bishop, John XXIII, human society is primarily spiritual in its *telos* or goal, and only secondarily material. The development of the potential of matter in economic life may be more foundational – for people must eat to live, but it is not what is ultimate in significance – for people do not live to eat. To paraphrase Pope John's words in terms of the 'transcendentals' – our primordial language for existence in its value-laden facticity – society should serve the access of persons to truth, goodness, and beauty.[4] Skilfully, the *Catechism* uses this teaching on the primacy of the spiritual, the personal, and even the interior (for without inner conversion to the true, the good and the beautiful: conversion of *heart*, all will be of null effect) not to depreciate the rôle of the structural processes of society, its stable yet labile, *arrangements*, but, rather, to underline them.

> The acknowledged priority of the conversion of heart in no way eliminates but on the contrary imposes the obligation of bringing the appropriate remedies to institutions and living conditions when they are an inducement to sin, so that they conform to the norms of justice and advance the good rather than hinder it.[5]

In a fallen world, 'progress' in such matters is possible only by God's grace, apprehended where social agents are moved by charity, which, so the *Catechism* provocatively declares, alone makes us capable of justice. Here its authors enter an *aide-mémoire*, reminding themselves (and their readers) that return

---

[4] Cf. John XXIII, *Pacem in terris*, 36.
[5] Paragraph 1888.

must be made to this topic if their subsequent remarks on 'participation in social life' are not to escape the meshes of a properly *theological* account of the social order.

The social template

For the ideas schematically stated under the heading of 'the person and society' in the foregoing merit some further exploration.

The *Catechism* makes its own a teaching as ancient as the New Testament Church itself when it describes authority – that quality 'by virtue of which persons or institutions make laws and give orders to men, and expect obedience from them'[6] – as God-derived. A practical advantage of such a view is its supplying a basis for the urgent requirement that those who govern should do so in the spirit of the divine governance, exercising 'in peace and gentleness' the power given to them, as the (late first century) *Prima Clementis* puts it.[7] Authority is given to men so that they may serve the legitimate good – the *common* good – of the communities committed to their charge. Social life is not possible without the recognition of authority as nurse of such a good. In addition, as St Thomas remarks, those who excel in knowledge and justice do so uselessly unless they can dedicate their gifts by some instrument for the benefit of others. The counsellors of the sovereign (be the latter individual or gathering) should always meet this 'job description'. That said, the mind of the Church can accommodate a weird and wonderful variety of political schemes: as in the mediaeval German-Roman *Reich*, kingdoms and urban republics may co-exist side by side. It is only régimes whose fundamental character is opposed to natural law, public order and the basic rights of persons that can never have her benediction.

The Church, however, is not just concerned with the overall aims of a State; she always wants to inspect the *means* whereby these aims are prosecuted: in a word policies, and not simply principles. Even when enshrined in law, morally illicit means

---

[6]Paragraph 1897.
[7]St Clement of Rome, *Letter to the Corinthians*, 61, cited Paragraph 1900.

do not bind in conscience. That is not to say, however, that
where citizens are left uncoerced, they have the duty to prevent
others from profiting by the provisions of unjust legislation.
For the rule of law itself is a good not lightly to be undermined;
'taking the law into one's own hands' is always a perilous
proceeding.

At the centre of what authority should aim at stands, for the
Catechism, the *common good*. Here our text sharply differentiates
itself from any scripture of liberalism, for which the lode-star
of law and State alike is individual autonomy, to be qualified
only when the liberty of another would suffer thereby. At the
same time, by insisting that the common good is itself oriented
in the last analysis to the good of persons (which includes,
then, the development of their nature by way of freedom), the
Catechism distances itself from all forms of collectivist thinking
likewise. The common good is meant to be fruitful in the life
of each person in the community, for their perfecting. The
common good entails a many-sided exchange, unavoidably so
when the fulness of social peace is its maximal form. Moral,
intellectual and artistic culture are aspects quite as integral as
the achievements of a system of justice, of public health,
communication, transport. Nor should the good of society be
too straitly enclosed within the concept of each single State.
The unity of the human race – a philosophical postulate
required by revelation where the message of salvation is
addressed to one and all – implies the existence of a universal
human good which the community – the 'concert' – of nations
could so order its affairs as to advance in various respects. (The
case of refugees and migrants is a well-chosen example.)

All must participate in the social co-inherence. This is not a
requirement that every citizen should study the political
columns of their daily newspaper. (Apart from any other
considerations, the *Catechism* is intended for more societies
than those where literacy – of a kind – is the norm.) In the first
place, this dictum refers to assiduity of attention in areas where
one has personal responsibility, for instance, in the education
of one's children and by 'conscientious work'. For these tasks
have ripples far beyond the breaking of the surface. And when
'social participation' does concern *public* life, one must bear in

mind how 'the manner of this participation may vary from one country or culture to another'.[8] The French monarchy of the *ancien régime*, wrote G. K. Chesterton, was based on the 'excellent principle that a cat may look at a king'.[9] The access of petitioners to a king available in a place as public as a modern park could be contrasted with the shielded remoteness of the leaders of a modern democracy. But the weightier conclusion is that, if participation is to be more than a gesture in a vaccuum, it not only needs, but makes no sense without, the vital continuity and institutional life of a social and political order. The *Catechism* pays tribute, with some words of the Second Vatican Council, to those societies which maximise the capacity of those who do desire to share in the political process. Still, its final word on 'participation in social life' breathes no easy optimism about democracy. In an age when counsels are frequently darkened, it is not run-of-the-mill politicians but philosopher-statesmen who are needed so as to provide generations to come with 'reasons for life and optimism'.[10] Not inappropriately, the *Catechism* cites those words on reaching the number that corresponds to the baleful year 1917.

'Social justice', which completes the *Catechism*'s 'template' for society as the Church would see it, does not correspond exactly to the use of that phrase in current secular discourse, since in line with the common good thinking percolating down from Scholastics and Neo-Scholastics, it refers more widely to that condition of things where both associations (civil society) and individuals (persons) can obtain what is due to their nature and (in the case of persons) to their *vocation*.

The philosophical difficulties attached to establishing the notion of the existence of rights anterior to society is well-known. In affirming such rights, the *Catechism* bases them on the dignity of the human creature, and the tacit appeal to the doctrine of creation found in those words shows up their character as paraphrase of the account of the divine imagehood in man which serves as *entrée* to the sub-book on ethics.

---

[8] Paragraph 1915.

[9] G. K. Chesterton, *What's Wrong with the World* (London 1912), p. 42.

[10] Paragraph 1917, citing *Gaudium et Spes* 31, 3.

Subsequently, in its treatment of equality, the *Catechism* will also appeal in so many words to the doctrine of the universal saving will of God, at the same time rendering the presence of the doctrine of the created image explicit. But while affirming the existence of certain human rights, the Church also wishes to unmask other alleged human rights either as bogus (the right to choose whether to permit an unborn child to live comes at once to mind), or at any rate insufficiently warranted. Indeed, the implausible expansion of rights-discourse to cover entire areas of potential human aspiration manifestly based on both the advanced state of Western economies and, all too often, a self-indulgent psychology, currently threatens to undermine the entire vocabulary of human rights altogether. In this context, the *Catechism*'s disclaimer may strike an echo from what has been termed

> a widespread dissatisfaction with the excessive individualism and materialism of rights-based interest group liberalism.[11]

But in any case the recognition of fundamental human rights – the acknowledgement, that is, of the inalienable dignity of other human beings and its entailments in various respects – does not become socially effective merely because lawmakers will have it so. Racism – the disparagement of that dignity and denial of those entailments on the ground of another's race – did not disappear in England with the passing of the Race Relations Act, since, as the *Catechism* recognises

> no legislation could by itself do away with the fears, prejudices and attitudes of pride and selfishness which obstruct the establishment of truly fraternal societies.[12]

The habitual manifestation of respect for the other as another self, *philadelphia*, is impossible without charity. Here the

---

[11] J. A. Nash, 'Catechesis for Justice and Peace in the *Catechism*', in B. L. Marthaler (ed.), *Introducing the 'Catechism of the Catholic Church'. Traditional Themes and Contemporary Issues* (Mahwah, NJ and London 1994), p. 128.

[12] Paragraph 1931.

Catechism marks the limits of what can reasonably be expected from any merely secular society. Legislation is but a barrier against barbarism; it does not convert hearts.

And if the *Catechism* shows itself sceptical of the rights industry as a panacea (while, however, providing a firm theological foundation for the central nucleus of human rights claims), it exercises a like discretion in judging that other shibboleth of modern *bien-pensant* politics, equality. For while there is such a thing as sinful inequality, where one's excess is another's deprivation of the necessities of life, and this the *Catechism* condemns without *arrière-pensées* of any kind, complete egalitarian parity is not, in its book, even a theoretically desirable, though practically impossible, ideal. Rather, the inequality of distribution of 'talents' (which can, as we have seen, be of many orders) belongs to the Creator's plan, since, with an explanatory reference to Catherine of Siena's *Dialogue*, God:

> wills that each receive what he needs from others, and that those endowed with particular 'talents' share the benefits with those who need them. These differences encourage and often oblige persons to practise generosity, kindness and sharing of goods …[13]

To this list the *Catechism* adds a quality which would scarcely have occurred to a fourteenth-century woman or man. The seemingly (but only seemingly) randomness of providential largesse should also lead *cultures* – and the term, thus used to signify particular schemes in the historical development of human powers is surely nineteenth-century in origin[14] – to open themselves to each other for their mutual enrichment. Here the *Catechism* takes up, implicitly, a position in a debate as old as the struggle between Enlightenment-driven cosmopolitanism, borne abroad on pikes by the armies of the Great Revolution of the West (1789–1815) and the Romantic nationalism which those invasive movements aroused from

---

[13]Paragraph 1937.

[14]For English, the *Oxford Dictionary* cites no example earlier than E. A. Freeman's *History of the Norman Conquest* of 1867–1876.

slumber. Yes, with the Romantics, cultures are valuable in their diversity; but No, with the Enlightenment, this must not be understood in so radical a fashion as to overthrow the unity of mankind. The *Catechism*'s solution is to regard the plurality of imperfect cultures as a providential incentive to reconstitute, by a process of reciprocal enrichment, the unity of the human race at a heightened level.

All of which shows the importance not only of subsidiarity – granting the human a local habitation and a name, for we must learn to love the primal decencies in household, village or neighbourhood, and country before we start to reform all the world – but also of its necessary corrective, the principle of *solidarity*, with which the *Catechism*'s brief theological ethics of human society comes to an end. Today one sometimes hears that the vocabulary of 'solidarity' entered Catholicism through the accident of a Polish pope conscious of the power of that word to mobilise the Christian masses in the Poland of the *Solidarność* movement. But the *Catechism*'s account begins and ends with quotations from Pope Pius XII who proclaimed the 'law of solidarity' binding all the nations into one in the apocalyptic moment of Europe's sliding into internecine war in October 1939. Solidarity is a conspicuous virtue, in that pope's teaching, since it unites not only those whose interests are the same albeit in different respects (for example, workers, or fellow-citizens). Its greatest triumph lies in bonding together those whose interests may be divergent, but who mutually adjust them for the greater good of a common cause (the nation, or, in another and even more fundamental regard, the human race as a whole). Such solidarity extends to the spiritual and supernatural order in the form of the *communio sanctorum* in a Church that is truly catholic – for all nations, and for all who are within those nations. That may sometimes bring benefits even in the temporal order, as when Christians are disinclined to wage the war of nations or classes against each other. Daringly, the authors find in the Church's achievements in this regard a proof of the word of Jesus in St Matthew's Gospel, 'Seek first his kingdom and his righteousness, and all these things shall be yours as well' (6:33).

Grace and morals

Pius XII gave a strictly soteriological, if additional, justification for the 'law of solidarity' when he described it as

> sealed by the sacrifice of redemption offered by Jesus Christ on the altar of the Cross to his heavenly Father, on behalf of sinful humanity.[15]

It was because the original draft of the *Catechism* contained an ethics too independent of the doctrine of salvation that it was decided to rework it wholly, and, in particular, to reserve for it the *Catechism's* fullest exposition of the theology of grace. As Archbishop Jean Honoré of Tours, the architect of the *Catechism's* fundamental morals, put it:

> While the [draft] Catechism succeeded in expressing the call to follow the Gospel and aim at perfection, it did not show (or at least not sufficiently) that this quest can only be accomplished by the baptized with the help of the gratuitous grace that heals and absolves them from sin and supports them along the way. In brief, because it had not been stated fully or with sufficient clarity, it was not immediately obvious that whatever Christians do in the order of salvation and holiness, they do not *do alone, but only with divine assistance.* In their effort to grow in virtue, all Christians, even the greatest saints, are justified and saved sinners.[16]

It chimes with a marked tendency of the pontificate of John Paul II that the authors of the *Catechism,* and their counsellors, wished to bring the natural law tradition of ethical reflection, which the Church, since the time of the early Apologists, has made her own, into the closest possible integration with evangelical and Catholic truth. The difficulty is that, where this process is allowed to come to full term, and ethics are entirely re-worked in the light of soteriological, Christological and even trinitarian doctrine, the Church ceases to have a vocabulary

[15]Paragraph 1939.
[16]J. Honoré, 'Reflections on the *Catechism of the Catholic Church, 11*', *L'Osservatore Romano,* 12 May 1993. Italics in original.

in which to recall those who are confessedly non-believers to the basic verities of the good life. And such power of address to all men of good will on the great and indispensable decencies is not something lightly to be surrendered. (Theologically considered, its possibility is a function of the mission of the angels who seek to clarify by their radiance the intelligence of every human creature, on the basis of nature, not Baptism, though at the same time the holy angels hold their own being and mission in dependence on the eternal Word who became man in Christ.)

What is needed, then, is a differentiated unity of an ethics of nature with an ethics of grace, where the latter holds a superordinate position *vis-à-vis* the former without, however, depriving that natural law component of all autonomy. (The call of theology to integrate philosophy within itself, whilst preserving the latter in its relative independence is the model: theological reason in its 'practical' mode must take its cue from the acting of its 'pure' counterpart.) Accordingly, the *Catechism* begins its account of the interrelation of law and grace by echoing the Sapiential Books of the Old Testament – the natural theology of the Hebrews. The moral law is, from first to last, in all its dispensations from creation to Christ, the 'work of divine Wisdom'.[17] The Wisdom of God is the single source of all law, whether this be the natural law, the revealed law of the Old Testament, or that New Testament law whose norm is Jesus Christ and whose primary vehicle is his Spirit. Even the civil and canon laws, where these are rightly framed, draw their justice, their *rectitudo*, from the rightness of divine Wisdom.

Before presenting the charter of the natural moral law, the *Catechism* establishes the theologically crucial point that

> The moral law finds its fulness and its unity in Christ. Jesus Christ is in person the way of perfection. He is the end of the law, for only he teaches and bestows the justice of God.[18]

[17]Paragraph 1950.
[18]Paragraph 1953.

'Christian ethics', wrote Hans Urs von Balthasar, 'must be modelled on Jesus Christ'.[19] They can be so modelled without prejudice to the continuing significance of the law inscribed on human hearts at the creation because, in the words of a student of Balthasar's own ethical contribution:

Man is one who awaits a Word that he cannot invent for himself, despite the thirst for the Absolute which haunts him. The norm of the Good inscribed in the nature of the first Adam orients him towards a gift and a renunciation of himself whose definitive measure is found in the second Adam. Balthasar does not fall into the 'christological narrowness' ... of Karl Barth because his doctrine of the analogy of being defends precisely the proper consistency of human nature even if it remains relative.[20]

In other words, just because the being of the creation which must include, then, the moral reason of mankind, was predisposed from the beginning by the grace of God towards the definitive revelation of God in Jesus Christ as its true centre and goal, the pattern of being of the world, and of ourselves within it, has from the outset constituted a provisional *but not for that reason misleading* sketch of the coming fulness in Christ. The natural law, consequently, cannot be the *whole* of Christian ethics, but it must be *part* of Christian ethics, awaiting its assumption by Christ so that its full implications may be known. The analogy of being in the cosmos and in man finds its fulfilment in the Word incarnate, who is, in his very selfhood, the living analogy of being. He holds the uncreated and the created together in his unique hypostasis, thus joining divine love to human freedom so as to become for us the 'concrete categorical imperative' – our ethical marching orders in person.

[19]H. U. von Balthasar, 'Nine Propositions on Christian Ethics', in J. Ratzinger, H. Schürmann, H. U. von Balthasar, *Principles of Christian Morality* (E.t. San Francisco 1986), I. 1.
[20]M. Ouellet, S.S., 'The Foundations of Christian Ethics according to Hans Urs von Balthasar' in D. L. Schindler (ed.), *Hans Urs von Balthasar. His Life and Work* (San Francisco 1991), translation slightly amended.

Of the natural moral law itself, the *Catechism* remarks, by way of summary of the classical doctrine, that it is termed 'natural':

> not in reference to the nature of irrational beings [i.e. what we have in common with the rest of the material creation], but because reason which decrees it properly belongs to human nature.[21]

Here we must be careful not to mistake the authors' meaning. *Recta ratio*, 'right reason' – to use Cicero's phrase which, following a long tradition of Christian humanism, the *Catechism* adopts in full consciousness of its pagan source – must evaluate all that we are, and the entirety of our environment. It is because human reason, limpid with the light of understanding placed in man by the Creator, *is* at home in our nature, itself related to the wider world around us, that judgments of reason can *also* extend to the significance of our bodiliness (and the lives of the other animals likewise, in their relation to ourselves).

The *Catechism* emphasises the universal extension of the natural law – there is no human being from whose heart its basic principles are absent, or to whose dignity they can fail to relate. It also stresses its abiding validity, which is of a culture- and generation-transcending kind. Through the 'variations of history', it subsists under the flux of ideas and customs, and supports their progress.[22] Essentially, then, the natural moral law has to do with the generality of our nature in its springing up from the wells of the divine creative act. As one Thomistic scholar has put it:

> We are not pure persons, but persons in human nature, and it is our nature which determines what kind of thing we are and what kind of actions we can perform. Without this reference we may speak in poetry, and yet not enter into an exchange of ideas with others; the apostolic function of theology would amount to no more than rhetoric. Now theology is a *civilis conversatio*, and this, as in

[21]Paragraph 1955.
[22]Paragraph 1958.

social life, requires agreement about norms which apply to what we have in common with others, namely our 'nature', not to what makes us distinct. The immediate interest does not lie in the springs of our personal activity, but in its specifically human structure we share in common with others, a structure which will be right by its 'lawfulness' in relation to a measure impersonally applied to all.[23]

The natural moral law specifies the distinctively human good at which human nature, with all its powers, instinctively aims, but which it cannot reach without the assisting interposition of rationality and freedom, mind and will. It does so by the formation of precepts which will govern right behaviour on a variety of aspects of life; and here, as the *Catechism* readily concedes, the question of its *application* to changing life conditions requires all the delicacy of which prudence is capable.[24] Yet all the goods which those precepts would identify and defend are themselves united in one utterly unchanging Good – the vision of God as the integral human fulfilment which is the true end of the human person.[25] It is to the validity of these deliverances of natural law that the Catholic Christian is committed when he or she enters the fray of civic debate on basic moral issues in society.

The *Catechism*'s treatise on fundamental morals does not itself tell us what whose precepts are: its exegesis of each of the Ten Commandments will do that. Instead, it claims on behalf of the *naturalia legis* – the deliverances of that law – a perpetual power of reviviscence. Even if men reject the natural law in its very principles, they will not eradicate it from the heart. It will

[23]T. Gilby, O.P., 'Natural Law', in idem, (ed.), *St Thomas Aquinas, Summa Theologiae, Volume 28. Law and Political Theory* (London 1966), pp. 167–168.
[24]Paragraph 1957.
[25]B. M. Ashley, O.P., 'What is the End of the Human Person? The Vision of God and Integral Human Fulfilment', in Gormally, *Moral Truth and Moral Tradition*, pp. 68–96. An important article defending the unity of the moral life, and so of all distinctively human aspiration, in the vision of God. That is assumed, one may say, by everything the *Catechism* will teach in its concluding section of spirituality: cf. Paragraph 2548.

rise again, both in individuals and societies: one thinks of Peter Geach's example of the Viking named 'Bairnsfriend' because he would not 'share in the popular sport of tossing infants from spearpoint to spearpoint'.[26] And so the natural moral law:

> provides revealed law and grace with a foundation prepared by God and in accordance with the work of the Spirit.[27]

But because without that revelation the natural law is *both* an incomplete reflection of the Creator's gracious will for his creatures in history *and*, to fallen creatures, known only with difficulty, uncertainty, and admixture of error, a *further* stage in the manifestation of divine truth to the moral sensibility of man is requisite indeed.

The words of St John's Prologue: 'The law was given through Moses; grace and truth came through Jesus Christ' (1:17) set the tone for what will follow. The Mosaic law contained many truths available to reason, yet by affirming them within the covenant of salvation it added something more. As the introduction to the treatise of Thomas on the Old Law in the Cambridge *Summa Theologiae* has it:

> Although the Old Law contained, over and above the universally binding principles of the Natural Law, certain special precepts applicable to the Jews alone, and designed for their special sanctification as the people of election and promise ..., still it has a permanent value even now that its binding force as law has been abrogated by the new dispensation of grace, because it foreshadows Christ and so deepens our knowledge of him. In this sense it is meant for the sanctification of us all, Gentiles as well as Jews.[28]

By presaging Christ's liberation of man from sin, providing images for the new life in the Spirit, and suffering reorientation,

---

[26]Geach, *The Virtues*, p. 32.
[27]Paragraph 1960.
[28]D. Bourke, 'Introduction', to idem and A. Littledale (eds.), *St Thomas Aquinas, Summa Theologiae, Volume 29, The Old Law* (London 1969), pp. xiv–xv.

via the wisdom writers and the prophets, to a new covenant, and the fulness of the Kingdom, the Torah is itself *praeparatio evangelica*, a preparation for the gospel. But what, then, of the Pauline teaching that the law remains nonetheless a 'law of bondage'? The *Catechism*'s explanation rehearses perfectly that given by Aquinas, showing yet again, if more evidence were needed, the indebtedness of this ethical sub-book at large to the Angel of the Schools. Like a tutor, the law showed what must be done. It restrained men from following their disordered inclinations and from idolatrous cultus, directing them rather to the worship of the one true God and the practice of justice and charity towards their neighbour. But it could not give the strength – the grace of the Spirit, as the *Catechism* paraphrases that word – to meet its own demands. In this sense, it revealed the deep-rootedness of sin from the Fall on. And yet it remains a 'first stage on the way to the Kingdom',[29] or what the Scholastics would call a subordinate cause of salvation. The Torah:

> removes the dispositions in man which are hostile to the reception of grace and binds the Jews to whom it is directed into a single community united in the worship of the one true God and the expectation of the fulfilment of the promise made to their forefather, Abraham.[30]

Christ is thus the 'end' (*telos*) of the law (Romans 10:4), not least in the Aristotelian sense of its final cause, the preordained goal to whom a principal Agent, God, is directing it beyond what any of the subordinate agents involved could have achieved by their own power.

In company with St Augustine, the *Catechism* centres its account of the New Law *qua* teaching on Jesus' Sermon on the Mount, the *Sermo Domini* of Augustine's influential commentary. Yet first and foremost, the New Law is not an exercise in didacticism at all. Rather is it that dispensation of the Spirit which defines the New Covenant; and this must mean the Spirit of the crucified and risen Christ overflowing from Jesus'

[29]Paragraph 1963.
[30]Bourke, 'Introduction', p. xv.

glorified manhood onto his corporate Body, the disciples of the Church. Here the *Catechism* brings together its dogmatic teaching on the economies of Son and Spirit in its first sub-book, on the Creed, with its account of the sacramental mysteries in its second sub-book, on the Liturgy, and links these with its account, in the sub-book now under consideration, of the place of Jesus' teaching in the New Law:

> The New Law is the grace of the Holy Spirit given to the faithful through faith in Christ. It works through charity; it uses the Sermon on the Mount to teach us what must be done, and makes use of the sacraments to give us the grace to do it.[31]

As prophet of the good life, Jesus is an ethical maximalist. But everything turns on how such 'perfection' should be understood. Jesus reaffirms the validity of the Ten Words, the foundational pillars of the moral life registered in inspired fashion by Moses on Sinai, but arising still more primordially (as we have seen) from the created pattern inscribed in the being of the human animal by its Maker. In the Sermon on the Mount, however, Jesus transforms the ethos of the law, the spirit in which these commands are to be received. The Beatitudes, in privileging such dispositions as humility, penitence, mercy, peacefulness, purity of heart, vulnerability for righteousness' sake, propose a new manner in which to obey the commandments, and so define ethical holiness in a novel, distinctively *evangelical*, way. For these qualities express, in a form appropriate to fallen creatures, their own archetypes in the attributes ascribed to God – his patient mercy and flaming justice – all summed up by the *Catechism* in a single phrase: the 'divine generosity',[32] for *both* mercy *and* justice are generous responses. Not that the life consequent on the New Law can be wholly expressed in moral terms alone: the *Catechism* takes the opportunity to speak here of the importance of prayer, fasting and almsgiving. And though, once the decision was made to allot a fourth and final sub-book to 'Christian

[31]Paragraph 1966.
[32]Paragraph 1968.

Prayer', the ascetical and mystical aspects of the specifically Christian dispensation were naturally allotted to the *Catechism*'s conclusion, we should bear in mind that Christian ethics is, in practice, inseparable from ascetic effort.

> The aim of asceticism is to transfigure our impersonal natural desires and needs into manifestations of the free personal will which brings into being the true life of love ... Asceticism checks the rebellion of our material nature and does not allow nature to become an end in itself – a second purpose within creation, different from that unique end which is the personal hypostasis of life, our participation in the life of trinitarian communion.[33]

Fasting, sexual continence, the participation of the body in prayer, humbling acts of service to others – all these play their necessary part in the restoration of God's overcast image in man to its primordial beauty.

The law of the Gospel, for the *Catechism*, is contained in a nutshell: and the sweet nut is the agapeic command, 'Love one another as I have loved you' (John 15:17). This is the *vita nuova* of charity which Augustine identifies with the 'new song' called for the Book of Psalms (149:1).

> Anyone who knows how to love the new life knows how to sing the new song. So for the sake of the new song we need to be reminded what the new life is. All these things, you see, belong to the one kingdom – the new person, the new song, the new testament or new covenant. So the new person will both sing the new song and belong to the new covenant ... The praise of the one to be sung about is the singer himself. Do you want to sing God his praises? Be yourselves what you sing. You are his praise if you lead good lives.[34]

To plot the contours of that good living in New Testament terms we are not, however, restricted to the gospel. The

---

[33]C. Yannaras, *The Freedom of Morality* (E.t. Crestwood, NY 1984), p. 110.

[34]*Sermon* 34, 1 and 6, in *The Works of Saint Augustine*, Part III: Sermons, II, translated by E. Hill, O.P. (Brooklyn, NY 1990), pp. 166, 168.

Catechism points to the rôle of moral catechesis in the apostolic preaching, thereby, implicitly, justifying the presence within its own pages of the topics now under discussion. The apostolic letters do indeed present a regular pattern in these matters. First, the convert to the faith is enjoined to abandon various vices recognised as such elsewhere in the ancient world – an important link to the law-of-nature idea. Next, he or she is invited to develop some typical virtues of the Christian life: gentleness, humility, generosity, purity, the readiness to forgive. Characteristically, the neophyte is then advised of the need to deal uprightly with one's pagan neighbours, to obey the lawfully constituted (State) authority (though without prejudice to the integrity of the faith), and he or she is reminded of the specially onerous time in which we now live: the 'last age' with its attendant responsibilities. The *Catechism* concentrates on the central panel of this triptych, doubtless considering that such virtues see off all vices, though it also refers to the paradigmatic way the apostles attempted to resolve hard cases or respond to 'limit situations' in the light of the twofold mystery of Christ and the Church. Faced with the modern invasion into conscience-formation of secular factors of an unevangelised kind, the authors of the *Catechism* can here be taken to sigh with Moses in the Book of Numbers (11:29), 'Would that *all* the Lord's people were prophets'!

In characterising the New Law as a law of love, grace and freedom, the *Catechism* may be said to remind us of how these qualities can cease to attach to Christian practice, as the old Adam puts in an unwelcome appearance in the forms of their opposites: fear, self-reliance and a mind-set dominated by rite and rote impervious to all spontaneity. At the same time, we can reflect how all that glitters is not gold: love, grace and freedom have, alas, their beguiling counterfeits, sentimental, anti-nomian, self-indulgent. Fittingly, then, the section on grace and morals is rounded off by a discussion of the evangelical counsels (poverty, chastity, obedience) which express better than anything else in the New Testament the exigence of charity, how its demands on us are *semper maior*, always seeking that we should give the more. If the precepts (or commandments) are incumbent on all Jesus' disciples, since they aim at the elimination of whatever is contrary to charity, the counsels go further by removing in addition whatever could hinder charity's perfect development (in other words, all the complexities of an encumbered life in the world). The way of the monk, or the consecrated virgin, is the more direct way, with the readier means. Though the *Catechism* passes over in silence (or, more probably, was composed too early to profit by) Pope John Paul II's suggestion in *Splendor Veritatis*, his encyclical on fundamental morals, that precepts and counsels are united in that the spirit of the latter must penetrate the exercise of the former for everyone in the Church,[35] its authors are conscious of the problem raised. Their solution is that of the seventeenth-century Catholic reformer and patron of writers Francis de Sales: it is charity itself which determines, as the concrete form of the will of God, who should keep which counsel as 'times, opportunities and strengths' may allow

> for it is charity, as queen of all virtues, all commandments, all counsels, and, in short, of all laws and all Christian actions, that gives to all of them their rank, order, time and value.[36]

Although the *Catechism* has already had occasion to touch on the infused aspect of the moral life – the sense in which moral performance originates in God himself – it has so far concentrated, despite the heading of 'Law and Grace', on what we are to do, rather than how we are to do it. Now it must investigate the grace of God in its own right: it would be ambiguous to say 'for its own sake', since grace is always for *our* sake. Its account unfolds in terms of two principal concepts, justification and sanctification, with emphasis on the fruits of the latter in meritorious deed and personal holiness. These furnish – as apt closing citations from the most heaven-oriented of the saints, Thérèse of Lisieux, and the most eschatologically minded book of Scripture, the Revelation of St John, illustrate – a foretaste of glory. Christian ethics is a proleptic eschatology.

---

[35] *Splendor Veritatis*, 16–24.
[36] *Treatise on the Love of God*, VIII. 6, cited Paragraph 1974.

Whether translucent or opaque, behaviour has windows that open onto heaven or, frosted, shut heaven out.

The ethical relevance of justification (once the latter is seen, with the Catholic tradition dogmatised at Trent as intrinsic, and not imputed only) is patent from the *Catechism*'s opening definition:

> The grace of the Holy Spirit has the power to justify us, that is, to cleanse us from our sins and to communicate to us 'the righteousness of God through faith in Jesus Christ' and through Baptism.[37]

Our justification means first of all our forgiveness and consequently – so radical is sin – our regeneration.

This comes about, so the *Catechism* explains, as a result of our participation in the paschal mystery of Christ. Completing in his atoning work what he had initiated in his incarnation, he changed places with the guilty. By a 'marvellous exchange' – the *mirabile commercium* of the Roman liturgy – he who knew no sin was 'made' sin so that in him we 'might become the righteousness of God' (II Corinthians 5:21).

Justification implies conversion, and so *repentance* as the *Catechism* now underlines. He who worked out our salvation in the cosmic acts of the assumption of our nature by the Logos, also struggled and suffered for us in his (now humanly energising) person. Our salvation cannot simply rest, then, on the objective metaphysic of the new life of grace communicated to us by the Church in her sacraments: I am called on personally to turn toward God and away from sin, by a heartfelt and demanding change of life whose force is admirably captured in Andrew of Crete's *Great Canon*:

> Have mercy upon me, O God, have mercy upon me. I
> have crusted over with passion the beauty of the Image.
> But seek me like the piece of silver, Saviour, and find
> me. Have mercy upon me, O God, have mercy upon
> me. I cry like the Harlot, I only have sinned, I have
> sinned against thee. Saviour, accept now my tears like
> hers as ointment. Have mercy upon me, O God, have

---

[37]Paragraph 1987, with an internal citation of Romans 3:22.

> mercy upon me. I have sinned like David and waxed
> wanton, and am deep in the mire. But wash me also,
>   Saviour, clean with my tears.

Such repentance entails the acceptance of forgiveness and 'righteousness', the acknowledgement, in the *Catechism*'s explanation, of the 'rectitude of divine love'.[38] Through God's merciful initiative, faith, hope and charity flood the heart, which, as in the prophecy of Ezekiel – 'I will give you a new heart and a new spirit I will put within you' (36:26) – becomes able, by grace, to obey the divine will.

The efficacious sign of our personal appropriation of the salvation won in and for our nature on the cross and its manifestation in the resurrection glory is, as the sub-book of the *Catechism* on the liturgical mysteries bears witness, holy Baptism in which we become 'new creatures'.[39] Contrary to what much Protestant evangelicalism would maintain, justification cannot be duly described without reference to the sacramental life of the Church. While in the saving passion, the God-Man acts exclusively in doing what only he can do, he also acts inclusively in standing in for us as our Head: the new Adam, whose Body, the Church, was even then, on Calvary, coming into being, as the figure of Mary standing by the crucified – the *ecclesia* embodied – attests.

Yet the Church, as the corporate, public and visible counterpart of the justification that is personal, hidden, invisible in its working, could in no way co-operate with the Redeemer unless she had first been totally dependent on his saving action. Over against all forms of Pelagianism, whether thoroughgoing or merely mitigated, the *Catechism* insists with Trent that the human 'contribution' to justification can only consist in the negative moment of non-rejection. Without God's grace we cannot by free will so much as move towards the condition of integral justice in God's sight. Here, truly, *tout est grâce.*

---

[38] Paragraph 1991.

[39] Paragraph 1227, occupied chiefly as this is with the vital Pauline testimony to this doctrine in Romans 6:3–4.

For the Italo-German philosopher-theologian Romano
Guardini in the modern Church, as for Augustine (cited by the
Catechism) in that of antiquity, this mystery is at least as equally
astounding as that of creation itself – the mystery that the world
arose from nothing. By a new creation, God draws man to
himself with all that he has done. He draws him into his
ineffable power, and man comes forth again renewed and
guiltless.[40]

The Spirit thus sanctifies our entire being – even, as the Paul
of Romans makes plain – the very limbs of our bodies. It is to
sanctification that the *Catechism* now turns.

Justification, as the *Catechism* has insinuated already, enables
a new kind of collaboration between God and ourselves. With
justification (but not before it) that co-operation between God
and man in the work of the Kingdom called by the Greek
Fathers *synergia* ('co-working') enters our range of possibilities.
Though the single grace of God ramifies so as to meet the
needs of his complex creature, man, the heart of the matter is
sanctifying or – as the *Catechism* will say, in deference to a
tradition chiefly but by no means exclusively Oriental – *deifying*
grace.[41]

The *Catechism*'s initial stab at a definition of grace calls it

the free and undeserved help that God gives us to respond
to his call to become children of God, adoptive sons,
partakers of the divine nature and of eternal life.[42]

In a little while the authors will affirm that this 'help' is, in the
single most important perspective on these matters, nothing
other than God himself in his self-gift. And yet a gift cannot be
called presented until it is received, and so the word 'grace' will
also refer to the transformation of our powers that such unique
receiving requires. The distinction between 'uncreated' and
'created' grace is already in view when the *Catechism* describes
grace as a 'participation' in the divine life – a finite sharing in

[40]R. Guardini, *Freedom, Grace and Destiny. Three Essays in the Interpretation of
Existence* (E.t. London 1961), pp. 124–131. Cf. Paragraph 1994.
[41]Paragraph 1999.
[42]Paragraph 1996.

the Infinite, the Infinite communicated to a finite reality rendered capable of giving it welcome.

But if this 'Infinite' is the 'Absolute' of the philosophical tradition in an ontological sense – that which is in no way dependent for its constitution on anything other than itself, it is certainly not the Absolute in an epistemological sense – that of which no further descriptive statements can be made. Rather is the 'life' of which grace is the 'participation' the holy and glorious Trinity. Our Baptism unites us by efficacious symbolism with the Crucified One at the moment of his resurrection when the Father is reunited with the Son in the latter's human nature, so as to form with him a single principle of spiration: from this source goes forth the Spirit into the Church and the redeemed world.[43] We therefore replicate, in a fashion wholly dependent on Christ, his relation as man to the Father, whilst simultaneously receiving, from the Spirit, the fruits of the perfecting of that relation in the sacrifice of the cross.

> As an 'adopted son' [the Christian] can henceforth call God 'Father', in union with the only Son. He receives the life of the Spirit who breathes charity into him and who forms the Church.[44]

Sharing the life of the Trinity, we begin to transcend the limitations endemic to our human way of knowing and loving, and through this transforming effect of the divine indwelling have access to the trinitarian Persons. This is what the *Catechism* means by introduction to the 'intimacy' of the trinitarian life.

And of course it can only be supernatural. This second gift, as different from the first gift of creation as creation itself is from nothing, does not simply make us better endowed human beings, even human beings with better endowments given in a supernatural way. It makes us more than human, indeed more than creaturely. Nature, what we are capable of by virtue of our own resources (not without God, but apart from his self-

---

[43]Cf. H. U. von Balthasar, *Mysterium Paschale. The Mystery of Easter* (E.t. Edinburgh 1990), p. 210.
[44]Paragraph 1997.

communication) is not grace: what we become capable of through that very self-communicating. The gifts of nature are given us as our own. The gifts of grace, by contrast, are bestowed as a sharing in what remains proper to God; and so reach us only through salvation history, with its power to change the form and goal of our natural lives.

Our engracement is both a stable disposition (unless rejected by mortal sin) and a very present help in trouble – divine assistance in time of need. For St Thomas, on whose limpid articulation of the doctrine of grace the *Catechism* tacitly depends – though its actual citations come chiefly from the 'doctor of grace', St Augustine – the 'grace that makes us gracious' (*gratia gratum faciens*) includes *both* an habitual gift, orienting us to the Father by the love we received freely in Christ, as poured out by the Spirit, and *also* what Aquinas terms the 'gratuitous moving of God', which later generations would call (like the *Catechism*) 'actual grace'. And this is grace to help with particular acts that the ethical and spiritual life calls for at different times, impulses that enable us to express, in particular, and perhaps highly unusual, contingencies, our new nature by living as befits the children of God.

In turning to the topic of grace and freedom, the *Catechism* is inspired by Augustine's maxim that the God who *completes* his work by co-operating with our will *began* that same work by so working that we might will such co-operation.[45] In other words, our will must be liberated from beyond itself if, in the perspective of salvation, it is to will effectively at all. Compared with the free will which is sufficient for many less significant options:

> This second order of human freedom transcends the power of natural human choice, it is a freedom which is elicited by the grace of God, and transfers the whole human being into a new order of human communion with the God of grace. In the one case we have a freedom to act within a region which is subordinate to the human will; in the other, we are given a freedom in a region where

---

[45]I paraphrase a famous passage from *On Grace and Free Will* 17, cited by the *Catechism* at Paragraph 2001.

the will itself is subordinate to God's higher purpose, where surrender to God in faith is elevation into a new realm.[46]

That the *Catechism,* and the wider theological tradition on which it draws, is not, by this emphasis on the irreplaceable divine initiative, proposing for us a destiny alien to us becomes clear when it goes on to speak of how God, from the moment of human nature's creation, 'has placed in man a longing for truth and goodness that only he can satisfy'.[47] The transcendental freeing of our will is experienced, accordingly, in the form of delight: delight, however, 'not as an exterior object of attraction [but as] the supreme spontaneity of the liberated will itself'.[48] There can be no question of compulsion when what is at work is that transcendent good for which the will was made.

But justifying and sanctifying grace are not the whole story of which the God of grace is the subject. The *Catechism* also speaks of *sacramental* grace: the (seven) particular ways in which the sacraments construct in human lives the régime of grace. The grace that brings righteousness and hallowing has ways of acting – cleansing, strengthening, nourishing, and so forth – discernible from the ritual structure of each sacramental sign. Then too the *Catechism* tells of those special graces called *charismata.* These may be highly dramatic and unusual, as with the extraordinary visitations comprised in authentically mystical visionary experience and the equally extraordinary gifts of prophecy, healing and speaking in tongues associated with the church at Corinth in the Pauline letters and a number of the lives of the saints, or more humdrum yet no less historically and spiritually effective, as with the vocations of the founders of the great Religious Orders, and of many lesser folk in their witness to this or that Christian truth or value. The *Catechism*'s insistence that all charisms, whatever their nature, are given both for the sanctification of the recipient and the upbuilding of the

[46]C. Ernst, O.P., *The Theology of Grace* (Dublin and Cork 1974), p. 42.
[47]Paragraph 2002.
[48]Ernst, *The Theology of Grace,* p. 44.

common good of the Church may reflect the influence upon its authors of the theological doctrine of Hans Urs von Balthasar, himself one of the presences surrounding the present commentary. Since all charisms are rooted in sacramental initiation, that connexion, highlighted by Balthasar, between charism and mission should remind us, with the *Catechism*, that grace befitting our state of life is never withheld by the good God from those 'representatives' and 'ministries' within the Church which also derive from the baptismal priesthood, and its extensions in Marriage and Order.[49]

Can grace be experienced? The *Catechism*'s answer is: in itself, no, except by faith; but its fruits may be. One thinks of the converting rôle played in the life of Edith Stein, Jewess and philosopher, by the narrative of grace which is St Teresa's autobiography, when she finished it with the words, *Dies ist die Wahrheit*, 'This is the truth'.

The crowning of the gifts

The *Catechism*'s final soteriological motifs are merit and holiness, and both of these naturally belong (but supernaturally so!) under the rubric of the crowning of the gifts of grace. The language of salvational merit is alarming to many Christians of the Reformation communities – unnecessarily. The *Catechism*'s exposition makes clear that the doctrine of merit as understood, above all, at Trent, is but a harmless inference from what has already been said about justification and grace. Where justification is concerned, the question of merit simply does not enter in: here we can only cry with Paul

> How great are God's riches! How deep are his wisdom and knowledge! Who can explain his decisions? Who can understand his ways? As the scripture says, 'Who knows the mind of the Lord? Who is able to give him advice? Who has ever given him anything, so that he had to pay it back?' For all things were created by him, and all things exist through him and for him. To God be glory forever! (Romans 11:33–36).

[49]Paragraph 2004.

Merit arises only with our justification, for it is an implicate of the fact that, as the *Catechism* puts it, 'God has freely chosen to associate man with the work of his grace'.[50] Our merits are God's gifts, but if they are truly his, then, since he has made us co-heirs with Christ, they are also truly ours. Just as it pleased God, who could have saved humankind by his own almighty *fiat*, to save us rather by the tree of one who was in all respects as we are, sin alone excepted, so too it is his joy to give us glory by crowning those deeds of ours which he himself inspires us to perform.

In identifying the *charity of Christ* as the source of all our merits, the *Catechism* tacitly regards holiness as a mediation of the grace poured in infinite abundance on the humanity of the Saviour. Here, then, in treating the saints, implicitly, as sub-mediators of Christ, the one and the only Mediator between God and man, it looks ahead to its own brief treatise entitled 'Christian holiness'.

That holiness is, as the text cited from the Letters to the Romans (8:28–30) testifies, Christologically founded, but ultimately, as the words of Jesus himself in St Matthew's Gospel (5:48) indicate, its model is paterological: in the Father's own perfection. The *Catechism*, following the teaching of the Dogmatic Constitution of the Second Vatican Council *de Ecclesia* teaches that each and every member of Christ's Church is called to the perfection of charity, and so to supernatural holiness. Sanctity, as the *Catechism* presents it, is always *mystical* sanctity; but it should at once be noted that the sense accorded to the term 'mystical' here is that of ancient, not early modern, theology. The holiness of Christians is 'mystical' because, in the first place, it derives from sacramental participation in the mystery of Christ, and, secondly, because it shares, through him, in the trinitarian mystery itself. This, then, is eminently 'objective mysticism'. For 'mystical life' we may read, with Dom Anselm Stolz, 'the full evolution of Christian being';[51] The question of what the *Catechism* terms 'the special graces or

---

[50]Paragraph 2008.

[51]A. Stolz, O.S.B., *The Doctrine of Spiritual Perfection* (E.t. St Louis, MO and London 1938), p. 215.

extraordinary signs of this mystical life ... granted ... to some
for the sake of manifesting the gratuitous gift given to all'[52] is
an altogether subsidiary – though not for that reason
unimportant – matter.

In any case mysticism and asceticism cannot be sundered,
and so the *Catechism* draws attention to that still point of the
turning world of Christian experience, the *cross.* Unconsciously
echoing the Russian theologian George Florovsky's emphasis
on ascetic effort as integral to Christian personhood, the
authors insist that without renunciation and spiritual battle
there can be no holiness.[53] *Without* these it would be presumption
to

> hope for the grace of final perseverance and the
> recompense of God our Father for the good works
> accomplished with his grace in communion with Jesus.[54]

With them, however, it is theological hope itself which makes
us look forward to our citizenship in that New Jerusalem which
the seer of the Apocalypse saw come down from God, as a bride
dressed for her spouse. It is with that word from the penultimate
chapter of the last book of holy Scripture that the *Catechism*
brings its soteriology to an end.

Morals and magisterium

One phrase which stands in grammatical qualification of that
'blessed hope' in the *Catechism*'s closing comment on grace
could easily be overlooked. The words 'keeping the same rule
of life' may not, *prima facie,* seem especially significant. They
signal, however, the intention to maintain a thesis: not simply
that all Catholic Christians should have the same ethical
aspirations, but that the norms in accordance with which they
act (or, through weakness of will, fail to act) in order to realise
these aspirations must also be the same likewise. And to this
(implicit) claim that Catholic Christians at large, if they be

[52]Paragraph 2014.
[53]Paragraph 2015.
[54]Paragraph 2016.

faithful, will agree on the concrete requirements of the natural moral law, subsumed, via the Old Law, into the law of Christ the *Catechism*'s remarks on morals and magisterium will inevitably be germane.

Rightly, the authors do not speak in this connexion of the magisterium of pope and bishops until they have situated Christian ethics in the corporate life of the Church at large. *From* the Church, the Christian learns the content of true moral teaching; *by* her, receives the sacramental grace that enables him to put the teaching into practice; and *in* her, contemplates the achieved models of holiness – the Blessed Virgin Mary and the saints – which give the moral life in its perfection a face and a name.[55]

Because the Church, as what the First Letter to Timothy calls 'the pillar and bulwark of the truth' (3:15), has the task of proclaiming saving truth, she also has the duty to teach authentic moral doctrine, since, as we have seen, the law of Christ and the grace of the Holy Spirit are inseparably conjoined in the single reality of gift and demand that is salvation. Normally, the teaching office of pope and bishops takes an unobtrusive part in the everyday *didaskalia*, or teaching activity that characterises the wider Church, as these sacramental office-holders themselves catechise and preach, or exercise pastoral oversight over others who do so in the name of Christ and of the Church – and so in *their* name since, in the words of Cyprian of Carthage, *ubi episcopus, ibi Ecclesia*: 'Where the bishop is, there is the Church.' The bishop is the first pastor of the local church, just as the pope is of the Church universal. We are not referring to anything exceptional or newsworthy, then, which we echo the *Catechism* and say:

> the ordinary and universal magisterium of the pope and the bishops in communion with him teaches the faithful the truth to believe, the charity to practise, the beatitude to hope for.[56]

---

[55] Paragraph 2030.
[56] Paragraph 2034.

The everyday pastoral activities in which a bishop recalls to the faithful their moral duties and responsibilities *are* the medium whereby, if on a rule of moral practice he concurs in his teaching with all his fellow bishops spread throughout the world *sub et cum Petro* – beneath Peter if also beside him – he participates in that charism of unerring truth given by the risen Christ to his Church through his Spirit.

But of course if a bishop is doing his stuff, then the resultant moral precepts will be far from anodyne. As the *Catechism* points out, there are in doctrine moral elements in whose absence the faith cannot be 'preserved, explained, or observed'.[57] Moreover, the rationale for the claim of the Church's magisterium to teach authentically – with due authority – the precepts of the natural law and, more widely, the law of God at large is, as the authors underline, *au fond* soteriological in kind. The observance of the specific precepts of the natural law, the norms which identify the good, is closely relevant to our salvation, as innumerable texts of both Old and New Testaments bear witness. And where the revealed law is concerned we are speaking of 'divine *saving* precepts', since the ethical teachings of the Saviour God 'purify judgment, and, with grace, heal wounded reason'.[58] And in this context the *Catechism* speaks not of the 'right' of the Church to teach, but of the 'right' of the faithful to learn. On the basis of baptismal initiation the faithful are entitled to everything in the Church's patrimony that can aid them to salvation, including, then, her ethical teaching in its fulness. Here, with discretion and serenity, the *Catechism* addresses those who question whether the Church *can* teach specific moral norms, rather than the most universal ethical principles; either on the grounds that, since faith and love determine salvation, specific moral practices are only secondary, or by appeal to the constantly changing concrete nature of humanity. But if the magisterium is itself to apply concretely the faith that works through charity, it has to teach specific norms. If it cannot be specific then it cannot teach

[57] Paragraph 2035.
[58] Paragraph 2037.

Christian morality in any challenging fashion. And on the matter of the historicity of morals: while the magisterium must teach with morally binding efficacy for the formation of conscience and the conduct of life, the quality of its teaching may be differentiated. On the one hand, it can teach some norm – arrived at by interpreting the law of the gospel or the natural law – as an absolute norm for all times and places; on the other, it can present some norm as the historical application of an indeterminate and dynamic gospel principle. In his commentary on Aristotle's *Politics* (an important treatise for morals), St Thomas points out that, as a society progresses, it may become more perfect through enrichment with new dispositions: for instance, a greater awareness of the need for education all round. There may not be progress in moral *behaviour*, but there can be a fuller explicit *awareness* of particular precepts of the natural law. That should not, however, lead us to the conclusion that all of the magisterium's moral norms are always historically conditioned in value, and hence changeable as cultures change. The *Catechism* may be alluding to this (rather than to the canons) when it speaks of

> the duty of observing the constitutions and decrees conveyed by the legitimate authority of the Church

since even these 'determinations call for docility in charity'.[59]

So far in the above the denotation of the phrase 'the Church teaching', has been the apostolic college of the bishops under their Petrine, papal head. The peculiar importance in the construction of Christian doctrine – including moral doctrine – of the episcopal order with, at its heart, the universal primate, justifies our calling its membership 'the teaching Church' in a uniquely strong sense. Yet many others teach, in various ways, and notably where the principled application of moral doctrine is concerned may have a thing or two to teach the (chief) teachers. The *Catechism* singles out in this connexion not only theologians but also, among the vast throng of the people of God at large, what it terms 'the humblest'. One might think in

[59]Paragraph 2037.

this connexion of the holy fools of Western and Eastern Christendom, who have played at different epochs an irreplaceable rôle in awakening hierarchs and Church-people to the evangelical demandingness of Catholic morals.[60] At any rate, the *Catechism*'s words strongly suggest that its authors would feel more confidence in looking in this direction than in that of 'experts'.

The final comments of the *Catechism* on the topic of magisterium and morals straitly conceived concern fraternity (or sorority) and sonship (or daughterhood). The exercise of conscience should be fraternal, in full consciousness of the truths, values and interests of our fellow Christians in the bosom of holy Church. And the moral life itself should be filial for the Church as teacher, *magistra*, is such only because she is first and foremost *mater*, our mother. Christian morals are not to be detached from the matrix of the sacramental and liturgical life of the Church which nourishes their growth.

It chimes perfectly with this, so the *Catechism* points out, that the 'precepts of the Church' listed, after those pertaining to the law of God in all traditional catechisms, have to do with that liturgical context of right living: assistance at Mass on Sunday, the weekly Easter; annual confession, which disposes us to eucharistic participation by continuing the work of baptismal conversion; the 'Easter duty' of receiving Holy Communion at the Pasch, the fount and origin of all liturgical (and Christian) life; keeping 'the holy days of obligation' which round off the Sunday observance by celebration of the chief feasts of Christ, the blessed Virgin and the saints; respecting the days of fasting and abstinence which ensure at least a modicum of that asceticism and penance needed for the worthy experiencing of festivity; and lastly, the duty of contributing to the Church's material needs – historically, her worship and her poor.

It fits with the situation of a catechism published in a decade of evangelisation that its final comments on the human vocation concern the interrelation of morale and mission. 'See how

---

[60]See J. Saward, *Perfect Fools. Folly for Christ's Sake in Catholic and Orthodox Spirituality* (Oxford 1980).

these Christians love one another' is an acclamation of that link. Good works done in a supernatural spirit are a converting ordinance. It was through the beauty of an ethos, an ethic, that Walter Pater envisaged the conversion of pagan antiquity in the shape of 'Marius the Epicurean'. Beginning with a reference to the Sacrifice of Christ, he wrote:

As if by way of a due recognition of some immeasurable divine condescension manifest in a certain historic fact, [Christianity's] influence was felt more especially at those points which demanded some sacrifice of one's self, for the weak, for the aged, for little children, and even for the dead. And then, for its constant outward token, its significant manner or index, it issued in a certain debonair grace, and a certain mystic attractiveness, a courtesy, which made Marius doubt whether that famed Greek 'blitheness' or gaiety, or grace, in the handling of life had been, after all, an unrivalled success. Contrasting with the incurable sipidity even of what was most exquisite in the higher Roman life, of what was still truest to the primitive life of goodness amid its evil, the new creation he now looked on – as it were a picture beyond the craft of any master of old pagan beauty – had indeed all the appropriate freshness of a 'bride adorned for her husband'. Things new and old seemed to be coming as if out of some goodly treasure-house, the brain full of science, the heart rich with various sentiment, possessing withal this surprising healthfulness, this reality, of heart.[61]

[61]W. Pater, *Marius the Epicurean. His Sensations and Ideas* (London 1892), II, pp. 120–121.

XIII

---

*The Ten Words**

The *Catechism* confirms the continuing validity of the Ten Commandments – the 'Ten Words' of the Hebrew Bible – for the Christian tradition, but also acknowledges how, with the incarnation, they look significantly different. The words of Jesus could hardly be plainer, 'If you would enter life, keep the commandments' (Matthew 19:17). Four factors, mentioned at the outset of the section entitled 'The Ten Commandments' ensure, however, that while the authority of those commandments is undiminished, the mode in which they are approached is altered. First, consult the dialogue with the Rich Young Man of St Matthew's Gospel where Jesus reiterates the continued pertinence of the Ten Words for salvation: a conversation that demonstrates how the context for keeping the commandments is now a life of discipleship centred on Christ himself. Secondly, the spirit in which the commandments are lived out has to be affected by the giving of the evangelical counsels – obedience, poverty, chastity – which accompany the Saviour's renewal of the Ten Words by a request for a more exigent self-stripping than the Mosaic law had ever demanded. Thirdly, there is also the little matter of that 'spirit' for whom we need in English a higher-case letter, the *Holy Spirit* who, in Jesus' reworking of the commandments in the Sermon on the Mount showed himself to be at work as a leaven in the letter of the Old Law. There he unfolds the hidden depths of the literal text of Scripture, as when Jesus explains the commandment

---

*=*Catechism*, Paragraphs 2052–2557.

'You shall not kill' to cover all anger with a brother, on pain of judgment. And fourthly, there is the Saviour's rabbinic-type determination of an inner hierarchy in the law as a whole, whereby the commands to love God with all one's heart, soul and mind, and one's neighbour as oneself emerge as the key principles on which every other precept must be made to turn. And these considerations, when taken *en bloc*, justify the *Catechism* in its claim that, though the Ten Words are integrally contained in the Sinai revelation, and could even – for 'the finger of God' writes them – be described as its incandescent heart, nonetheless it is only

> in the New Covenant in Jesus Christ that their full meaning will be revealed.[1]

Some words of Pope John Paul II in *Splendor Veritatis* constitute a miniature commentary of their own upon these words: For there the pope wrote:

> Jesus brings God's commandments to fulfilment, particularly the commandment of love of neighbour, by interiorizing their demands and by bringing out their fullest meaning. Love of neighbour springs from a loving heart which, precisely because it loves, is ready to live out the loftiest challenges. Jesus shows that the commandments must not be understood as a minimum limit not to be gone beyond, but rather as a path involving a moral and spiritual journey towards perfection, at the heart of which is love.[2]

However, it would be entirely wrong to give the impression that the *Catechism* is so much as touched by Marcionitism, the deliberate disprizing of the Old Testament revelation. The exodus, the Sinai theophany, the new life in the land, the covenant (without whose recalling the Decalogue is never transmitted): all these structuring events of the Jewish religion are crucial if the gift of the Ten Words is to be read aright. It cannot be irrelevant to their construal that they form part of

[1]Paragraph 2056.
[2]*Splendor Veritatis*, 15.

(1) a divine liberating event, which comes to its climax in (2) a manifestation of the divine glory, accompanied by (3) the promise of a renewed existence, itself inseparable from (4) the self-committal of the people to the mutual fidelity treaty offered by God. Taking their cue from the interpretation of the Decalogue by that good Hebraist Origen of Alexandria, for whom the Ten Words amount to a divine reversal of Adam's passage from 'the paradise of freedom to the slavery of this world',[3] the authors of the *Catechism* see the commandments as expressing:

> the implications of belonging to God through the establishment of the covenant. Moral existence is a *response* to the Lord's loving initiative. It is the acknowledgement and homage given to God and a worship of thanksgiving. It is co-operation with the plan God pursues in history.[4]

But though the setting of the gift of the Ten Words is *popular*, and therefore, corporate, all of this is *for me*. As the *Catechism* insists, the pronominal form for the addressees of each commandment is singular: 'thou'. Here archaic English makes succinctly a point on which contemporary English is inarticulate. The divine will is made known at one and the same time to 'us' and to 'me'.

What of the Decalogue in the Church's tradition? The authors report its historic importance. Professor John Finnis has summed up in this respect the results, arrived at by both Jewish and Christian scholars, of recent research.

> Explicitly and implicitly, the New Testament and the Apostolic Fathers, the earliest witnesses to the completed revelation in Christ, resort spontaneously to the Decalogue. Indeed, the Decalogue is referred to more frequently in the New Testament than in the whole of the Old Testament, and the zeal with which Christians preached it (as the one element in the Law still valid in the New Covenant) seems to have provoked its suspension from

[3] *Homilies on Exodus*, 8, 1, cited Paragraph 2061.
[4] Paragraph 2062.

use in Jewish daily worship and sabbath morning prayers
within a few decades after Pentecost.[5]

But the place of Augustine was pivotal for Western Catholicism,
and that not only for the use he made of them in setting forth
the ethical code required of the newly baptised, and for his
manner of numbering them (followed by Lutherans, but not
used in the Christian East, to whose reckoning the Reformed
communities also adhere). Of peculiar interest to the *Catechism*'s
authors is his notion of 'the twin tablets': the first (comprising
three precepts) corresponding to Jesus' command to love
God, the second (the remaining seven precepts) answering to
the accompanying command to love one's neighbour. Mixing
its metaphors rather badly, the *Catechism* speaks of the reciprocal
irradiation of the two tables of the law, and calls theirs an
'organic unity'. And that step is crucial to its claim that the
Decalogue 'brings man's religious and social life into unity'.[6]
But, as if to echo Finnis' judgment on the place of the Ten
Words in the apostolic and subapostolic age, the laying of such
weight on the Ten Words in the instruction of Christians is no
mere Augustinian theologoumenon. It is co-witnessed among
the Greek Fathers by St Irenaeus, and in the Middle Ages by St
Bonaventure, while the Council of Trent provided the Second
Vatican Council with its source for the firm teaching that
salvation comes through 'faith, Baptism *and the observance of the
Commandments*'.[7] But while asserting that no one can dispense
from the Ten Commandments which always oblige us even if,
in a particular case, the matter be minor, the authors take care
to ensure that the final comment in the preamble to their
exposition of each of the ten, is a reminder that their fulfilment
is made possible *by the grace of Christ.*

The First Commandment, on the reckoning normal in the
Latin church, embraces two precepts: to have 'none other
gods', and to abstain from idolatry. In point of fact, the
Catechism's account of the command to worship only the one
true God is more biblicist than has been customary in Christian

[5] Finnis, *Moral Absolutes*, p. 6.
[6] Paragraph 2069.
[7] *Lumen Gentium*, 24. Italics added.

history where, from an early date, the self-description of that God by reference to the events of the exodus (of interest in the first place, of course, only to Jews) was often rewritten to incorporate allusion of more universal scope to the divine action involved in creating. Though in original context the Ten Words were received by human beings perhaps monolatrous rather than monotheistic, the forward movement of divine revelation rapidly transformed Judaism into a faith whose conscious object was the unique Source of all that is. Still, the exodus remains a founding event for Judaeo-Christianity, and one to which the Isaianic school would look precisely for their description of the creation, as a liberation, then, not from Egypt but from chaos. This is the one God, the only Creator and Redeemer, whom alone we are bidden to worship and to serve. To shoot forward more precipitously than the *Catechism* itself (which makes a halt at the apologist Justin Martyr's dialogue with a Jewish interlocutor, Trypho), this is he in whom the *Catechism of the Council of Trent* encourages us to place our faith, our hope, our love.

The *Catechism* explains the content of the First Commandment using strategies both positive and negative. Negatively, the faith, hope and charity of which the authors have already spoken in each of the *Catechism*'s three sub-books can be undermined in ways the Commandment adjures us to avoid. For these are *theological* virtues which dispose us towards that selfsame divine Reality the First Commandment would have us adore. Where faith is concerned, we are to avoid 'voluntary doubt', as distinguished from those involuntary doubts or 'difficulties' of which Cardinal Newman once remarked that a thousand do not equal a single one of their voluntary soul-mates; the 'incredulity' which would wilfully refuse or at least neglect the claims of revelation; the 'heresy' which obstinately denies, after our Baptism, some truth of the faith; and even more so the 'apostasy' which would repudiate them all wholesale. Finally, among sins against faith the Catechism places *schism*, presumably because it is a rejection of the ecclesial communion which faith brings into being and on which the articulation of the truths of faith depends. Where hope is at stake, we need to shun despair (that might seem tautologous, but the *Catechism* defines it strictly as a ceasing to hope for personal salvation from God, or help with attaining such salvation, or, most particularly of all, for the forgiveness of one's sins); and also presumption, either of a Pelagian sort, where I would lift myself up to heaven by my own bootstraps, or of an antinomian kind, where I expect to be saved without ever really being converted. And where love (charity) is in question I can fall into the same sins *vis-à-vis* God as may afflict me *vis-à-vis* my human friends – indifference, ingratitude, lukewarmness, though in the case of my relation with God these are all, for the *Catechism*, ways of selling short above all the *grace* of God – whether by failing to consider how the divine goodness always takes the initiative, or by lacking in responsiveness to it, either totally or in part. Then there is that *accidie* identified by the monastic tradition and defined in the *Catechism* as a spiritual sloth that 'goes so far as to refuse the joy that comes from God and to be repelled by divine goodness',[8] and, more alarmingly still – and for the depiction of this one needs the imaginative powers of a Dostoevsky or a Baudelaire – the hatred for God which presumes to curse him as he who forbids sin, and punishes those who choose evil.

As charity should animate the exercise of justice in general (in the Christian dispensation) so in particular it ought to inform that virtue whereby we give God himself his just due as Lord. And here, reflecting the deepest faith instinct of the Church, the *Catechism* places before all else in its account of our cultic duties the act of sheer adoration: 'you shall *worship* the Lord your God' affirms the Lucan Jesus (4:8) in the words of Deuteronomy (6:13). The *Catechism* will not speak of the liturgy of the heart (prayer) or the public liturgy of the *polis* (sacrifice) until it has made this clear. Hans Urs von Balthasar wrote:

> No liturgy designed by men could be 'worthy' of the subject of their homage, of God at whose throne the heavenly choirs prostrate themselves with covered faces, having cast off their crowns and ornaments before offering

[8]Paragraph 2094.

adoration. The attempt to return to him who 'created all according to his will' the honour that all creatures received must *a priori* compel to its knees an earthly community of sinners. *Domine, non sum dignus!* If such a community, meeting for praise and worship, should have anything else in mind than adoration and self-oblation – for example, self-development or any other project in which they place themselves thematically in context next to the Lord who is to be worshipped, then they naively deceive themselves. This topic can be touched only with fear and trembling.[9]

Woe betide us if the posture of the Muslim, touching his forehead to the ground in adoring submission, seems something unfit for Christians to practise.

The *Catechism* singles out, among the signs of loving respect for God's *maiestas*, faithfulness to promises made to God, whether in our sacramental self-engagement in Baptism, Confirmation and Marriage, or in that extension of the baptismal vows which is the religious life, or in any way in which we have solemnly undertaken some good thing in a spirit of divine homage. Though acknowledging, in small print and few words, that 'in certain cases and for proportionate reasons' the Church can dispense from many such vows and promises,[10] the *Catechism* is surely right to place its finger on fidelity to promises as a litmus test of the quality of Christian believing. The inability to sustain marriage vows or the vows of religious profession is, for a Catholic population, a warning light of imminent cataclysm to come.

No one may be forced into the profession of faith, but that is not to say that the worshipful recognition of the true God is purely a private affair. While not reneging on the declaration of the Second Vatican Council that each human being has a right – albeit a circumscribed one – to immunity from external restraint in matters of religion, the *Catechism* also proclaims the

[9]H. U. von Balthasar, 'The Grandeur of the Liturgy', *Communio* 5, 4 (1978), p. 344.
[10]Paragraph 2103.

crown rights of the Redeemer, Jesus Christ, to his social reign – and not to that in individual hearts alone. In a Christian society, the drawing of boundaries between those rights founded on the salvific work of the Logos incarnate and the rights not of error but of *conscience* founded ultimately on the image of the pre-existent Logos in each human being, is a matter for the governmental prudence of statesmen to decide, albeit in reference to the principles of the Church. That, however it may commend itself to certain Hindus, the practice of ritual murder by devotees of Kali cannot be covered by such immunity, would be conceded by all. That the public mockery of the Judaeo-Christian revelation comes into the same category of the objectionable is a harder pill for liberalism to swallow. But the claim that the State cannot be indifferent to the dissemination of falsehood in religious and moral matters, since the very object of freedom is truth and goodness, is precisely what distinguishes the Catholic understanding of liberty from that of liberals.

The honouring of God has many aspects which the *Catechism* now tries to bring out. Far from contenting themselves with simply listing such forms of deviation as superstition, idolatry, divination and magic – all of which they place under the heading of 'perverse excess of religion'[11] – the authors seek to show in what precisely the malice of such practices consists. Thus the evil of superstition (on this account) lies in a false trust in ritual performance; that of idolatry in the disintegration of human life caused by missing the unitary goal of all human aspiration in adoration of the one God; that of divination in the desire to manipulate history and other men, and to conciliate occult powers; of magic in the attempt to harness such powers to one's service and enjoy a more than natural influence over others, even when this is attempted for their good. In its comments on superstition the *Catechism* appears to have in mind possible malpractice by Christians themselves; in speaking of idolatry it names both false pagan religions and the moral surrogates of their idols in erroneous life-goals; and as to

[11]Paragraph 2110.

divination and magic, while the New Age movement in such countries teetering on the brink of de-Christianisation as England has, doubtless, breathed on the dying embers of witchcraft and caused them to glow, serious belief in say, astrology and sorcery should probably be associated, rather, with others of the myriad societies for which the *Catechism* was made.

By contrast to these vicious excesses in religion, the *Catechism*, in its Aristotelian mood, identifies as corresponding deficiencies which also miss the just mean irreligion, atheism and agnosticism. Irreligion consists in demeaning the respect and trust due to God through 'tempting' him: 'putting his goodness and almighty power to the test by word or deed';[12] in treating unworthily what has been consecrated to him ('sacrilege'), or even attempting to exercise proprietorship of a commercial kind over the things of God by buying and selling spiritual goods ('simony'). Seen *sub specie aeternitatis* – and the *Catechism*'s confidence here in relation to late-twentieth century secular culture is truly breathtaking! – atheism belongs with such (rather more colourful, or even frankly bizarre) failures to strike *le juste moyen* in the matter of religion. Agnosticism shares the same company. The authors consider it to be, often enough, simply practical atheism. Interestingly, they are inclined to treat a principled atheism as more upright than (much) agnosticism since the latter can express simply

> indifferentism, a flight from the ultimate question of existence, and a sluggish moral conscience.[13]

Catholic Christianity is an iconic religion, where visual images play a large part in the portrayal and worship of the divine. So the First Commandment's prohibition on 'graven images' will inevitably undergo reinterpretation. In what sense, after the incarnation when God made himself portrayable in the flesh-taking of his consubstantial Image and Son, can this precept of the opening commandment of the Decalogue still bind? Only in regard to literal idolatry where the deity is strictly identified with the cult-object in its sheer materiality, for

---

[12]Paragraph 2119.
[13]Paragraph 2128.

otherwise it is *périmé*, outdated. The *Catechism* softens the shock
by suggesting lines of thought and devotion in the Old
Testament which converge on an image-using religion issuing
from the New. Thus in the Book of Deuteronomy it is human
presumption in taking the initiative by providing a 'form'
where none had been offered in the Sinaitic revelation that is
condemned, while in the Sapiential literature the God who is
greater than all his works (and thus not pictured in any of
them) is nonetheless the author of *beauty*. Furthermore, the
Israelite cultus was not totally aniconic. The ark of the covenant
with its attendant cherubim, the serpent of bronze lifted up
apotropaically in the wilderness: the guardians of the Mosaic
tradition did not regard these with the malign eye that they cast
on the bovine effigies of the Strength of Jacob in the Northern
Kingdom. But when all that *can* be said along these lines *has*
been said, the sea-change which overcame the biblical tradition
is called the incarnation: 'By becoming incarnate, the Son of
God introduced a new "economy" of salvation.'[14] If the present
author be allowed to cite some words of his own:

> The appearing of a supreme image throws open the way
> for the creation of a theological art apt to serve as exegesis
> of this new situation of the embodied disclosure of God in
> man. If God has elected to show himself definitively in the
> form of a human life, then may not the artist shape and
> fashion visual images which will add up to an exegesis of
> revelation?[15]

Christian iconography, indeed, does not only help us to grasp
the meaning of God's self-revelation in Christ, inseparable as
the figure of the latter is from those of the Blessed Virgin Mary
and the saints of Scripture and beyond. It also assists us to enter
into communion with them, as the *Catechism's* little *catena* of
texts – from St Basil, as read in the conciliar tradition, and St
Thomas Aquinas – makes clear.

[14]Paragraph 2131.
[15]A. Nichols, O.P., *The Art of God Incarnate. Theology and Image in Christian Tradition* (London 1980), p. 48.

The Second Commandment prescribes reverence for the divine Name. Considered as due respect for the holy Name, observance of this precept belongs, like obedience to the First Commandment, with the virtue of religion – itself, we noted, the Godward aspect of justice. In this perspective, to respect the divine Name is to give God his due in our inhabiting of language, and man is in not the least of his constitutive dimensions the language-using animal. As the *Catechism* puts it:

> The gift of a name belongs to the order of trust and intimacy. 'The Lord's name is holy.' For this reason man must not abuse it. He must keep it in mind in silent, loving adoration. He will not introduce it into his own speech except to bless, praise and glorify it.[16]

By its own choice of tropes, heightened and warmed beyond the clinical, cool idiom of justice, the *Catechism* prepares us for the introduction of a subtheme. And here, with *the sense of the sacred*, at any rate in the presentation of the latter in the self-conscious guise of Newman's sermons, we confront a contribution of the Romantic movement to the nineteenth-century Christian revival. For the shaking of the sacred canopy which, inherited from the ancient world, had sheltered traditional Christendom produced a more reflective realisation of what earlier ages had taken for granted.

> Are these feelings of fear and awe Christian feelings or not? ... They are the class of feelings we *should* have ... if we literally had the sight of almighty God; therefore they are the class of feelings we *shall* have, *if* we realize his presence.[17]

The conclusions which the *Catechism* draws are a cocktail of positive and negative ingredients. Positively, one must bear witness to the name of God and of Christ, while letting reverence

---

[16]Paragraph 2142, with a part citation of Zechariah 2:13, and the Psalm texts 29:2; 96:2 and 113:1–2.

[17]J. H. Newman, *Parochial and Plain Sermons* V. 2 (London 1907), pp. 21–22, cited Paragraph 2144.

for the holy Name of Jesus permeate one's speech when
catechising (or, for the ordained, preaching). In promising to
others in the Name of God one adds an extra obligation to
perform one's covenant as made, having thus committed
God's honour. Negatively, the Second Commandment forbids
all abusive naming not only of God and his co-eternal Son
made man, but also of those human persons on whom his
holiness resists, above all, our Lady and the saints. And of
course, that commandments covers outright blasphemy,
whether in the classic form of speaking hatefully of God to
others or in the heart (and this the *Catechism* extends to all
malevolent naming of God's Church, his holy ones, and other
'sacred things' (presumably the sacraments and sacramentals),[18]
or by using the divine Name as a cloak for criminality, especially
the enslavement of others, their torture, or murder. Brief
consideration in this context of oath-taking and the possibility
of a magical abuse of the Name of God leads the authors to
confront the apparent unwillingness of Jesus that his disciples
should swear oaths of *any* kind at all. There is no difficulty in
establishing the malice of false oaths, and notably of that
deceptive promising on oath called perjury. These actions
destroy respect for 'the Lord of all speech'.[19] The difficulty
arises when the oath-taking is true and faithful. Taking its cue
from the adjudication of these matters by Paul, Catholic
tradition has not regarded the words of Jesus about oath-taking
as literal or exceptionless prohibitions comparable with his
rejection of divorce. Rather has the Church seen his words as
a call for the honouring of God's presence and truth in *all* our
use of language, as well as to a certain discretion in calling on
God, though for 'grave and right reasons', such as in court, this
is not illegitimate.[20]

Because the Name of God is a revelation of his identity,
Baptism, whereby the Christian enters sacramentally the mystery
of that identity's self-manifestation in time, is carried out in the
threefold Name. It is also when the Christian man or woman

[18]Paragraph 2148.
[19]Paragraph 2152.
[20]Paragraph 2154.

(or child) receives a new name, or in the case of a baby, a name *tout court*: this name may be taken from one of the Church's saints (who will henceforth be a 'model of charity' for their namesake), from some aspect of the mystery of salvation (as, in Latin countries, Pasqualina or Asuncion), or a Christian virtue (such as Hope or Eirene, 'peace'). And that leads the *Catechism* to two further thoughts, which concern the continuing Christian life and final destiny of the named human being baptised in the trinitarian Name. First, just as, in the words of Tertullian, Christians no more can live outside Baptism than fish outside water, so by the sign of the cross in the triune Name we recall each day, and at the main significant moments of that day, our own baptismal dedication and its power. Secondly, though the name of each human person is sacred – their 'icon', the *Catechism* calls it, since it is the disclosure of the unique *prosōpon* (personhood, face) which God addresses and contemplates in his utterly particularised dealings with them, still our true 'name' is that which the Christ of the Apocalypse promises to the victory in the spiritual combat, the new name written on a 'stone' (possibly the *tessera* given to the gladiator) in the 'letter' to the church at Pergamum (Apocalypse 2:17).

The Third Commandment, rounding off the trio of God-centred precepts on the first 'table' of the Decalogue, is the command to keep holy the sabbath day. In Jewish tradition, the setting aside of this day to the Lord is for the recalling of the original creative act, the remembering of the exodus deliverance from Egypt, and a sign of the unbreakable covenant which binds Israel to God. The *Catechism* underlines its personal and social bearing: man is to rest, and let others rest, especially the poor. It is 'a day of protest against the servitude of work and the worship of money'.[21]

Still, the sabbath law is not primarily pragmatic, nor was Jesus' freedom of spirit in dealing with the sabbath a matter of taking liberties in order to make life more convenient, if less differentiated, for everyone. As the *Catechism* puts it, he did not fail to respect its holiness, for God's 'rest', which the sabbath memorialises, is God himself as the fulness of life and, by

[21]Paragraph 2172.

derivation, that condition of enjoying God and God's goodness
for which the people of God were destined from the beginning.
Jesus's authority to suspend, modify or reapply the sabbath law
is in view of the object of that law: the enjoyment of the creation
in union with God's own rest. His message was not human
liberalism, but divine liberality.

The Christian Sunday is the fulfilment of the sabbath not its
displacement to another day. As the *Catechism* explains in a
well-crafted formulation:

> Because it is the 'first day', the day of Christ's Resurrection
> recalls the first creation. Because it is the 'eighth day'
> following the sabbath, it symbolizes the new creation
> ushered in by Christ's Resurrection. For Christians it has
> become the first of all days, the first of all feasts, the Lord's
> Day (*hē kuriakē hēmera, dies dominica*) – Sunday.[22]

Cardinal Joseph Ratzinger, in an essay on the relation of
sabbath and Sunday, shows how it was possible for Sunday,
without loss of its resurrectional – and so eschatological –
novelty to take up what the *Catechism* calls the 'rhythm and
spirit' of the Old Law's Third Commandment.

> The Resurrection joins together beginning and end,
> creation and restoration. In the great hymn to Christ of
> the Letter to the Colossians, he is characterised both as
> creation's First-born (1:15) and as the First-born from the
> dead (1:18), through whom God wished to reconcile all
> with himself. Precisely at this point do we find the synthesis
> which lay concealed in the 'date' of the first day and which
> for the future would stamp the theology of the Christian
> Sunday. To this extent, the entire theological content of
> the sabbath could pass over, in renewed guise, into the
> Christian celebration of Sunday. Indeed, the passages
> from sabbath to Sunday mirrors in a most exact way the
> continuity and novelty of what is Christian.[23]

[22]Paragraph 2174.
[23]J. Ratzinger, 'Auferstehung als Grundlegung christlicher Liturgie – Von der
Bedeutung des Sonntags für Beten und Leben der Christen', in idem, *Ein neues Lied
für den Herren. Christusglaube und Liturgie in der Gegenwart* (Freiburg 1995), p. 92.

Not surprisingly, then, the *Catechism* stresses the intimate link between the observance of Sunday and the celebration of the Holy Eucharist. For the Mass, the presence of the Risen One who was crucified, the renewal of his sacrifice as accepted at Easter by the Father, is a foretaste of that day without end of which the resurrection triumph is the first-fruits. The *Catechism* emphasises the role of the parish as the primary locus for the common sharing of the faithful in the Eucharist within a given 'particular church' (diocese). And it meets a hoary objection (Why go to church when you can pray at home – perhaps nowadays, follow the Mass by television?) with the words of that great early Byzantine preacher Chrysostom who points out how at the *synaxis* there is something more: accord of minds, souls, hearts, and not least, given the high Catholic doctrine, Eastern and Western, of the ordained ministry, the prayers of the priests.

In what setting should this jewel be housed? Echoing the felicitous formulation of the Latin Code of Canon Law, the *Catechism* calls the faithful to observe Sunday (and the other holy days) by refraining from

> work or activities that hinder the worship owed to God, the joy proper to the Lord's Day, the performance of the works of mercy, and the appropriate relaxation of mind and body.[24]

Though in modern society conditions will not always be easy to meet, a space should be created for that 'reflection, silence, cultivation of the mind and meditation' which foster the interior life of Christians, and not simply for the jollification which also befits the 'assembly of the first-born who are enrolled in heaven' (Hebrews 12:22).

The *Catechism* must now turn to the second diptych of the law, those precepts which express the command to love one's neighbour as oneself. After its lengthy disquisition on fundamental morals the authors expect us to have grasped the nature of the unity that binds together the two primordial imperatives: Love God! Love your fellow! In brief: our neighbour

[24]Paragraph 2184.

is the image of God, though it takes the eyes of faith to see this; the love of God itself urges us to love those whom God loves, and in loving our neighbour with the same love by which we love God we hope to bring him or her to love God also.

And the first of our neighbours to be mentioned in this connexion are those biologically closest to us. The Fourth Commandment reads, 'Honour your father and your mother'. Yet though the *Catechism*'s exposition will have much to say about the nexus of nature and nurture which is the family, it soon becomes clear that human biology is not in fact its principal presupposition. Rather do parents illustrate the moral fact that

> we are obliged to honour and respect all those whom God, for our good, has vested with his authority.[26]

Although the *Catechism* does not presuppose the modern Western 'nuclear' family – it speaks in almost Chinese terms of the Fourth Commandment's requiring 'honour, affection and gratitude toward elders and ancestors'[27] – it nonetheless singles out for special mention the all-important nucleus *of* the family: namely, the relation between spouses considered as parents and their children or child. The weight given to the family as the primary social cell, today frequently minimised by the interventions of well-meant but ill-advised State intervention, will come as no surprise to anyone at all familiar with the much-publicised stance on such issues of the Catholic Church. The family is the hearth where the most basic values of human and Christian living are focussed and whence they must radiate. Husband and wife are called to share their common love in a fruitful giving of self which has its first but not its only object in children. Their mutual support should sustain them in a call to shape a cell of civilised living – where the word 'civilised' must be taken not in its modern sense, which has connotations of fashion and *snobisme* – but in the sense of all that which through culture and grace, makes a being most human. The lifelong

---

[25]Paragraphs 2186–2188.
[26]Paragraph 2197.
[27]Paragraph 2199.

dedication of spouses to each other, and the sturdy acceptance of responsibility for how their children grow up, is the foundation on which all else can be built, creating the confidence which is a necessary condition for the successful transmission of values.

Much of what the *Catechism* has to say about the family has been touched on earlier. Its discussion of the nature of Christian marriage in the sub-book on the sacraments could hardly avoid speaking of the family as the 'domestic Church', the most microscopic yet vital kind of baptismal communion. Now, in the fresh context of the Fourth Commandment, the authors underline at once the supernatural presuppositions and the empirical consequences of the Christian family. They stress how the common life of spouses and child mirrors the fruitful love of Father and Son in the Holy Spirit; they also insist on the 'affinity of feelings, affections and interests' which should arise from family life, giving force to the family institution as an instrument of social agency.[28] In speaking of the family as the 'original cell of social life' the *Catechism* is in danger of simply repeating what it has already said in discussing the 'corporate context' of the good life as a whole.[29] The need to assuage those critics of the draft *Catechism* who regarded its ethical sub-book as excessively focussed on the individual in his or her biographical setting compelled the authors to treat of such matters as family, society and State, not only (as was traditional) under the heading of the Ten Commandments but also, by way of anticipation, in a sustained section by way of preamble to the Ten Words. Here, however, much more is said about the virtues that should animate family life, the duties to which it gives rise, and the manner in which it can illuminate other social relationships.

Those who composed the *Catechism* were not only theologians but also pastors. Their remarks at this juncture declare an interest in strengthening the classical structure of the family which (they are evidently aware) is undermined in contemporary Western society by the combined effect of a

---

[28]Paragraph 2206.
[29]See above, Chapter XII.

series of factors political, social, economic and cultural in kind. As they stalwartly assert:

> Authority, stability and a life of relationships within the family constitute the foundations for freedom, security and fraternity within society. The family is the community in which, from childhood, one can learn moral values, begin to honour God and make good use of freedom. Family life is an initiation into life in society.[30]

So much might have been said by the ancient Romans, though these statements are none the worse for that. A more distinctively Christian note is struck, however, when the *Catechism* goes on to single out the practice of care for the more vulnerable neighbour (young, old, sick, handicapped, poor) as a peculiar hallmark of the Catholic family. Not all families can be self-supporting; those that are so lucky should lend a helping hand to the others, and first of all directly, while only in the second place does the *Catechism* mention on the rôle of the State. Following the principle of subsidiarity, where a family proves helpless or incompetent, the task of the civil authorities is to aid and support, not supplant.

A particularly subtle point is that, inhabiting the family microcosm, we come to see the social and ecclesial macrocosms in its light – namely as human communities made up of *persons,* not simply legal parties to the social contract. The idea that the pervasiveness of the familial analogy is an index of social health might be regarded as a sophisticated restatement of Sir Robert Filmer's characteristic arguments for the king's cause in the English Civil War, of which the best-known expression is the posthumously published *Patriarcha.* Authority in the civil community is one of the *Catechism*'s preoccupations in considering the Fourth Commandment.

The *Catechism* balances the duties of children and parents, which include, in a Christian context, the evangelical or missionary charge of father and mother in their offspring's regard, with the gospel's own insistence that family ties are not to be seen as absolutes. Divine vocation can call a family

[30]Paragraph 2207.

member from out of the 'domestic Church', not in order to form another such micro-church, but precisely to be free of family ties in consecrated virginity. This includes, of course, the call to celibate priesthood, the predominant way of understanding spiritual equipment for the presbyteral order in the Latin church.

Everything the *Catechism* says about the macrocosmic mirror of the reciprocal responsibilities of parents and children – that is, their correlates in the wider sphere or action of the State, where 'parents' become 'civil authorities' and 'children' 'citizens' (or 'subjects') – assumes that the fundamental moral formation in the family setting has worked. If at the family hearth such qualities as 'tenderness, forgiveness, respect, fidelity and disinterested service, ... self-denial, sound judgment and self-mastery'[31] have truly been acquired, then there is some possibility that the 'exercise of authority' will succeed in giving 'outward expression to a just hierarchy of values in order to facilitate the exercise of freedom and responsibility by all'.[32]

A real symmetry aligns the parent-child and ruler-citizen relation. The source of human fatherhood is the fontal divine parenting, just as 'those subject to authority should regard those in authority as representatives of God'.[33] And exactly as the duty of filial obedience to father and mother ceases when the child is convinced in conscience that some particular order of its parents is wrong, so too the 'loyal collaboration' of the ruled

> includes the right, and at times the duty, to voice their just criticisms of that which seems harmful to the dignity of persons and to the good of the community.[34]

Isometric with the teaching that families must be seedbeds of the ancient pagan pieties yet also launching-pads of specifically Christian charity is the *Catechism*'s affirmation that not only are the duties suggested by patriotism – from paying taxes to the

[31]Paragraph 2223.
[32]Paragraph 2236.
[33]Paragraph 2238.
[34]Ibid.

defence of the realm – incumbent on citizens but also, in more
biblical idiom

> the more prosperous nations are obliged, to the extent
> that they are able, to welcome the foreigner in search of
> security and the means of livelihood which he cannot find
> in his country of origin.[35]

And as one of the premier duties of parents is to be – whether
themselves or by proxy – Christian educators, so that they are
obliged to select schools for their children consonant with this
end, so too citizens *qua* citizens are not dispensed from the
responsibility of giving a Christian stamp to the form of their
civil society:

> Every institution is inspired, at least implicitly, by a vision
> of man and his destiny, from which it derives the point of
> reference for its judgment, its hierarchy of values, its line
> of conduct. Most societies have formed their institutions
> in the recognition of a certain pre-eminence of man over
> things. Only the divinely revealed religion has clearly
> recognized man's origin and destiny in God the Creator
> and Redeemer. The Church invites political authorities
> to measure their judgments and decisions against this
> inspired truth about God and man.[36]

And if this statement, with its resonances of Jacques Maritain's
theocentric political humanism, suggests the ideal of a 'new
Christendom', albeit one of a more spacious kind than the
European and Europe-inspired *anciens régimes*, any
misinterpretation of the authors' intentions along the lines
of a Church-State hybrid is at once ruled out when they warn
that the Church is never to be confused with any political
community. By her supra-political character, indeed, she points
to the transcendence of the human person over the organised
communal life of city and country alike.

[35]Paragraph 2241.
[36]Paragraph 2244.

The Fifth Commandment states, most simply, 'You shall not kill' (Exodus 20:13; Deuteronomy 5:17). And as the instruction *Donum Vitae*, work of the Congregation for the Doctrine of the Faith, glosses that text:

> no one can under any circumstance claim for himself the right directly to destroy an innocent human being.[37]

As usual, the original commandment, while retained, is also exceeded in the teaching of Jesus, which therefore adds to this a prohibition on anger, hatred and revenge, and not only this but the precept to *love* one's enemies.

Before describing the four principal forms of encompassing the death of another which the commandment proscribes (intentional homicide, abortion, euthanasia or assisted suicide, and suicide itself), the *Catechism* clears away a difficulty. Does the Fifth Commandment entail that no one, whether individual person or the moral person of the State, can ever deal a lethal response to deadly aggression? The Catholic tradition has not understood this command to rule out those acts of self-defence in which the death of another is not willed for its own sake but as, in particular situations, the inevitable consequence of self-defence. Not only is this a right – based on the right to life – in one's own case, even more important (for the exercise of such a right may be waived by the martyr) there can be a 'grave duty' of lawful offence for someone who is 'responsible for another's life, the common good of the family, or of the State'.[38] That covers both military action against external aggressors, and judicial action against aggressors from within. Although the capital penalty, of its very nature, by abolishing (on earth) the morally sick person along with their disease, renders the medicinal or therapeutic function of punishment vain, the Church does not hold the corrective reform of the criminous individual to be the *prime* purpose of judicial penalty. The latter consists rather in what the *Catechism* calls redressal of the 'disorder' caused by their offence. Though such a theory of

[37]*Donum Vitae*, 'Introduction', 5, cited Paragraph 2258.
[38]Paragraph 2265.

retributive justice will no doubt be stigmatised as illiberal by
the politically correct it rests in fact on a deeper respect for
human dignity – for the responsibility of the person in choosing,
whether well or ill – than does its rival for that place of honour.
For it treats the person not as a moral minor but as an adult,
with all the gravity which attaches to the moral action of the
one who has achieved majority in the moral sense. This
consideration leads the *Catechism* into an apparent antinomy:
for on the one hand, in cases of 'extreme gravity', the civil law
need not exclude the capital penalty which may the better fit
the crime; on the other hand, the very dignity of the person
which the objective theory of disorder-redressal would serve is
itself better expressed in the choice of 'bloodless means' for
protecting public order and the safety of persons wherever
possible. The antinomy is *only* apparent, for it can be resolved
in one of two ways. First, where the State is too weak or primitive
to detain the most dangerous criminals securely, that choice of
bloodless means may in practice be unavailable. And secondly,
in stronger or more developed States, the sovereign authority,
so as to indicate the extreme turpitude of offences may impose
the death penalty, yet subsequently commute it in the name of
mercy. Though the *Catechism* does not say so there is a peculiar
fittingness in that synthesis of justice with mercy for the ethos
of a confessional, Christian State.

It will astonish no one to discover that the Catholic Church
is opposed to murder and self-murder, the slaughter of the
unborn, and the assisted murder called, impiously, by its
advocates the 'good death' (*eu-thanasia*). Some nuances, and
explanations, may however be underlined. First, on *homicide*
the *Catechism* notes the unique horror of infanticide, fratricide,
parricide and the murder of a spouse: reference to its earlier
remarks on the family as the matrix of human communion
explains why. It rejects outright appeal to eugenic or public
health factors as legitimations of murder. It interprets the Fifth
Commandment to include not only the direct but also the
*in*direct encompassing of another's death, whether by exposing
another needlessly to grave danger or refusing to assist one
who has succumbed to such. Under the latter heading it
includes, packing a political punch, 'usurious and avaricious

dealings' which 'lead to the hunger and death of their brethren in the human family'.[39] Secondly, on *abortion* it affirms the incompetence of the civil law to derogate from the right of the embryo to live, whether by positively enshrining the (pseudonymous) 'right to choose' in law or by declaring immunity to parents or doctors involved.

> These human rights depend neither on single individuals nor on parents; nor do they represent a concession made by society and the State; they belong to human nature and are inherent in the person by virtue of the creative act from which the person took his origin.[40]

It follows that the production of embryos for the purposes of medical experimentation is absolutely unacceptable. In reflecting the clear teaching of the Roman magisterium on this point, the *Catechism* speaks also (tacitly) in the Name of the Saviour who himself at the Annunciation took flesh as a human embryo in the womb of Mary and at the Visitation was heralded while still an embryo by his foetal cousin. Thirdly, on *euthanasia*: death brought about so as to eliminate suffering is, whatever the subjective good faith of those involved, rank murder, an offence against man and, as Pope John Paul II's letter on the 'culture of death' *Evangelium Vitae*, brings out more fully than the *Catechism* itself

> a rejection of God's absolute sovereignty over life and death, as proclaimed in the prayer of the ancient sage of Israel, 'You have power over life and death; you lead men down to the gates of Hades and back again'.[41]

Though medicine can be overzealous, it can also refuse a palliative care of the terminally ill that is its duty: thinking perhaps of the financial factors which increasingly drive the movement to legalise euthanasia, the authors of the *Catechism*

---

[39]Paragraph 2269.
[40]*Donum Vitae* III, cited Paragraph 2273.
[41]*Evangelium Vitae*, 4, with an internal citation of Wisdom 16:13.

call such palliative medicine 'a special form of disinterested charity'.[42] And fourthly on *suicide*, while the Church prays for those who take their own lives, in the hope that God can offer them (in the moment of death, no doubt) opportunity for repentance, the *Catechism* roundly declares self-murder contrary to the love of God. Breaking the onerous ties of solidarity which rightly bind us to others, it is especially pernicious when carried out as an example to the young, in the service of some false ideology.

Much of the foregoing depends on the principle that the dignity of the human person is inalienable, and, in so being, rules out certain courses of action. Moral judgment comes into strenuous play when we are called upon to decide what should count as such respect: for defective judgment, euthanasia is dying with dignity; for sound judgment, to die with dignity is to accept one's own death, however it come. The *Catechism* now investigates what such respect entails in five areas: respect for the souls of others; for health; for the integrity of the person in the context of scientific research; for the integrity of the body; and for the dead. Respecting the souls of others involves not giving 'scandal', interpreted by the *Catechism* in generous terms to include the actions of those who

> establish laws or social structures leading to the decline of morals and the corruption of religious practice ...[43]

Respect for health means taking all reasonable care for the body, not a 'neo-pagan' worship of its perfection. Respect for the person *vis-à-vis* scientific experiment disqualifies any experimentation that would expose the 'subject's life or physical and psychological integrity to disproportionate or avoidable risks' – with or without their consent, though without is grosser.[44] Respect for the integrity of the body excludes such practices as terrorism, kidnapping, and any form of mutilation of the body save for strictly therapeutic reasons, as well as

---

[42]Paragraph 2279.
[43]Paragraph 2286.
[44]Paragraph 2295.

torture, a topic on which the *Catechism* takes the opportunity to apologise for the historical fact that in her own tribunals the Church at one time adopted the more permissive prescriptions of Roman law on that topic. The assumption that torture could be necessary for the maintenance of public order was ill-founded. Recent studies on the Spanish Inquisition show the rôle played by that particular tribunal in pioneering the practice of examining suspects without recourse to physical duress – much ahead of its time in early modern Europe – though the *Catechism* does not advert to this. Finally, respect for the dead extends from care, both physical and spiritual, for the dying to proper respect for the bodies of the departed, something which is not only retrospective, as the mortal temples of the once living, but also prospective, 'in faith and hope of the Resurrection'.[45] The free gift of bodily organs after death can be positively meritorious, in sharp contrast to the authors' warning of the premature removal of such organs from the dying. As to cremation, it is not encouraged but only permitted, with the proviso that no such licence exists where the introduction of the practice implies denial of the article of the Creed in the resurrection of the flesh.

In the teaching of Jesus the Fifth Commandment, as we have seen, so expands as to govern our attitude towards not only killing but anger, hatred and vengeance likewise, and the *Catechism* must deal with these themes. Peace is, in a celebrated adage of Augustine's, *tranquillitas ordinis*, 'the tranquillity of order'.

> Peace cannot be attained on earth without safeguarding the goods of persons, free communication among men, respect for the dignity of persons and peoples, and the assiduous practice of fraternity ... Peace is the work of justice and the effect of charity.[46]

But the gospel does not promise any *naturalistic* peace on earth; earthly peace is not just the image but the *fruit* of the

[45]Paragraph 2300.
[46]*De civitate Dei*, XIX. 13, 1, cited Paragraph 2304.

peace of Christ, which is supernal. Here utopian expectations are out of place. The *Catechism*, therefore, has no option but to proceed to a discussion of the way, in a fallen world, recourse to arms may be a cruel necessity. However, it prefaces its account of the conditions of a just war by commending those who renounce unconditionally the use of violence (one thinks of the example, in the East, of the Kievan princes saints Boris and Gleb, or, in the West, of the servant of God, Charles of Habsburg, who refused to regain the iron crown of Stephen of Hungary by the shedding of blood in the two restoration attempts of 1921). Still, this must not extend to the impairing of the rights and obligations of others: the Catholic Church is no pacifist organisation, though she honours the peacemakers as blessed.

And just as the *Catechism* rigorously restricted the conditions on which armed resistance to political oppression may be legitimate, so here too, in the case of struggle between nations the Church's moral theologians are agreed on the need for the utmost discretion in releasing the hounds of war.[47] The traditional elements of just war doctrine are enumerated; reminder is given that armed conflict entails no suspension of the moral law, since no human development can annul perpetual moral truth; the blanket destruction of entire cities or populations is stigmatised a crime against man and God. Realistically, the *Catechism* comments:

> Because of the evils and injustices that accompany all war, the Church insistently urges everyone to prayer and to action so that the divine Goodness may free us from the ancient bondage of war.[48]

In these words the authors dismiss as a chimaera the notion that the invention of high precision tools of war can render warfare as clinical and sanitised as a doctor's surgery. The theatre of war will never be in *that* sense a theatre of operations.

---

[47]Compare Paragraphs 2243 and 2309.
[48]Paragraph 2307.

The topic of the Sixth Commandment, adultery, enables the *Catechism* to set forth its sexual ethic. For, on the Catholic view, all sexual transgressions are, essentially, insults to a bride and groom, offences against matrimony.

> Sexuality, in which man's belonging to the bodily and biological world is expressed, becomes personal and truly human when it is integrated into the relationship of one person to another, in the complete and lifelong mutual gift of a man and a woman.[49]

Gender identity and therefore gender differentiation – what the *Catechism* calls 'difference and complementarity' – are ordered to the 'goods of marriage and the flourishing of family life'.[50] When the sexed person, *precisely as such*, makes a gift of him- or herself, that self-gift is always, then, nuptial in character: it is a wedding-present.

Since sexuality conditions affectivity – the capacity of the human individual for emotion, love, bonding – whether inside marriage or outside it, its powers are to be neither denied nor untrammelled. Both courses would end in moral shipwreck. Instead, these powers are to be husbanded. The ability to do this is called *chastity*. Chastity involves an 'apprenticeship in self-mastery', a 'training in freedom'. As an intrinsic aspect of human integrity, it belongs with the well-ordered beauty of the first creation now restored by grace: for this reason, the authors see it as covenanted by the baptised in their promise of discipleship at Christian initiation. But that promise – summed up in the repudiation of not only fallen world and fallen angel but also fallen *flesh* – is mere vibration of the air unless it wills the means to chastity:

> self-knowledge; practice of an ascesis adapted to the situations that confront [one], obedience to God's commandments, exercise of the moral virtues and fidelity to prayer.[51]

---

[49]Paragraph 2337.
[50]Paragraph 2333.
[51]Paragraph 2340.

Since fallen sexuality is pandemic, the authors are under no illusion that this is hard labour, requiring not only special effort during certain periods such as pubescence but also help from the social environment, what they term a 'cultural effort'. Fortunately, the virtue of chastity can have its infused aspect, where human trying elicits divine assisting. But the prize of this spiritual labour is great: enhanced capacity for the gift of self; for spiritual communion with others, and for friendship, which is chastity's flower. In a sex-drenched and sex-obsessed culture, friendship withers away, for no intimate relation not leading to concourse can be envisaged. In this perspective, the *Catechism* goes so far as to say that the credibility of chastity is bound up with that of immortality itself.

> It shows the disciple how to follow and imitate him who has chosen us as his friend, who has given himself totally to us and allows us to participate in his divine estate. Chastity is a promise of immortality.[52]

Offences against chastity are lust (sexual pleasure sought in deliberate abstraction from the unitive and procreative dimensions of the act whose exercise it accompanies), masturbation, fornication, pornography, prostitution and rape. In any case, *pleasure* is never the proper end of human acting, but, rather, the proper accompaniment of action befitting human ends. The auto-eroticism of masturbation is closely connected with lust since it reinforces an attitude of seeking immediate satisfaction rather than self-giving. It is in fact an enacted parable of lust itself. Fornication falsifies the unitive aspect of sexuality by rendering it *punctual*, 'point-like', thus disabling it from fostering bonds of communion which provide the context for a whole life. Pornography authorises lust by freeing it from moral scruple, denying the elements of modesty and shame essential to sexual desire and so denaturing it, till it becomes merely interest in another body without awareness of another soul. Prostitution does not only, like lust, confound sexual pleasure with the essence of the act whose pleasure it is; it actually transforms one of the contracting parties into the

sheer instrument of such pleasure, though the *Catechism* here
records, mindful of the corporate context of such sale of
human powers, how the 'imputability of the offence can be
attenuated by destitution, blackmail or social pressure'.[53] Rape
reduces the sexual act to a compulsive discharge of no intrinsic
moral significance, negating (like pornography) the very nature
of sexual desire as longing to be united with another person.

Homosexuality, to which the *Catechism* devotes a distinct
section, can be thought of as either condition or activity. As
condition it issues (by a causal chain on whose nature there is
no general consensus) from the diffused character of early
erotic feeling: in fallen human nature, sexual instinct is highly
pliable and therefore potentially polymorphous. As activity, it
lacks the full complementarity of the man-woman relationship,
as well as procreative openness to new life. Even if taking place,
then, within a simulacrum of the monogamous relationship,
the Church cannot regard it as a legitimate expression of the
sexual inclination in man. The virtue and gift of chastity are as
available to those who experience themselves as having an
affective disposition oriented primarily to those of their own
gender as it is to all those other sorts and conditions of human
being of whom St Ambrose, cited by the *Catechism*, writes that
in their different manners of realising chastity (he singles out
the married, those widowed, and virgins), they constitute the
'richness of the discipline of the Church'.[54]

What the *Catechism* has to say on marriage itself rehearses, in
the new context of ethics, its teaching on the sacrament of
matrimony in the second sub-book, just as, so we have already
noted, its remarks on the family as the basic social cell echoed
its earlier sacramental doctrine on the *ecclesia domestica* as
marriage's ecclesiological fruit and significance. The authors
reiterate the indissoluble connexion in marriage between
union and procreation, for this notion of *nuptial creativity* is the
key to the entire (biblical and) Catholic sexual ethic. It is

[53]Paragraph 2355.
[54]*On Widows*, IV, 23, cited Paragraph 2349.

because the Creator has so arranged things that the sexual act is simultaneously both *per se* generative and *per se* expressive of intimate oblative love that artificial contraception (which would exclude the first) and the conception of children by artificial procreation or fertilisation (which would exclude the second) are incompatible with the moral understanding of Catholicism.

The *Catechism* ends its account of the Sixth Commandment with a quintet of issues where the good of marriage is menaced in peculiarly direct ways: adultery, divorce, polygamy (or polyandry), incest (with which it connects child abuse) and 'free union'. As we might expect, these transgressions of the ethics of marriage attack either the nuptial covenant of the spouses or the family life which their union creates, or both of these together. They undermine both that sign of the covenant of salvation which is (sacramental) marriage and the flourishing of the society to which salvation is addressed. Mindful, though, of the difficulty in negotiating orderly transition from a state of things constructed on the basis of one partner taking numerous spouses at one and the same time, the *Catechism* asserts that

> the Christian who has previously lived in polygamy has a
> grave duty in justice to honour the obligations contracted
> in regard to his former wives and his children.[55]

The Seventh Commandment, which we last encountered in the company of Chesterton's Father Brown, states, 'You shall not steal' (Exodux 20:15; Deuteronomy 5:19; Matthew 19:18). It concerns, then, respect for the goods of others (and, in the case of the poor, their lack of them). Following a consistent Catholic tradition, the *Catechism* teaches the universal destination of the goods of creation: they are meant for the whole human race to enjoy, while also affirming that

> the appropriation of property [i.e. private property] is
> legitimate for guaranteeing the freedom and dignity of
> persons, and for helping each of them to meet his basic
> needs and the needs of those in his charge.[56]

[55]Paragraph 2387.
[56]Paragraph 2402.

Since we have allowed Chesterton to introduce the Seventh
Commandment, we may also invite him to explain it:

> Property ... means that every man should have something
> that he can shape in his own image, as he is shaped in the
> image of heaven. But because he is not God, but only a
> graven image of God, his self-expression must deal with
> limits ... The average man cannot cut clay into the shape
> of a man; but he can cut earth into the shape of a garden;
> but though he arranges it with red geraniums and blue
> potatoes in alternate straight lines, he is still an artist;
> because he has chosen. The average man cannot paint
> the sunset whose colours he admires; but he can paint his
> own house with what colour he chooses; and though he
> paints it pea green with pink spots, he is still an artist;
> because that is his choice. Property is merely the art of the
> democracy.[57]

The *Catechism*, however, does not quite draw Chesterton's
conclusion that the limits of personal (or familial) property
must therefore be 'strict and even small', but contents itself
with maintaining that:

> those who hold goods for use and consumption should
> use them with moderation, reserving the better part for
> guests, for the sick and the poor ...[58]

an attractive imperative which conjures up the vision of a
society marrying the merits of the Ithaca of Ulysses to the
France of St Vincent de Paul.

Much of what the *Catechism* has to say about the right to
ownership, itself ordered to the common good, is in any case
enshrined in legal enactments in decent society: thus the
avoidance of theft and the keeping of contracts belong both
with that commutative justice recognised by the Church and
with the law of property and the law of contract at large. Not,
however, all. For the Church, there can be no theft where
refusal of what is sought by another is 'contrary to reason and

---

[57]Chesterton, *What's Wrong with the World*, pp. 47–48.
[58]Paragraph 2405.

the universal destination of goods' as for instance in the case of those desperate for food, shelter, clothes.[59] Paying unjust wages, and forcing up prices through exploitation of the ignorance or hardship of others are equally forbidden by the Seventh Commandment, though the civil law may not agree.

More widely, that commandment enjoins respect for the integral order of creation. It sets its face, therefore, against all treating of persons as merchandise (of which slave trading is the 'purest' example), and all contempt for the animal creation which by its simple existence blesses and glorifies God. While not ascribing rights to animals, the *Catechism* speaks of what is their due (above all, kindness which, if we are to take seriously the etymology of the English word, means our sense of *kinship* with them). Yet the relief of human misery always takes precedence over animal welfare: this is how the authors interpret, with the entire Judaeo-Christian tradition, the Genesis entrustment of animals to the stewardship of those, namely human beings, God created in his own image. It is the *needless* suffering or death of animals that the Seventh Commandment forbids as theft of the creation's riches.

The remainder of the *Catechism*'s treatment of the commandment furnishes a moral theory of economic life, whether on the micro-level, at the individual's workplace, or on the macro-level, in the affairs of peoples. As the authors make clear, the Church's social doctrine found articulation in the nineteenth century as agrarian and industrial revolution, fortified by the mobilisation of society in the name of the liberal State, detached individuals from those moral codes and institutions – family, Church, local community, artisanal workplace – that once empowered them. At the same time, however, the *Catechism* claims for that social doctrine a profound consonance with ecclesial tradition, and hence a real authority. In one sense, the Church's social teaching is an anti-economism, since:

> any system in which social relationships are determined entirely by economic factors is contrary to the nature of the human person and his acts[60]

[59]Paragraph 2408.
[60]Paragraph 2423.

a statement made *a priori*, prior to any perusal of the particular economic factors involved. But then, descending to the *a posteriori* criticism of given economic systems tried in history:

> regulating the economy solely by centralized planning perverts the basis of social bonds; regulating it solely by the law of the marketplace fails social justice, for 'there are many human needs which cannot be satisfied by the market'[61]

– an allusion to Pope John Paul II's letter in celebration of the first hundred years of magisterial guidance in this territory of the 'dismal science', *Centesimus Annus*.[62] More positively, the Church's portrait of economic activity in its authentic development is a humanism: economic life should satisfy human need, bestow dignity on the world of work (without removing its asceticism which is proper to a time of pilgrimage), encourage economic initiative, find mechanisms for reducing the conflict of interests by mutual adjustment, allow the State to serve as guarantor of freedom and property, sound money and efficient public services, even though

> primary responsibility in this area belongs not to the State but to individuals and to the various groups and associations which make up society.[63] The Church is not so foolish as to decry the profit-motive as such, since only profit makes possible the investment that secures employment, yet she insists on the determination of a just wage, and allows workers a (limited) resource to the weapon of the strike; but only if this be peaceful, linked to working conditions (rather than wider political objectives) and compatible with the common good.

The fabric of a good national order is replicated on a global scale in the texture of the international order. Here the *Catechism* speaks of a duty of solidarity (at the natural level) and (on the supernatural, for Christendom societies) one of charity also. Consequently:

[61]Paragraph 2425.
[62]*Centesimus Annus*, 34.
[63]Paragraph 2431.

rich nations have a grave moral responsibility towards
those which are unable to ensure the means of their
development by themselves or have been prevented from
doing so by tragic historical events.[64]

And where better to end, in a treatise on property, than with
love of the poor? Though the advent of liberation theology –
not unattended by infelicities, both doctrinal and political, as
this was – has sharpened the Church's sense of the privileged
place of the poor in her midst, the heart of the matter is already
there in such Scriptures as the Letter of James and patristic
exhortation like the homily of Chrysostom on Lazarus, both
cited by the *Catechism*. The Church's love is for them first and
foremost, as the lives of saints too many to enumerate attest.

The Eighth Commandment forbids the misrepresentation
of the truth. The Names of all the trinitarian Persons are truth-
related. If the Father is the Source of all truth, the Son presents
himself as both the truth and the One come to bear witness to
the truth: for he alone is sent by the Father to make him known.
Moreover, the Father's interpreter, Jesus, is himself interpreted
by the Spirit of truth, who leads the disciples into the fully
eschatological truth, at once rounding off the interpretation
of the Father given by the Son and yet opening out that
interpretation to endless submediated explanation until the
end comes. In the light of all this, stated in simplest terms by the
Catechism,[65] drawn out in all its manifold connexions by Balthasar
in his twin studies 'Truth of God' and 'The Spirit of Truth',[66]
Christian disciples will naturally have a special devotion to the
truth – the truth in words but also the truth in deeds. They are
to engage in the work of truth in person, and this entails *veritas
vitae*, truth of life. As the *Catechism* puts it

Truth as uprightness in human action and speech is
called truthfulness, sincerity or candour. Truth or
truthfulness is the virtue which consists in showing oneself

[64]Paragraph 2439.
[65]Paragraphs 2465–2466.
[66]H. U. von Balthasar, *Wahrheit Gottes* (= *Theologik* II. Einsiedeln 1985); *Der Geist
der Wahrheit* (= *Theologik* III, Einsiedeln 1987).

true in deeds and truthful in words, and in guarding against duplicity, dissimulation and hypocrisy.[67]

But this is not merely self-consistency; it is the reference of all we say and are to the Truth himself.

Quite properly, then, the *Catechism*'s first task in commenting on the Eighth Commandment is to speak of bearing witness to the gospel. Here the martyr stands as paradigm. As the Greek word *martys* proclaims, the martyr is the witness *par excellence*. He bears witness to 'the truth of the faith and of Christian doctrine'.[68] So here we are dealing centrally with the truth of propositions, wrongly depreciated in some contemporary theology, for Truth gives himself in truths, and the formulation thereof is a glory of the human mind. And yet in the moment of the martyr's dying the 'archives of truth' are written in 'letters of blood'.[69]

The centrality of truth to Christian revelation and its registration in Christian thinking and living leads on the *Catechism* to its next topic, offences against truth, which are, after all, the central focus of the commandment: 'You shall not bear false witness against your neighbour' (Exodus 20:16; Deuteronomy 5:20). The authors select for particular disapprobation false witness in the forensic sense of perjury, above all when this would lead to the condemnation of the innocent, the setting free of the guilty, or the increased punishment of one accused. Then too the Commandment rejects all destruction of the neighbour's reputation and honour by calumny (false report) and detraction (true report, but made without objectively valid reason to a hearer ignorant of the facts). Good counsel for those who would be perfect in charity is the advice to interpret a neighbour's thoughts, words and deeds, so far as be possible, in a favourable way. The flattery of another's perversity, malicious caricature, and just plain straightforward bragging and boasting all offend against the Eighth Commandment. Most directly of all, it is the lie which

[67]Paragraph 2468.
[68]Paragraph 2473.
[69]Paragraph 2474.

gives the lie to this commandment. The *Catechism* characterises lying as profanation of speech, violation of the virtue of truthfulness, and insists on the morally obligatory nature of reparation for all offences made against justice and truth by such sins of word. Charles Kingsley, had he taken this *Catechism* between his hands, would not have found occasion to cast his famous aspersion, 'Truth for its own sake need not be, and on the whole ought not to be, a virtue with the Roman clergy', that irritant which brought forth, as a pearl in an oyster, the *Apologia pro Vita sua* of John Henry Newman.[70]

Kingsley's complaint, however ill-founded, was not entirely unprovoked: the Catholic Church, with a fuller patrimony of moral reflection than Kingsley's own communion, also maintains, in the *Catechism*'s words, that 'the right to the communication of the truth is not unconditional'.[71] Sometimes it may be no loving deed to reveal the truth, for some truth could subvert another to nil purpose.

> The good and safety of others, respect for privacy, and the common good are sufficient reasons for being silent about what ought not to be known, or for making use of a discreet language ...[72]

– though 'silence' and 'discretion' are not, *pace* Kingsley, the same as a lie. The seal of priestly confession and the professional secrets of others are, respectively, inviolable, and to be divulged only when the gravest harm can be avoided in no other way. The modern 'social communications media', to whose corporate itchy ears this message will be no music, are told that the content of their communiqués must always be true – but not always need it be complete – for justice and charity may determine otherwise.

[70]For a good account of the controversy, see I. Ker, *John Henry Newman. A Biography* (Oxford and New York 1988, 1990), pp. 533–559.
[71]Paragraph 2488.
[72]Paragraph 2489.

It was an inspired thought on the authors' part to end their account of the Eighth Commandment by speaking of the truth of art, for truth divorced from beauty lacks attractive power, and is soon carelessly separated from goodness as a result. The *Catechism* addresses itself first to the realm of art as a whole.

> Beyond the search for the necessities of life which is common to all living creatures, art is a freely given superabundance of the human being's inner riches. Arising from talent given by the Creator and from man's own effort, art is a form of practical wisdom, uniting knowledge and skill, to give form to the truth of reality in a language accessible to sight or hearing.

And they go on to say

> To the extent that it is inspired by truth and by love of beings, art bears a certain likeness to God's activity in what he has created. Like any other human activity, art is not an absolute end in itself, but is ordered to and ennobled by the ultimate end of man.[73]

This passage shows remarkable convergencies with the 'hymn of praise in gratitude for the joys and consolations and general usefulness of art' sung by Iris Murdoch in the teeth, rather deliberately, of philosophical detractors of art, both ancient and (post-) modern. The differences are also striking.

> Art is informative and entertaining, it condenses and clarifies the world, directing attention upon particular things. This intense showing, this bearing witness, of which it is capable is detested by tyrants who always persecute or demoralise their artists. Art illuminates accident and contingency and the general muddle of life, the limitations of time and the discursive intellect, so as to enable us to survey complex or horrible things which would otherwise appal us. It creates an authoritative public human world, a treasury of past experience, it

[73]Paragraph 2501.

preserves the past. Art makes places and open spaces for reflection, it is a defence against materialism and against pseudo-scientific attitudes to life. It calms and invigorates, it gives us energy by unifying, possibly by purifying, our feelings.

And Miss Murdoch concludes:

> In enjoying great art we experience a clarification and concentration and perfection of our own consciousness. Emotion and intellect are unified into a limited whole. In this sense art also *creates* its client; it inspires intuitions of ideal formal and symbolic unity which enable us to co-operate with the artist and to be, as we enjoy the work, artists ourselves. The art object conveys, in the most accessible and for many the only available form, the idea of a transcendent perfection. Great art inspires because it is separate, it is for nothing, it is for itself. It is an image of virtue. Its condensed, clarified presentation enables us to look without sin upon a sinful world. It renders innocent and transforms into truthful vision our baser energies connected with power, curiosity, envy and sex.[74]

In these two aesthetics we find the same emphasis upon the gratuity of art, its form-giving yet cognitive power, its semi-divine graciousness. But note also the more palpable presence in the Catholic aesthetic of an objective ontological reference (art gives 'form to the truth of reality'), based on the doctrine of creation and the *philosophia perennis*, as also Iris Murdoch's failure to reach a true version of transcendence (signalled by her statement that art like virtue is 'for nothing, ... for itself'). But the God of the Catholic faith, being true transcendence, is not in competition with any creaturely perfection which can, therefore, point to him without detraction from itself.

Such an aesthetic of created nature, which art at large prolongs, is the presupposition of that sacred art we call Christian iconography. When the uncreated divine beauty enters into composition with its own creation in the flesh-

---

[74]Murdoch, *Metaphysics as a Guide to Morals*, p. 8.

taking of the Word and the outpouring of the Spirit, the capacity of art to speak of the primordial glory is indefinitely enhanced. In the icons of Christ, of his Mother and the saints we glimpse the union – whether hypostatic or, in dependence on that personal bond of divinity and humanity in the God-man – adoptive between the Father and his sons and daughters, and thus the foundation of the redeemed cosmos, the transfigured world where the angels are not sundered from the material creation but ascend and descend upon the Son of Man. It is, the *Catechism* points out, a serious responsibility of the episcopate to ensure that Christian sanctuaries are filled with such a *theological* art, drawing men to adoration, prayer and love.[75]

There remain only the two Commandments, briefly treated in the *Catechism*, which speak of 'coveting' – whether one's neighbour's wife, or anything that is his own. In the Church's catechetical tradition, these precepts proscribe lust and covetousness, prescribe purity of heart and detachment from earthly goods. Weaving a tissue of moral, ascetical and mystical references, the authors bring the sub-book on morals to a fitting close, at once challenging the commonplace assumptions of a flawed self and environment and renewing the reader's hope of eternal life, that, in George Herbert's words, 'as [Christ's] death calcined thee to dust, / His life may make thee gold, and much more just'.[76]

> It remains for the holy people to struggle, with grace from on high, to obtain the good things God promises. In order to possess and contemplate God, Christ's faithful mortify their cravings and, with the grace of God, prevail over the seductions of pleasure and power.[77]

> On this way of perfection, the Spirit and the Pride call whoever hears them to perfect communion with God.[78]

---

[75]For the current difficulties faced by such a programme, see my 'On Baptising the Visual Arts: A Friar's Meditation on Art', in Nichols, *Scribe of the Kingdom*, pp. 183–195.

[76]G. Herbert, 'Easter'.

[77]Paragraph 2549.

[78]Paragraph 2550.

It is that 'call' which the *Catechism* will explore in its final sub-book, on prayer.

PART THREE

THE TREASURES OF MERCY

SPIRITUALITY

Almighty, ever-living God,
whose love surpasses all that we ask or deserve,
open for us the treasures of your mercy.
Forgive us all that weighs on our conscience,
and grant us more even than we dare to ask.

Oratio **of the Roman rite for the**
Twenty-Seventh Sunday of the Year

XIV

---

*The Revelation of Prayer**

The fourth sub-book of the *Catechism*, entitled 'Prayer in the Christian Life', should not be considered a mere tail-piece. Rather do the authors see it as arising in organic fashion from everything that has preceded it, giving the earlier books, in a sense, their supreme rationale. This is how the opening paragraph of the spirituality sub-book expresses things.

> 'Great is the mystery of the faith!' The Church professes this mystery in the Apostles' Creed (Part One) and celebrates it in the sacramental liturgy (Part Two), so that the life of the faithful may be conformed to Christ in the Holy Spirit to the glory of God the Father (Part Three). This mystery, then, requires that the faithful believe in it, that they celebrate it, and that they live from it in a vital and personal relationship with the living and true God. This relationship is prayer.[1]

The statement does not only situate the *Catechism*'s theology of prayer in relation to its fundamental and dogmatic theology, its liturgiology and sacramentology, and its theological ethics. It also serves as a preamble to the author's[2] initial stab at describing what prayer is.

---

*=*Catechism*, Paragraphs 2558–2649.
[1]Paragraph 2558.
[2]The use of the singular is justified by the account of the Abbé Jean Corbon's unique rôle in the preparation of this section of the *Catechism* in J. Ratzinger and C. Schönborn, *Introduction to the 'Catechism of the Catholic Church'* (E.t. San Francisco 1994), p. 23.

The Service of Glory

He begins from the celebrated definition of the eighth-
century doctor of the Church, St John of Damascus: 'the
raising of one's mind and heart to God, or the requesting of
good things from God'.[3] Actually, Damascene's summary
suggests the complexity of the subject, since between
contemplative union (the raising of mind and heart) and the
prayer of petition (seeking good things) is fixed, if not a great
gulf, then at least an appreciable difference. The question of
the unity of prayer is one the *Catechism* will not be able to avoid,
but it is not so fundamental as those which it now tackles. And
these concern precisely the *foundations* of the act of prayer,
both human and divine.

The most basic human attitude in prayer is mendicancy:
only those with arms outstretched and open hands can pray.
For the psalmist the main precondition of prayer, on the
manward side, lies in a 'humble and contrite heart (Psalm
130:1) which, recognising that, in the words of the Paul of
Romans we 'do not know how to pray as we ought' (8:26)
approaches prayer as what it really is, the *gift* of God. For the
deeper foundation of prayer is not human at all, but divine. It
is God who has the primacy in initiating prayer; and this is true
whether we think of prayer in its more existentially exalted,
contemplative, state, or in its everyday condition as asking for
things. In a spiritual interpretation of the conversation of Jesus
with the Woman of Samaria in chapter four of St John's Gospel,
it is God in Christ who comes to meet the human being at the
well of the world, who establishes the encounter that leads to
union, just as it is the same God in his incarnate Word who
begins by asking us for something, and so puts in place that
relationship on which we later capitalise by the prayer of
petition. 'God thirsts that we may thirst for him', and 'our
prayer of petition is a response to the plea of the living God'.[4]

If, however, prayer is essentially *responsive* (to God, that is),
we still need to ask whence its response comes. Commonly, the
Scriptures identify the locus of prayer as the human heart,

[3] *On the Orthodox Faith*, III. 24, cited Paragraph 2559.
[4] Paragraphs 2560, 2561.

which is, for the anthropology found or presumed in most of the Bible, the centre of man.

> The heart is our hidden centre, beyond the grasp of our reason and of others; only the Spirit of God can fathom the human heart and know it fully. The heart is the place of decision, deeper than our psychic drives. It is the place of truth, where we choose life or death. It is the place of encounter, because as image of God we live in relation ...[5]

The accumulation of predicates combines the language of Scripture with that of philosophy and depth psychology. But its intent is not simply to evoke the metaphysical conjunction of the Creator Spirit with the human spirit. For that passage comes to its climax in calling the heart the 'place of covenant': the meeting place not only of Creator and spiritual creature but also of God as Redeemer, as Author of the missions of Son and Spirit in redemption history and of man as the historical animal, open to transcendence not least as the latter comes to greet him in historical time. And this leads the author to as good as *identify* prayer with the covenant relationship inaugurated by the biblical God with humankind, not just at the creation or in the cosmic covenant summed up in Noah, or with Israel in Abraham, Moses and David, but also, and above all, in Jesus Christ.

> Christian prayer is a covenant relationship between God and man in Christ. It is the action of God and of man, springing forth from both the Holy Spirit and ourselves, wholly directed to the Father, in union with the human will of the Son of God made man.[6]

Since the aim of the divine saving economy is the communion of man with God by the insertion of human persons into the fellowship of the inner-trinitarian life itself, so, in the final analysis, prayer cannot be defined – even provisionally, as here – without calling the language of communion to one's aid. The life of prayer is made possible

[5]Paragraph 2563.
[6]Paragraph 2564.

by a communion of life described by the fourth-century Cappadocian Father St Gregory the Theologian as 'the union of the entire holy and royal Trinity with the whole human spirit'.[7] And that communion brings us within its embrace when the coinherence of Father, Son and Spirit extends itself through Jesus Christ into his mystical Body, the Church, whereof by baptismal initiation we are members. Prayer cannot be divorced from these sacramental and ecclesial dimensions, nor, *a fortiori* from the mystery of Christ whose loving outreach into the cosmos alone sets prayer's limits.

Having thus ensured that, when we come to search the sources of revelation for instruction about prayer, we have some rough idea, at any rate, of what it is we are looking for, the *Catechism* turns to deal in so many words with the 'revelation of prayer'. It begins with a warning, though one that, Janus-like, points in two opposite directions at once.

God reveals prayer to man, but would man hear the Word of God revealing unless he were already listening out for him? Yet if man is seeking God even before God seeks out man, what becomes of the claim that in matters of prayer it is God who acts first? Evidently, it must fall to the ground unless man's very seeking of the (potentially) self-revealing God is itself a response to God's call. And this – we might term it a Catholic answer to Barth, that mighty Neo-Orthodox Protestant theologian of the divine primacy – is the door on which the *Catechism*'s account of the 'revelation of prayer' swings. We must neither deny that man is truly and impressively in search of God, nor that it is God who calls man first. By creation God has sent out his call, calling man into existence from nothing, and if we think that too obviously a play of words with the lexical item 'call', this is no *mere* wordplay, for our creation leaves us with a *desire* for the One who calls into being, a set of antennae attuned, however imperfectly, to the divine wavelength. Thus 'all religions bear witness to men's essential search for God'.[8] Such seeking is, for post-lapsarian humanity, inefficacious for salvation unless it be

---

[7]Gregory of Nazianzus, *Orations*, XVI. 9, cited Paragraph 2565.
[8]Paragraph 2566.

somehow taken up and given imperishable worth by the God of grace. And thanks to the universality of God's saving will

> the living and true God tirelessly calls each person to that mysterious encounter known as prayer.[9]

As in the history of revelation God discloses step by step who he is and, *pari passu*, shows man who man is, so a 'covenant drama' unfolds, of which the essence is the divine-human relationship itself, namely, prayer.

The *Catechism* divides its materials for an account of prayer in biblical revelation along the line of articulation of the two Testaments, but within the New it treats first the prayer of Jesus (with a coda on the prayer of Mary) and then the prayer of the (apostolic) Church.

What, then, of prayer in the *Old* Testament? In the Genesis history of human beginnings, human relation with God in the midst of creation is mediated by sacrificial cultus, through an offering from the shepherd's flock, with Abel; invocation of the divine Name, as with Enosh; and that straightforward rectitude, called by the Genesis writer 'walking with God' which, in Noah's case, leads the Lord to renew his creation covenant with the earth and all it contains.

But the prayer of Israelite faith proper begins with Abraham as the latter is called forth, by the Lord's Word, as was deemed, from Haran and Ur of the Chaldees, cities of the rich 'land between the rivers' (Mesopotamia), into the rough existence of a pastoralist along the caravan routes through Palestine to Egypt. The *Catechism* does not attempt to reconstruct the historical setting of the theophanies to Abraham which first made Palestine the *holy* land: that is not its task. Instead it draws out the spiritual message about Godward relationship they embody. Those theophanies provide the *Catechism* with five themes of Abrahamic prayer: the precedence of the heart's attentiveness (obeying God's will) over prayer in words; prayer as pleading before God – the expression of how faith in God's fidelity to his promises is tested; prayer as hospitality to the divine guest, as Abraham offered hospitality at the oaks of

Mamre; confident intercession for others; and, in a *tour de force*
of spiritual exegesis of the offering of Isaac, when Abraham,
father of all believers in both Jewish and Christian tradition, is
'conformed to the likeness of the Father who will not spare his
only Son' but 'delivers him up for us all', the revelation of
prayer as

> [restoring] man to God's likeness and [enabling] him to
> share in the power of God's love that saves the multitude.[10]

Before leaving the topic of the prayer of the patriarchs, the
Catechism notes the importance to the spiritual tradition of the
wrestling of Jacob with the angel of Yahweh at the fords of
Jabbok: here prayer shows faith's agonistic element but also
how it can persevere and triumph.

The promise to Abraham began to be fulfilled in the time of
Moses. As mediator between the people and the God of the
fathers Moses is a type of Jesus Christ, and as the prayer of
Christ is pre-eminently mediatorial intercession so too
intercessory praying is the hallmark of Mosaic spirituality in
the Exodus and Sinai traditions. The *Catechism*'s portrait of
Moses finds the clue to his mediatorial rôle in that episode
which has etched itself on the imagination of the Church:
God's call to Moses from out of the burning bush – 'one of the
primordial images of prayer in the spiritual tradition of Jews
and Christians alike'.[11] The bush that burns but is not consumed
signals the uncreated energies of the divine Being, in whose
presence Moses must take off his shoes, for the ground on
which he stands is holy (Exodus 3:1–10). But this mystical grace
is also a missionary charge. Integral to Moses' contemplation
is learning what God desires for his people. The *Catechism*
stresses in this connexion the rôle of the prophet's clamant
questioning, in answer to which God confides to him his
ineffable Name, the tetragrammaton YHWH, drawing attention
as this does to the uniqueness of the divine mode of existence

---

[10]Paragraph 2572 – a *relecture* of the allusion to the sacrifice of Isaac in Romans
8:16–21.
[11]Paragraph 2575.

and his sovereign freedom. Like the Cappadocian doctor Gregory of Nyssa, the author of the *Catechism*'s treatise on prayer regards the life of Moses as a study in contemplation, not only because he speaks to God face to face, but also because he passes on the fruit of contemplation.

> Moses converses with God often and at length, climbing the mountain to hear and entreat him and coming down to the people to repeat the words of his God for their guidance.[12]

Though David and Elijah are also singled out by the *Catechism*, following the lead of the Hebrew Bible itself, as models of prayer, these archetypal figures do not receive quite the accentuation given to Abraham and Moses. Instead, the author's treatment of the rest of the Old Testament sources trifurcates into a treatment of, first, ark and temple (both closely related to the Davidic dynasty); secondly, the prophetic movement in Israel; and thirdly, the prayer of the Psalter. On the first, the person of David binds together these twin foci of Israelite devotion the ark of the covenant, which he brings into the citadel of Zion, and the temple, the house of prayer projected yet unrealised until the work of Solomon his son. To the theme of intercession are added, by the portrayal of David in the Books of Samuel, those of repentance and praise, and not in terms of some general religious attitude, merely, but in a manner specific to the covenant of God with the people.

> His prayer, the prayer of God's Anointed, is a faithful adherence to the divine promise and expresses a loving and joyful trust in God, the only King and Lord.[13]

The fuller sense of David's praying will be disclosed only in the prayer of *the* Anointed, the Saviour: the *Catechism*'s theology of prayer is marked by 'Christological concentration'. Not irrelevant to the final outcome of Israel's experience of saving

---

[12]Paragraph 2576; cf. A. J. Malherbe and E. Ferguson (tr.), *Gregory of Nyssa. The Life of Moses* (New York 1978).

[13]Paragraph 2579.

history in Jesus Christ is the 'Name theology' associated with the Jerusalem temple: the invocation of the divine Name in that unique sanctuary is made possible by God's 'sending' his Name to 'dwell' there – a way of symbolising the divine presence which looks ahead to the incarnation when that Name will become one with a nameable human being, Jesus Christ.

The prophets, as interpreted by the *Catechism*, contribute to the unfolding pattern of biblical spirituality a deepened sense of the need for education in faith, and for conversion of heart. But despite the rich pigments employed in the painting of a verbal icon of Elijah, the prayer of that 'father of the prophets' on the mountains of Israel is depicted as above all pointing on, like David's, towards its own fulfilment in the divine Man, Jesus Christ.

> Taking the desert road that leads to the place where the living and true God reveals himself to his people, Elijah, like Moses before him, hides 'in a cleft of the rock' until the mysterious presence of God has passed by. But only on the mountain of the Transfiguration will Moses and Elijah behold the unveiled face of him whom they sought; 'the light of the knowledge of the glory of God [shines] in the face of Christ', crucified and risen.[14]

In dealing last with the Psalter, the *Catechism* which is following a broadly chronological path through the history of the Elder Covenant, implies that the Psalms are, *im Grossen und Ganzen*, the work of the post-exilic period: the Psalter, if not simply the prayer book of the Second Temple, is indebted to Israel's worship both at the Jerusalemite centre and in communities more on the periphery, indeed into the Diaspora itself. But whatever the providential particularities of the origins of the Psalms there is nothing constrictingly particular about their purview which

---

[14]Paragraph 2583, with internal part-citations of I Kings 19:9 and 13 (the cave of Elijah on Horeb); Exodus 33:22, and of II Corinthians 4:6.

embraces all creation. Their prayer recalls the saving events of the past, yet extends into the future, even to the end of history; it commemorates the promises God has already kept, and awaits the Messiah who will fulfil them definitively.[15]

The *Catechism* presents the Psalter as an exercise in incipient Chalcedonianism. The inspired writers find words for God in his complex yet unified pathos towards his covenant partner: love and wrath, mercy and justice; but equally they provide a language for the human response. In the God-man, the two are united, the quality of the divine address is perfectly replicated in the human reply. With the incarnation of the Word in Jesus, the Psalter is to be prayed *in* the mystery of Christ where its two chief voices, God's and man's, enter into perfect harmony for the first time.

The Psalter's diversity is emphasised: in terms of the gamut of human situations, and their appropriate emotions, here is something for everyone. And yet this is not incoherence, for certain 'constant characteristics' appear throughout, and these are well summed up as:

> the desire for God himself through and with all that is good in his creation; the distraught situation of the believer who, in his preferential love for the Lord, is exposed to a host of enemies and temptations, but who waits upon what the faithful God will do, in the certitude of his love and in submission to his will. The prayer of the Psalms is always sustained by praise ...[16]

And so we come to the prayer of Christ himself. The *Catechism*'s approach to the prayer of ancient Israel has prepared us for its assertion that in the Word incarnate, who is Emmanuel, God with us, the 'drama' of prayer is for the first time fully revealed. Consonant with the way it highlighted the theophany of the burning bush in Exodus, it now presents the glory made flesh, Jesus Christ, as the true Burning Bush, where the creation

[15]Paragraph 2586.
[16]Paragraph 2589.

is hypostatically united to the Creator – not, then, a transient manifestation of the divine, however wonderful, but its abiding sacrament, the human face of God. Still, the *Catechism* gives a special place, despite the permanence of the Word's indwelling among us, to 'his witnesses ... in the Gospel'. It is in the company of the New Testament writers (and their sources) that we are to contemplate the 'holy Lord Jesus', hear his teaching about prayer and so come to understand how he in turn receives the prayer of his disciples.

How does Jesus himself pray? By absorbing utterly the prayer of Israel which is already revelation from the Father, but transforming that inheritance through the absolute novelty of his own filial attitude as only Son of the Father, who, even at twelve years old must be in his Father's house (cf. Luke 2:49). There, in the grace of the union which conjoins the Logos in definitive fashion to the (Israelite) manhood taken from Mary we have the foundation of Jesus' prayer.

But when we espy in action the prayer of Jesus what is it that we see? What is the *mode* and *content* of that prayer which, as the only-begotten Son now living out to the full the vocation of God's servant Israel, he both embodies and is? Here the *Catechism* mentions first the decisive importance prayer takes on in Jesus' mission. It precedes, evidently of set purpose, all the really determinative moments of his life and ministry: baptism, transfiguration, passion, and the events, so crucial for the communication to the future of that life and ministry, which brought into being the mission of the apostles – their election and calling, and Peter's establishment as primus of the apostolic college. The *Catechism* draws the Christological lesson in terms redolent of the defence of the doctrine of the two wills of the Redeemer made in the wake of the Lateran Synod of 649 by St Maximus the Confessor.

> Jesus' prayer before the events of salvation that the Father has asked him to fulfil is a humble and trusting commitment of his human will to the loving will of the Father.[17]

[17]Paragraph 2600.

Contemplation of the praying Jesus must have been uniquely beautiful, powerful, persuasive. It convinced the first disciples, devout Jews though they were, that in comparison with their Master they could barely be said to pray at all. 'Lord, teach us to pray' (Luke 11:1) is the request that elicits the *Pater*, a commentary on which will close the *Catechism* as a whole.

The *Catechism* brings to its readers' attention three main aspects of that prayer life which was thus so momentous for its own divine-human subject. First, Jesus prayed in solitude, on hillsides, frequently at night. It is supposed, on the basis of the Lord's assuming all humanity with the created nature personalised in the Logos, that such prayer was for all men, offering all to the Father of all. And here the *Catechism*'s approach to the mystery of Jesus could be termed 'oratiocentric', prayer-centred, since it speaks of his words and works as the exteriorisation of his secret prayer. Secondly, the book before us draws out the prayer of Christ *to the Father* in the 'Johannine thunderbolt' of the Synoptic Gospels (Matthew 11:25–27, Luke 10:21–23); at the raising of Lazarus (John 11:41–42), and on the cross, in the 'Seven Words' of the Four Gospels taken cumulatively as, with the third-century Syriac writer Tatian, a 'diatessaron'. The lesson the *Catechism* would have us learn from the prayer of the incarnate Son to the Father is that here 'prayer and the gift of self are but one'.[18]

> Jesus' prayer, characterised by thanksgiving, reveals to us how to ask: *before* the gift is given, Jesus commits himself to the One who in giving gives himself. The Giver is more precious than the gift; he is the 'treasure'; in him abides his Son's heart; the gift is given 'as well'.[19]

Finally, in the wordless cry with which, in Mark (15:37), Jesus dies (the *Catechism* alludes also to its interpretation, or perhaps *better remembering*, in John where it appears as *tetēlestai*, 'It is accomplished': 19:30b), we are to find all the 'petitions and intercessions of salvation history' caught up in the Logos, and accepted by the Father who answers them beyond all human

---

[18]Paragraph 2605.
[19]Paragraph 2604.

imagining of good in the resurrection of the Son, presaging as this does the transfiguration of the world. St Augustine, commenting on Psalm 56, remarks that Christ did not really pray for himself but for us who were impersonated in him. He is the form, and therefore the linguistically of the relation between man and God. Before God we found our speaking part in him.

What, then, of Jesus' actual *teaching* about prayer? As the *Catechism* presents matters, Jesus set out his teaching, in dependence on the capacity of his audience to 'hear' him, along a trajectory linking the most exoteric proclamation, based in part on what was already familiar in the Old Testament, to a reserved, esoteric instruction circling around the two chief theological mysteries of New Testament believing: his relation to the Father, and to the Spirit.

> Addressing the crowds following him, Jesus builds on what they already know of prayer from the Old Covenant, and opens to them the newness of the coming Kingdom. Then he reveals this newness to them in parables. Finally, he will speak openly of the Father and the Holy Spirit to his disciples who will be the teachers of prayer in his Church.[20]

The key word in the *Catechism*'s version of the content of Jesus' teaching is 'filial'. We could render that in more Anglo-Saxon English as 'son-like'. But better, so as to displace from a position of centrality the concept of imitation ('like') and, following the *Catechism*'s own *Tendenz*,[21] replace it in this context with that of incorporation, we might call it 'son-*ly*'. We are *filii in Filio:* 'sons *in* the Son'. At the heart of Jesus' doctrine of prayer we find notions of filial conversion, filial faith, filial boldness. The prayer he teaches is for sons, not slaves. And this corresponds to the new era of grace he proclaims as inaugurator of the Father's Kingdom.

But since that Kingdom has not yet come in its fulness, the vigilance or watchfulness which Jesus bade his disciples practise

---

[20]Paragraph 2607.
[21]See above, p. 114.

against the day of his trial and vindication as the Son of Man has lost none of its actuality. It will remain a hallmark of the Christian attitude:

> In prayer, the disciple keeps watch, attentive to Him Who Is and Him Who Comes, in memory of his first coming in the lowliness of the flesh, and in the hope of his second coming in glory. In communion with their Master, the disciples' prayer is a battle; only by keeping watch in prayer can one avoid falling into temptation.[22]

Finally, if urgent, patient, humble prayer, such as Jesus recommends in his parables (respectively those of the importunate friend, the importunate widow, and the Pharisee and publican) might be considered as intensifications of the Old Testament's witness to prayer, given new sharpness by the imminence of the Kingdom's arrival, those aspects of the prayer of Christ which touch on the Father and the Spirit are altogether unparalleled – in their meaning, if not in every respect in their language. Prayer in the name of the Son, by faith in him, introduces us to the knowledge of the Father, since only the Son is the Father's self-expression, his 'exegesis', and thus the way, the truth, and the life. Abiding with the Son in the Father's bosom, we receive the second Paraclete, the Holy Spirit; we enter the joyous circumincession, beyond the distinction of seriousness and play, of the holy Trinity.

And the divinity of the Son, which belongs to Jesus through the hypostatic union, means that we can properly address our prayer to him, as indeed his contemporaries did in their own beseeching. They prayed to him in silent gesture: as with the bearers of the paralytic at Capernaum, or the *haemorrhissa*, or the woman in the house of Simon who anointed his feet with tears and nard. They prayed to him in words: as when the leper called on him, and Jairus for his daughter, and the good thief to be with him that day in Paradise. The Church has turned the plea of the blind beggar at Jericho into her own 'Jesus Prayer', especially beloved of the Byzantine-Slav East, 'Lord Jesus Christ, Son of God, have mercy on me.' And this is a prayer also

---

[22]Paragraph 2612.

recommended to those renewing their contrition in the sacrament of Penance in the West.

For Catholicism, the Son is not found far from the Mother, and so this Christological account of prayer does not come to an end without reference to the prayer of Mary.

In three dense paragraphs we are given the materials for a lifetime's reflection on this subject. Her prayer is co-operation with the Father's loving plan: for Christ's personal conception as man at the Annunciation, for his ecclesial conception in the Church, his mystical Body, at Pentecost. And this perfect balancing of the Christological and ecclesiological dimensions of our Lady's praying is maintained when the *Catechism* speaks of her rôle in the public ministry. At Cana she asks her Son to meet the needs of a bride and groom in distress. But his miracle, the first of that 'book of signs' embedded within St John's Gospel, signalises the joy of the divine nuptials, when at the wedding feast of the Lamb he 'gives his body and blood at the request of the Church, his Bride'.[23] And since, then, the Atonement is the precondition *par excellence* for the life of the Church, when we see Mary again in that Gospel it is as the *adiuvatrix* at the foot of the cross where Jesus declares her the new Eve, Mother of all the living. This intimate linkage between Mary's rapport of prayer with her sacrificed Son, and her rôle in the coming to be of the Church which is the fruit of his sacrifice explains, for the *Catechism*, the special genius of the Canticle of Mary, the *Magnificat* or as, conscious of the Church's Eastern 'lung' it insists on adding, in Greek as well as Latin, the *Megalunei.* The *Magnificat*

is the song both of the Mother of God and of the Church; the song of the Daughter of Zion and of the new People of God; the song of thanksgiving for the fulness of graces poured out in the economy of salvation and the song of the 'poor' whose hope is met by the fulfilment of the promises made to our ancestors.[24]

It remains only to consider, under the heading of 'the revelation of prayer', the last chapter in revelation's giving, the

[23]Paragraph 2618.
[24]Paragraph 2619.

story of the New Testament Church. The *Catechism* finds five great forms of prayer in the canon of the Younger Covenant: the prayer of blessing and adoration; of petition; of intercession; of thanksgiving, and of praise. And these will remain normative for the life of the Church, not simply because they are given *in* the inspired and inerrant Scriptures but also because, more deeply, they are given *by* the speech-bearing Spirit who is that canon's Source.

The sub-book of the *Catechism* on the Liturgy has already offered a theory of doxology, a theology of blessing. Here it suffices, with a handful of references to the Pauline corpus, to indicate the two 'directions' in which blessing can move: in the Spirit through Christ to the Father, as we bless him for having blessed us; and from the Father through Christ by the Spirit to us, as God renews his blessing. On adoration, the paired term in the title of this first major mode of New Testament prayer, the *Catechism*'s references are in fact chiefly to the Psalter but these are Christianised thanks to an implicit trinitarian reference: it is 'adoration of the thrice-holy and sovereign God of love [that] blends with humility and gives assurance to our supplications'.[25] New Testament Greek has a rich store of vocabulary for, next, the prayer of petition, which prayer is singularly well-fitted for expressing our most fundamental relation to God.

> We are creatures who are not our own beginning, not the masters of adversity, not our own last end. We are sinners who as Christians know that we have turned away from our Father. Our petition is already a turning back to him.[26]

Perceptively, the author notes the striking absence of prayers of lamentation in the New Testament, in sharp contrast to the Old. Here is an important clue, Arthur Conan Doyle's dog that did not bark. The solution is that 'in the risen Christ, the Church's petition is buoyed by hope',[26] even if the whole creation, including ourselves, still groans in travail for its liberation. Though the *Catechism* agrees with a long tradition

[25]Paragraph 2628.
[26]Paragraph 2629.

that any and every need, no matter how small, can be made the object of petitionary prayer, it also insists on a principle of hierarchy. Praying for fine weather for a *fête champêtre*, that we may not miss the downtrain from Waterloo, or that Sikkimese Diamond may win the local cats' show is not beneath the dignity of the disciple of the Christ who 'assumed all things in order to redeem all things'.[28] Nonetheless, we are to pray first for the Kingdom, and then for 'what is necessary to welcome it and co-operate with its coming',[29] which means in the words of the Liturgy of Saint John Chrysostom, for 'the peace of the whole world, the good estate of the holy churches of God, and the union of all'.

And that inevitably means in turn a *glissando* in the music of prayer which brings us to the *Catechism*'s third movement, prayer of intercession. According to the Paul of Philippians, in prayer one's petition should extend to considering the interests of others (2:4), a seemingly commonplace, not to say banal, observation which, however, has unsuspected depths in the doctrines of the (heavenly) intercession of the exalted Christ, and the (interior) intercession of the Spirit, for these are in fact the models which intercessory prayer follows, the inspiration by which it endures. Intercession expresses the communion of saints in both the 'only Holy One', Christ, and the 'unity of the Holy Spirit', as the Roman church confesses in the Gloria of the Mass-ritual.

Fourthly, the prayer of thanksgiving can hardly be sundered, in a Catholic context, from that ecclesial prayer which we call above all others *the* thanksgiving, the Holy Eucharist. Still, as with petitionary prayer itself 'every event *and need* can become an offering of thanksgiving';[30] the italicising of two words in that proposition is necessitated by the extraordinary daring of this doctrine, which is, however, soundly rooted in Pauline theology:

[27]Paragraph 2630.
[28]Paragraph 2633.
[29]Paragraph 2632.
[30]Paragraph 2638.

Rejoice always, pray constantly, give thanks in all circumstances; for this is the will of God in Christ Jesus for you. (I Thessalonians 5:18)

There remains the prayer of praise, to which the *Catechism* awards the palm, on the grounds that

it lauds God for his own sake, and gives him glory, quite beyond what he does, but simply because HE IS.[31]

As the most theocentric mode of the five types of New Testament praying, (for, as we have seen, the *Catechism* only integrates adoration into the prayer of blessing by way of texts from the Old), praise

embraces the other forms of prayer and carries them toward him who is prayer's source and goal.[32]

In that prayer the Father is lauded for the marvels of Christ and the actions of the Holy Spirit, not as a lonely Monad surgically clean of entanglement with history. The consummation of all things, the final destiny of the cosmos, is borne along, in the closing book of the Bible, by the songs of the heavenly liturgy (cf. Apocalypse 4:8–11, 5:9–14, 7:10–12), and the Church struggling on earth sings these same songs in communion with the glorified Church, even in the midst of her trials.

[31]Paragraph 2639.
[32]Ibid.

XV

Prayer in the Church *

Under the rubric 'The Tradition of Prayer', the *Catechism* offers its synthesis of the ascetic and mystical doctrine of the post-apostolic Church, while setting the same within the context of a well-ordered Catholic environment and meeting some common objections and difficulties. As its own principal author, writing elsewhere, explains:

> The *Catechism* does not adopt any one school of spirituality, but rather develops biblical spirituality in the light of the common experience of the spiritual writers of East and West.[1]

The section opens by making two quite basic points. First, in the realm of prayer, intellectualism is not enough. One must not just know what has been revealed about prayer; one must actually learn to pray. Secondly, however, this caveat should not itself be taken in an anti-intellectualist sense. The 'tradition of Christian prayer' has profound value for our understanding of the faith; it is one of the moving forces of doctrinal development, as the Dogmatic Constitution of the Second Vatican Council on Divine Revelation makes clear.[2]

What are the resources the Catholic Christian can bring to the life of prayer, or find at hand? First and foremost, that

---

*=*Catechism*, Paragraphs 2650–2758.

[1] J. Corbon, 'Reflections on the *Catechism of the Catholic Church* 13, *L'Osservatore Romano* (English edition), 26 May 1993.

[2] *Dei Verbum* 8, allusively cited in Paragraph 2651.

245

interior font, the water given by Jesus and welling up to life eternal, which is the Holy Spirit. He is the life-giving Spring, our personal source of renewal and growth in the Christian life; and therefore in prayer. The *Catechism* speaks of the missions of Son and Spirit as mutually enabling: the Spirit leads us to Christ who sets this source flowing, just as Christ enables us to drink of this Spirit. And this coheres with the triadology of the *Catechism*'s sub-book on the Creed, where the saving outreach of the holy Trinity, there conceived in more dogmatic idiom, is described in just this fashion.[3]

Our second resource is Scripture, read not simply by way of study but in *lectio divina*, that is: study accompanied by prayer. To meditate is, in the first place, to rehearse the biblical text, constantly repeating, murmuring, its words. The mediaevals called this *ruminare*: as a cow chews the cud, so a Christian digests the Word of God, tranquilly engrossed. If the biblical Word is to be a seed of life that can germinate within us, we must let it sink down and enter the heart. Such *meditatio* turns naturally into prayer, my response of self-surrender to God in Christ via this text – what, on the classical mediaeval scheme, cited by the *Catechism*, is called *oratio*. Finally, such prayer tends to become the silent adoration of God's presence, *contemplatio*. The movement is not of course inevitable, but it is self-correcting. When distractions take over, the person has a remedy: returning to the text, he or she lets the language pour over them again until the prayerful and contemplative spiral resumes.

Then thirdly, we have the sacramental Liturgy, which the heart can internalise and make its own. The *Liber Graduum*, the earliest Syrian treatise on the Church, speaks of a perpetual liturgy celebrated in the temple of the heart. It should be a typical by-product of the Mass and the Divine Office that they move people to continue to pray even after the rites are concluded, as the early Dominicans did, scattered round their churches at altars and images when Compline was over. Part of responding to the *Ite, missa est!* of the eucharistic dismissal is that we take the spirit of prayer, learned in the Liturgy, into the rest of our lives. That is one major reason why to judge the

[3]Nichols, *The Splendour of Doctrine*, pp. 104–105.

Church's worship by its immediate 'feel-good' impact is wrong. And, as the phenomenon of the Christian hermit shows, no matter how physically separated from the common assembly a person may be, his or her prayer remains the prayer of the Church. There is no such thing as an extra-ecclesial disciple.

The final 'bank-deposit' on which we can draw in the life of prayer consists in the theological virtues of faith, hope and charity, already discussed by the *Catechism* under various aspects in each of its sub-books hitherto. Succinctly, the *Catechism* shows their relevance to the present subject. Prayer is a very pure example of the exercise of faith:

> It is the Face of the Lord that we seek and desire; it is his Word that we want to hear and keep.[4]

Prayer is also carried out through the medium of hope, since the Spirit teaches us to celebrate the Liturgy – both that of the *synaxis* and that of the heart – in 'joyful hope for the coming of our Saviour Jesus Christ', as the English translation of the embolism of the Mass of Paul VI has it. And as for love, it is the summit of prayer. A point made with both clarity and amplitude by St Francis de Sales in his *Treatise on the Love of God*, though the author of the *Catechism*'s euchology prefers to cite another figure of the *Ecole Française*, the Curé d'Ars.

And all drinking at the wellsprings of prayer goes on in the biblical 'today', which is the historically introduced yet now ever-present moment of salvation. There is, as the seventeenth-century Jesuit spiritual theologian Jean-Pierre de Caussade saw, a 'sacrament of the present moment', for self-abandonment to divine Providence is not something that can be done retrospectively, or prospectively for that matter. It is *in actu*, or it is nothing. We meet the God who comes to meet us not chiefly in the formulation of heady, world-historical objectives, but in the immediacy of now. Or as the *Catechism* itself puts it, rather more serenely:

> It is right and good to pray so that the coming of the Kingdom of justice and peace may influence the march of

[4]Paragraphs 2656.

history, but it is just as important to bring the help of prayer into humble, everyday situations; all forms of prayer can be the leaven to which the Lord compares the Kingdom.[5]

Turning from the *sources* of prayer to the actual structure of prayer, the *Catechism* appeals to the ecclesiological distinction between the many (local or regional) churches and the single Church in order to speak of the simultaneous multiplicity and unity of the *way* of prayer. The 'ritual churches' of Catholicism (Latin, Byzantine, Chaldaean, Maronite, and so forth) are the most manifest examples of what the *Catechism* calls here the manner

each church proposes to her faithful, according to her historic, social and cultural context, a language for prayer: words, melodies, gestures, iconography ...[6]

Yet *mutatis mutandis*, something similar could be said of the regional or local variations within those ritual churches, and notably in the far-flung Western patriarchate. And yet, as always in matters of Catholic pluralism, it is not enough to say, Let a thousand flowers bloom! Lest variety fall into anarchy and incoherence, we need to know that variations are on themes, that the same common principles are everywhere at work. That discernment pertains to the Church's magisterium to carry out: just as the unity of Christian believing, sacramental life and ethical practice is assured by the pastors of the Church, with the supreme pastor, the Roman pontiff, at their head, so here too. The consonance of different ways of praying with apostolic faith must be tested and, as far as possible, proved.

Once so tried and proved as gold, catechists have the job of explaining the meaning of such ways of prayer, and this they should do, the *Catechism* goes on, *in relation to Jesus Christ*. And the text gives a perfect ostensive definition of what it has in mind by reviewing not only the Christological dimension of prayer in this light (that would of course be tautological), but

---

[5]Paragraph 2660.
[6]Paragraph 2663.

prayer's relation likewise to the Father and the Spirit, as well as to the Mother of God. For the *Catechism* would hold that Christian prayer is *always* carried out in communion with the Blessed Virgin Mary, the God-bearer. Here the potent influence of Byzantine Christianity is palpable. In the words of Nicolas Zernov, once Spalding Lecturer in Eastern Christian Studies in the University of Oxford:

> whenever [the Christian] lifts up his heart, he meets her who never ceases her intercession for suffering and struggling mankind.[7]

Thus, to take first the first trinitarian person, the *Father* is to be approached only through Jesus Christ our Lord, and more especially via the sacred humanity of Christ. Furthermore, the Liturgy, while addressed primarily to the Father, also teaches us to address the *Son* directly, and the fruit of this is found in devotion to the Name of Jesus, whose invocation the *Catechism* considers the simplest and best way of fulfilling the Pauline injunction to 'pray always'. At the same time, the reality that Name signifies is further revealed in his sacred heart and on his way to the cross, which also serve then as foci of prayer to Christ. And lastly, in the trinitarian schema, the most venerable and widespread form of praying to the *Spirit* is, once again, Christocentric in character: a prayer through Christ that the Father will send the Comforter on Christ's faithful, as the Saviour promised. However, the *Catechism* notes the complete legitimacy of direct petitioning of the Spirit also, of which splendid examples are the Pentecost Sequence, *Veni Sancte Spiritus*, of the Roman Liturgy and the wonderful troparion, beginning 'Heavenly King, Consoler Spirit, Spirit of truth' originally found in Byzantine Vespers for Whit Sunday and subsequently in the Greek Manual as part of the morning prayers of the devout.

And if such Christologically ordered trinitarian praying is everywhere different and yet everywhere the same, for the

[7]N. Zernov, 'Explanatory Notes', *A Manual of Eastern Orthodox Prayers* (London 1945; 1977), p. xi.

same catholic spirit animates all the ritual families of the Church, so it is too with prayer in union with Mary.

The sub-book on prayer has already spoken of the prayer *of* Mary as a facet of the biblical disclosure of the mystery of man's relations with God at large. Now it considers prayer *to* Mary, seen all the time in the perspective of the *Catechism*'s Christological concentration. As in the Eastern icons that go by these generic names, Mary is *Hodegitria*, the one who shows us the way to Jesus, and the 'Mother of God of the Sign' (cf. Isaiah 7:14), *Bogomater Znamenie*, with the Redeemer in her womb.

The *Catechism* underlines the sheer profusion of forms that the Christian imagination has put forth in devotion to Mary. The cultus of the Virgin is indeed enormously varied in Catholicism. Its simplest form is a cry for assistance, as in the very early (possibly third century) prayer *Sub tuum praesidium*:

> We seek refuge under the protection of your mercies, O Mother of God; do not reject our supplications in need but save us from perdition, O you who alone are blessed.

But then it can also take complex forms, as in the Psalter of Mary, the Rosary. The *Catechism* makes an heroic effort to introduce order into the staggering luxuriance of Mary's rose-garden. Marian prayer, it proposes, follows a twofold movement (thus replicating, in miniature, the general pattern of that New Testament 'prayer of blessing' the author has already described[8]). First, it thanks God for what he has done in Mary, and through her for us; secondly, it asks Mary to continue in us the work which, through her, God has begun.

In its commentary on that most commonplace Marian prayer of Latin Catholicism, the Ave Maria, the *Catechism* tries to show how this is so. In the first part of the prayer, the 'Hail Mary' proper, we place ourselves in the 'shoes' of Gabriel and Elizabeth to contemplate with them the *mirabilia Dei* in Mary; then, in the second part, the 'Holy Mary', we do not simply *greet* her with them, but *plead* with her, entrusting ourselves to her intercession. And this is for both the 'today' of the present moment, and for the 'hour of our death', where we hope she

[8]See above, p. 241.

will attend, as she did on Calvary, and demonstrate her spiritual motherhood in the moment of our greatest crisis. Both the 'Hail Mary' and the 'Holy Mary' undergo Christological reinterpretation: thus we greet Mary as 'full of grace' because she is to be filled with him whom she will give to the world; we plead with her as Mother of mercy in the hope, above all, that she will 'lead us to her Son, Jesus, in paradise'.[9]

The learned principal author of this section of the *Catechism* moves with ease from Latin to Byzantine, Syrian to Armenian, yet his fundamental conviction is that

> in the *Ave Maria* [Latin], the *theotokia* [Greek], the hymns of St Ephrem [Syriac] or St Gregory of Narek [Armenian], the tradition of prayer is basically the same.[10]

Recognising that Mary is the *Orante*, the very figure of the praying Church, allows the *Catechism* to make a smooth transition to the next aspect of its subject.

And this is what I called, in the introduction to this chapter, an evocation of a 'well-ordered Catholic environment' for the activity of prayer. The milieu must be our novice-master. This appears to be the *Catechism*'s *Leitmotiv* in its approach to 'guides for prayer'. That environment is many-layered. In the first place it must be understood hagiologically: we are surrounded by the intercession of the saints, as by the continuing vitality of their example, and the testimony of their writings. As the Roman Preface for the feasts of holy pastors puts it:

> You inspire us by their lives
> instruct us by their preaching,
> and give us your protection in answer to their prayers.

But secondly, our prayer environment can also be analysed historically, in terms of the origin and development of the various spiritualities recognised by the Church. The *Catechism* finds that those take their rise either from the charisms of particular holy men and women who passed on a share in their

---

[9]Paragraph 2677.
[10]Paragraph 2678.

particular spirit to their successors (thus for example, Franciscan or Ignatian spirituality) or from some 'point of convergence of liturgical and theological currents' (as perhaps with Byzantine spirituality). These spiritualities must not be thought of as rivals so much as 'refractions of the one light of the Spirit': as a diverse humanity, in a Church with varied missions to perform, grows in the love of God and neighbour against the vast backcloth of the historic revelation, it is hardly surprising that no one 'school' can equal the total richness of the tradition of prayer.[11]

Then thirdly, the environment for praying is also, and most simply, an empirical, human affair. We need other people, whether as individuals or groups, in order to learn to pray. A vital prayer environment is constructed by the efforts of many people: the *Catechism* singles out for special mention three sets: families; priests; and monastics. If the family is the domestic church, then it has a duty to pray together, and this must mean not simply at the common liturgy of the parish but in the form of family prayers. The child begins its prayer life at the bedside and the board or, as we shall see, in some special place within the household set apart for this purpose. The priest's rôle is also crucial; ordained to serve as minister of Word and sacrament, as well as to pastor the flock of God in a local place, he must bring the faithful to those sources of prayer that are the Word of God, the Liturgy, and the life of faith, hope, charity. Monks and nuns are extremely important figures in the creation of a Catholic environment of prayer. Familiarity with some religious community where the vowed life is lived with real seriousness, or acquaintance with a truly holy nun or brother, means access to people for whom prayer not only has been, but still is, valid.

Groups too have their part to play here, and the *Catechism* makes special mention of 'prayer groups' as of the institution (possibly quite elementary in structure) of the catechetical 'school' itself. Catechists should ensure that certain Catholic prayers pivotal to the devotional life are learned by heart; but

[11]Paragraph 2684.

also that their hearers come to 'savour' their meaning: this must be no mere routine. Sometimes catechists may come across a popular piety that is untutored: and here is an opportunity for its redressal and complementation (the *Catechism* does not make the mistake of supposing that such piety is an enemy to be eliminated in the name of a sanitising enlightenment). Prayer groups or 'schools of prayer' are commended, but the caveat is entered that the wells from which they drink must be pure, and any sectarian tendency to close themselves off from the wider tradition of the Church (the excesses of some manifestations of the Charismatic Renewal are clearly in mind) avoided. Last mentioned is the 'institution' of spiritual direction, though it is not one that can be organised since it is the *Holy Spirit* who

> gives to certain of the faithful the gifts of wisdom, faith and discernment for the sake of this common good which is prayer.[12]

And finally, the environment of prayer is unashamedly material for we are enfleshed spirits. The church of bricks and mortar is simultaneously God's house, the locus not only of liturgical prayer but also of that eucharistic devotion to the Christ of the tabernacle which is its natural overflow. Every home should have a prayer corner, with sacred images and the holy Bible. And the uprooting of self from one plot of earth to travel to another on pilgrimage, by way of visiting monastery or shrine prevents our settling down too comfortably in Zion, when we should always be stirring ourselves for the onward journey to the New Jerusalem of heaven.

For ultimately what is important is our relation with God himself, and the *Catechism* confronts this most directly when it considers 'the life of prayer', which it does positively, by way of examining its main expressions and negatively through looking at its difficulties, at the spiritual combat.

Just as, say, Dominicans are called to be permanently studious, but this does not mean (on the contrary!) that they should read no particular books, so the Christian, in being called to 'pray

---

[12]Paragraph 2690.

254 The Service of Glory

always' is not dispensed (far from it!) from the onerous duty to pray at certain times. For the concept of 'praying always' must be well understood. It is a matter of the 'memory of God', *memoria Dei, mnēmē tou Theou*, as a continuous *tacit* presence in the depths of the graced consciousness of the baptised person, just as the natural ego likewise is hiddenly energised by the transcendental 'I'. The rationale of set periods of prayer (as of the Hours of the Divine Office, at any rate in a monastic or personal, as distinct from cathedral and public, context) lies in the way regular, determinate times of explicit prayer can render this tacit presence ever more palpable throughout the whole of daily life. And this is possible not only for contemplative monks.

> If each day you give some moments to the prayer of simplicity; if you know how to separate yourself interiorly, in some degree, from persons and things in order to enter into yourself, and not allow yourself to be dominated by them; if, in your thinking and reading, you bring with you a certain pre-occupation with God and attentiveness to his presence; you are already beginning to live the contemplative life, even if you are still in the world.[13]

The *Catechism* speaks of the life of prayer as borne forward by certain fundamental rhythms: the liturgical year with its feasts; the liturgical week, with its hebdomadal Easter, Sunday; the liturgical day with not only the Liturgy of the Hours but also prayers of rising and retiring, before meals and after them. What these rhythms sustain is, in one sense, individual to each person. Pray as you can, not as you can't, as Dom John Chapman told his *dirigés*. That said, we can still maintain that, for all and sundry, prayer will surely have, in broad outline, three main expressions. And these are: vocal prayer; meditation; and contemplative prayer. Each is a manner of keeping the Word in the heart and pondering it, after the fashion, we can

---

[13]A Monk of the Eastern Church, *Orthodox Spirituality. An Outline of the Orthodox Ascetical and Mystical Tradition* (London 1945; 1974), p. 28.

add of the Blessed Virgin Mary, whom St Luke presents in his infancy Gospel as the model of attentiveness to that Word.

Vocal prayer corresponds especially well to our basic nature as speech-using animals for whom, moreover, nothing is in the intelligence that was not first in the senses. When the Word became flesh, the flesh became eloquent with the Word. If the Logos, the Foundation of all meaning, himself stooped to form phonemes, whereby to praise and supplicate the Father, who are we to depreciate the prayer of the lips?

> He not only prayed aloud the liturgical prayers of the synagogue but, as the Gospels show, he raised his voice to express his personal prayer, from exultant blessing of the Father to the agony of Gethsemani.[14]

In this sense no great abyss separates the child praying in its mother's hearing for a box of delights at Christmas from the prayer of the heart of a Carthusian in his hermitage. It is important, as the author remarks, that our bodily being should be initiated into prayer along with the soul, for we can be described not only as embodied soul but also as ensouled body. In vocal prayer, the body pays its Maker and Redeemer homage; the more so when certain words suggest certain gestures. The *Nine Ways of Prayer of Saint Dominic* exemplify this.[15]

'Methods' of *meditation* are legion, as many as the spiritual masters (and mistresses) themselves, but their common aim is the *mobilisation of faculties* – thought, imagination, emotion, desire – for the fuller empowerment of faith, repentance and the will to follow Christ. For the *Catechism*, meditation takes the form of a *quest*, and this differentiates it from the manifold prayer of the lips (in blessing and adoration, petition, intercession, thanksgiving, praise) on the one hand, and the simple prayer of union which is contemplation on the other. Like theology, meditation seeks understanding, a grasp of the 'way and how of the Christian life'.[16] It proceeds by juxtaposing two kinds of 'text'. The specifically revelational 'text' – not only

[14] Paragraph 2701.
[15] S. Tugwell, O.P. (ed.), *The Nine Ways of Prayer of St Dominic* (Dublin 1978).
[16] Paragraph 2705.

found in the Word of God in Scripture, and especially the
Gospels, but also in the liturgical prayers, the holy icons, the
writings of the spiritual fathers of the tradition, all illuminated
by the self-manifestation of God in creation and history – is
brought together with the 'text' of my life, as unfolding in the
midst of the world, and from the confrontation of these two
deeper insights arises. In meditation, I turn over my life, letting
it run through my hands, not, however, in some purely
introverted or self-referential way, but consciously in relation
to the self-communication of God in his own outpouring in
revelation. And from this (and short of private revelation there
can be no other way) I look to discern what it is the Lord is
calling me to do and to become. As one student of the
influence of meditation methods on the English poets of the
Catholic Reformation has put it:

> St Ignatius intends meditation to be a localised ordering
> – with lasting effects – of the entire personality: to be more
> exact, a Christocentric ordering of the personality.[17]

In this, Ignatian method is hardly alone, though its
Christological concentration is especially intense.

And so to the prayer of *contemplation*. This is a subject on
which there is a vast corpus of Christian reflection. Though the
Catechism cites the Carmelites of the sixteenth century, as well
as Ignatius, for the Latins, and Isaac of Nineveh for the
Orientals, its freight of references is light, its desire not to
discourage readers by brandishing the contents of a technical
armoury palpable. What, after all, could be more straightforward
than its opening definition, borrowed from St Teresa?
Contemplation is (in the older translation of Allison Peers):

> friendly intercourse, and frequent solitary converse with
> him who we know loves us.[18]

[17]A. D. Cousins, *The Catholic Religious Poets from Southwell to Crashaw. A Critical History* (London 1991); cf. L. L. Martz, *The Poetry of Meditation* (New Haven and London 1954).

[18]*The Life of the Holy Mother Teresa of Jesus*, VIII, in *The Complete Works of Saint Teresa of Jesus* (London 1946), I, p. 50. Actually, as the *Catechism* admits, she speaks of 'mental prayer', but context and content make plain that it is not precisely meditation that is at stake.

Here meditation may still happen, but it is not the heart of the matter, which is *attention to the Lord himself.* That knowing quest not this time for *understanding* but for a *Person* – Jesus, and, in Jesus the Father – is the soul's loving search for her true Bridegroom, as a venerable tradition of spiritual exegesis of the Song of Songs, reaching far back into the pre-Nicene Church, affirms.

The terms in which the *Catechism* fills out its initial Teresian definition of contemplation are deceptively, but attractively, simple. Contemplation is the gathering up of the heart, recollection prompted by the Spirit, self-offering to God that we be purified and transformed. Contemplative prayer is the praying of the spiritual child, of the contrite sinner, it is freely confessed poverty and humility. It is the gift of the Spirit for obedience to the Father and union with the Son. It is that communion with the Trinity which conforms us to their likeness. It is looking and hearing, but also silent love. It consents to abide in the night of faith. The *Catechism* has avoided the specialised vocabulary of 'acquired' and 'infused' contemplation, of the 'ligature' and the prayer of union, the night of the sense and the spirit, transforming union and spiritual marriage. Leaving aside the *verba*, the terms, it has not abandoned the *res* in which the words terminate, for all of these are globally contained in its account. Nor is this surprising for though as terminology the words belong specifically to Western Catholicism, and notably to the Carmelite-Thomist synthesis of the data of the Latin Middle Ages and the seventeenth-century golden age, it must not be thought that they fail to correspond to anything in the Eastern tradition.

Thus an Orthodox witness has pointed out the parallels in the Eastern tradition with the stages of contemplative prayer established (if with a greater attempt at precision) by the Western writer from whom, in these matters, the *Catechism* sets forth: the great Teresa, she of Avila. The prayer of simple regard, the prayer of quiet, and the prayer of full union, where distractions fall away and the powers of the soul seem bonded to God, correspond to varying intensities of that *hēsychia* ('quiet' or 'rest') which is 'in some form of other, the introduction to Eastern contemplation'. Again, the 'ecstatic' union where the soul (literally) stands out from itself is mirrored in accounts of the prayer of the Desert Fathers, as well as Dionysius the Areopagite's own teaching on (precisely) *ekstasis* and the 'circular movement' which brings back the soul to God. Finally, the 'transforming' union or spiritual marriage is echoed by those in the East who conceive the spiritual life as *theōsis*, 'deification', or as the nuptials of the soul with her Lord – Origen, for instance and Methodius of Olympus. What is, perhaps, more characteristic of the Greeks (over against the Latins) is their supposal that

> an imperceptible transition, an unbroken chain of intermediate shades, links these states one to the other. Thus it happens, in Orthodox practice, that the Name of Jesus (which is really the heart and the strength of the 'Jesus-prayer') may be used, not only as the starting-point, but also in continuous support of mystical states ranging from *hēsychia* to *ekstasis*.[19]

What, I suggest, the author of the *Catechism*'s treatise on prayer has done is to recast these imposing themes of the contemplative ascent into a more evangelical and personalist idiom less likely to overawe. He has made of them, in fact, a kind of *little way of spiritual childhood*, thus betraying the influence upon him of another practitioner of 'Christocentric concentration', the little Teresa, she of Lisieux.[20]

Certainly, the Christological character of the *Catechism*'s account of contemplation is most marked, not least in its climax when it speaks of contemplative prayer as a generative love that endures darkness in conformation to the pattern of Jesus' paschal *triduum*, for:

> the Paschal night of the Resurrection passes through the night of the agony and the tomb.[21]

Agonistic and sepulchral, such nocturnal imagery prepares us for the possibility that there may be difficulties in prayer,

---

[19]A Monk of the Eastern Church, *Orthodox Spirituality*, pp. 28–29.

[20]C. de Meester, *Dynamique de la confiance. Génèse et structure de la voie d'enfance spirituelle chez Ste Thérèse de Lisieux* (Paris 1969).

[21]Paragraph 2719.

and these the *Catechism* treats under the ancient name of the
spiritual conflict, 'the battle of prayer'. Its account is robustly
traditional.

> Prayer is a battle. Against whom? Against ourselves and
> against the wiles of the Tempter who does all he can to
> turn man away from prayer, away from union with God.[22]

This is the true voice of the desert, the tones of existential
authenticity for the Christian man in a world of angelic warfare.
But the difficulties to which prayer is subject are of more than
one sort. The *Catechism* begins with *intellectual* obstacles. Some
view prayer, we hear, as of purely psychological value – one
might think here of the 'non-objective' view of prayer of the
Cambridge religious philosopher Don Cupitt; others as a way
to reach a 'mental void' – the 'no-mind' of Zen, or perhaps the
'transcendental meditation' of the followers of the Maharishi
Mahesh Yogi? Others again reduce prayer simply to ritual
activity, conceivably a reference to the practice of white magic,
and to features of the New Age movement. However, the
Catechism moves on at once to speak of *Christian*
misunderstandings, so we may be meant to suppose that ill-
instructed Catholics too can share these ideas. At any rate,
closer to home are the 'many' Christians who disregard prayer
as practically impossible in an activity-filled life, or, attempting
it a few times, abandon it as too difficult, not realising that its
source is the Holy Spirit and not just themselves. Prayer can be
undermined by false ideologies all too pervasive in the
contemporary secularised milieu. Such are rationalistic
scientism, always seeking verification, yet prayer is 'a mystery
that overflows both our conscious and our unconscious lives';
a consumeristic materialism for which its apparent non-
productivity and unprofitability render it useless; and hedonism
where 'sensuality and comfort' become

> the criteria of the true, the good and the beautiful;
> whereas prayer, the 'love of beauty' (*philokalia*), is caught
> up in the glory of the living and true God.[23]

[22]Paragraph 2725.
[23]Paragraph 2727.

Or is prayer a flight from an activist world? The gratuitous assertion that it is meets a gratuitous negation from the *Catechism* to the opposite effect.

Then there are also *spiritual* obstacles to prayer. These are not recondite, but altogether familiar to anyone who has tried seriously to pray. The *Catechism* mentions first discouragement, arising from, for instance, the experience of dryness in prayer, a sense that we have not made a complete gift of ourselves to God but are always holding much back, disappointment at the refusal of our petitions, and the like. But even those who resist the subversive effect of such factors continue to meet distractions, on which the *Catechism* offers eminently sensible advice:

> To set about hunting down distractions would be to fall into their trap, when all that is necessary is to turn back to our heart: for a distraction reveals to us what we are attached to, and this humble awareness before the Lord should awaken our preferential love for him and lead us resolutely to offer him our heart to be purified.[24]

That is a topic to which the author returns under the title the temptation of faithlessness: we have too many preferences, and have not clarified in our hearts whom we shall serve.

But if in that perspective distractions are a less superficial lesion of the tissue of prayer than might be thought, the *Catechism* nonetheless devotes more space, cumulatively at any rate, to aridity, *accidie* or spiritual depression, and the question of unanswered petitionary prayer. Dryness can be a sign of poor progress, or of much progress. It requires, respectively, reconversion or the confidence that we are privileged to enter the night of Christ's strange work. *Accidie* – boredom at one's own spiritual good – is treated more sharply as the result of 'lax ascetical practice, decreasing vigilance, carelessness of heart'.[25] The making of petitionary prayer is pleasing to God since he has given his children the dignity of freedom in which such prayer unfolds. But, as we remember from the *Catechism*'s

[24]Paragraph 2729.
[25]Paragraph 2732.

treatment of liberty in its sub-book on morals, freedom is not merely the negative capacity to determine ourselves towards this or that end; it is also the positive ability to choose our proper end. So here too, with the help of the Spirit who is the liberator of our will from within, we must pray to be free enough to seek what God wants for us, our true good. Petitionary prayer makes a real difference to the world, granted that sometimes at least people do ask for what is, concretely, the will of God: God has willed that such prayer be an absolutely integral aspect of the causal action of continuing creation. It is, as the *Catechism* puts it, 'co-operation with his providence'.[26] Not that a purely *philosophical* doctrine of this will suffice, for crucial to it is the intercession before the Father of his Son, Jesus Christ. The *Catechism's* profoundest *theological* comment on petitionary prayer comes when it says that:

> If our prayer is resolutely united with that of Jesus, in trust and boldness as children, we obtain all that we ask in his name, even more than any particular thing: the Holy Spirit himself, who contains all gifts.[27]

And that thought is the best possible incentive to perseverance in prayer, which, conscious of the inseparability of praying from Christian living at large, the *Catechism* also calls 'persevering in love'.

The *Catechism's* euchology has kept the best wine till the last: its exegesis of the High Priestly Prayer of Christ at the Last Supper in St John's Gospel. Because that moment is *par excellence*, his 'hour', which defines his mission and therefore his personal identity, the *Catechism* considers that this prayer which sums up the creation and redemption, as well as his own death and resurrection, remains abidingly Jesus' own. It is eternally reiterated before the throne by the Lamb who was slain not only on Golgotha, but in the Father's predestining mercy, before the foundation of the world. In it everything is recapitulated in Christ, and thus our prayer too belongs *here*.

---

[26]Paragraph 2738.
[27]Paragraph 2741.

The prayer of Jesus which is his crucifixion, his absolute renunciation of himself in love to the Father, is the eternal relationship of Father and Son made available as part of our history, part of the web of mankind of which we are fragments, a part of the web that gives it a new centre, a new pattern ... Prayer then, whatever stage we are at, is an entry into the mystery of the crucifixion of Christ, a sharing into the eternal exchange between Father and Son.[28]

[28]H. McCabe, O.P., 'Prayer', in idem., *God Matters* (London 1987), pp. 220, 224.

XVI

Commenting the Pater

That would have been a pretty good note on which to bring the
Catechism to a close. But no great *Catechism* has ever lacked a
commentary on the *Pater*, the Lord's Prayer, given to the
disciples by Jesus as the summation of what they were to say to
his Father and theirs.[1] Recited thrice daily as early as the
Didache, and so, in all probability, within the New Testament
period itself, its donation to new Christians (the *traditio orationis
dominicae*) early became an integral part of preparation for
Baptism while in the fourth century, in both East and West, it
comes to occupy a place of the greatest honour in the eucharistic
Liturgy itself. Many Fathers and early ecclesiastical writers
devoted tractates or extended homilies to its exposition: in the
West, Tertullian, Cyprian, Cassian, Chromatius of Aquileia,
Peter Chrysologus, Augustine, Caesarius of Arles, Ambrose,
Jerome, Venantius Fortunatus; in the East, Origen, Theodore
of Mopsuestia, Cyril of Jerusalem, Gregory of Nyssa, John
Chrysostom, Cyril of Alexandria, Maximus Confessor. The
authors of the *Catechism of the Catholic Church* were faced with an
embarras de richesse, and they do in fact draw copiously on most
of these sources.

What these ancient teachers will be invited to address are, in
essence, three great themes which the close of the previous

---

*=*Catechism*, paragraphs 2759–2865.
[1]Much information in S. Sabugal, *El Padre nuestro en la interpretación catequética
antigua y moderna* (Salamanca 1982).

section, on the Lord's High Priestly Prayer before his saving sacrifice, has already stated. For there the *Catechism* presents the great prayer of the Supper as fulfilling 'from within' the chief petitions of the *Pater*:

> concern for the Father's name, passionate zeal for his Kingdom (glory); the accomplishment of the will of the Father, of his plan of salvation; and deliverance from evil.[2]

These points will now be developed, by way of rounding off the entire *Catechism* through a concentrated presentation of its own essential motifs. For the Lord's Prayer is, in words of the North African Tertullian, cited here, 'truly the summary of the whole Gospel'.[3]

Not only, then, does the *Pater*, in some words of Augustine to a correspondent, contain the essential elements of all the prayers in Scripture.[4] More than this, it is the distinctively evangelical prayer by which Jesus teaches us how to ask for what the *vita nuova* of the gospel comprises. As the only-begotten Son, the Saviour can communicate to us the 'words' he has received from the Father; and as One in our flesh, made like us, he knows whereof we are made, our weaknesses and needs. He can be, then, at one and the same time, our prayer's master and its model; and this he is in that prayer which is uniquely his, the *Lord*'s prayer.

The prayer is not given to the disciples simply as a formula to be recited. For Jesus also promises, and subsequently, at Easter, gives them the Holy Spirit by whom the prayer is animated, and through whom the words of the humanised Son become themselves 'Spirit and life' (John 6:3). It is

> this indivisible gift of the Lord's words and of the Holy Spirit who gives life to them in the hearts of believers [that] has been received and lived by the Church from the beginning.[5]

[2]Paragraph 2750.
[3]Tertullian, *On Prayer*, 1; cited Paragraph 2761.
[4]Augustine, *Letter* 130, xii, 22, cited Paragraph 2762.
[5]Paragraph 2767.

And if for this reason, the solemn giving of the *Pater* to catechumens and neophytes in the mystagogy of Christian initiation signifies 'new birth into the divine life', the recitation of the *Oratio dominicalis* between the canon of the Mass and Holy Communion

> sums up on the one hand all the petitions and intercessions expressed in the movement of the epiclesis and, on the other, knocks at the door of the Banquet of the Kingdom which sacramental communion anticipates.[6]

The Lord's Prayer has, accordingly, an inescapably *eschatological* dimension: it is a prayer made in the Spirit poured out in the last days on all flesh, and looking to the Parousia of the Son which will consummate all things in glory.

The prayer opens by placing us in the presence of the heavenly Father. The *Catechism* stresses how this cannot be taken for granted. God is the *mysterium tremendum et fascinans* whom Moses could not approach in the burning bush till he had bared his feet in a sign of creaturely humility and penitence. Not even Jesus himself could enter as man the presence of that incandescent holiness until he had made purification for the sins he assumed as the scapegoat. It is only in the Spirit of the crucified and exalted Son that we can say *Abba*, 'Father!' Similarly, it is only with *filial* boldness, created in us by the Spirit poured into our hearts, that we can begin the *Abba* prayer at all. The *Catechism* warns, therefore, of the danger of domesticating this prayer, of taking the All-Holy for granted. Before praying it we must in all humility cleanse our hearts from false images of the divine Fatherhood, based on aberrant projections, it may be, of our own personal cultural experience of fathers at large. Implicitly sidelining the radical-feminist critique of the naming of God as Father (for here we do not have to do with any patriarchal hierarchy on earth), the author affirms:

> To pray to the Father is to enter into his mystery as he is and as the Son has revealed him to us.[7]

---

[6]Paragraphs 2769–2770.
[7]Paragraph 2779.

In praying to the Father we are exclusively beneficiaries of the revealing and sanctifying missions of Son and Spirit. Here the Homeric apostrophe of Zeus as father of gods and men is irrelevant: it is as inserted by the Spirit into the unique relation of the Son to the Father that we say this prayer. The *Pater* is the distinctive utterance of those adopted and regenerated as sons of God. Thus it discloses to us with peculiar force that new Christian dignity of ours which the *Catechism*'s sub-book on morals took as its departure-point for an account of the specifically Christian 'good life'. Praying to the Father, moreover, should create in us the desire to be like him, and John Chrysostom will note how this means above all some imitation of the Father's mercy and loving-kindness, for these are the very divine attributes which the name 'Father' signifies in the teaching of the Son.[8] At the same time, this prayer defines us as, precisely, children (in the best sense of that word, with its connotations of openness, spontaneity, uncalculatingness), and in this emphasis the author rejoins his earlier account of contemplation, where the theme of spiritual childhood is, as suggested above, perhaps the primary tonality.

The Father is *our* Father. The *Catechism* sees this plural pronoun as in the first instance a confession that the Old Testament promise of a new and everlasting covenant has been fulfilled: we have so become God's own people that he is in indefeasible fashion *our* God. And these are the tones of the Apocalypse: the triumph song of those redeemed by the Lamb in the city of the end. But is not the God of the Christian more than simply the Father? What of Son and Holy Spirit? The *Catechism*'s response, which integrates the fatherly orientation of the prayer within the entire trinitarian life, appears to draw on the dogmatically sophisticated commentary on the *Pater* by the seventh-century Byzantine theologian Maximus the Confessor.

> For Maximus, ... when we invoke the Father, his 'Name' and his 'Reign', it is Father, Son and Spirit, respectively, whom we are invoking. They exist *from* the Father and *with*

[8]John Chrysostom, *On the Lord's Prayer*, 3; cited Paragraph 2784.

him, as well as *in* him, in a fashion which is 'above cause and reason'.[9]

With this we can compare the *Catechism*'s words:

> When we pray to 'our' Father, we personally address the Father of our Lord Jesus Christ. By doing so we do not divide the Godhead, since the Father is its 'source and origin', but rather confess that the Son is eternally begotten by him and the Holy Spirit proceeds from him. We are not confusing the persons, for we confess that our communion is with the Father and his Son, Jesus Christ, in their one Holy Spirit. The Holy Trinity is consubstantial and indivisible. When we pray to the Father, we adore and glorify him together with the Son and the Holy Spirit.[10]

The 'we' of the *Our Father* is the communion of the Church where alone the triune Name is believed on, blessed and preached. For this reason, praying the *Pater* commits us to the ecumenical reconstitution of the unity of all Christians in the single Church; abnegates individualism because for the *koinōnia* of the Church all hypostases – all human persons – are mutually implicating and co-involved one with another, in the image of the trinitarian communion; and, since all human beings are potentially members of Christ's mystical Body, leads us to bring before God every human soul, and indeed – so the *Catechism* adds, thinking perhaps of the reach of God's providence in the preaching of Jesus or those saints who, like Cuthbert of Lindisfarne, made a point of blessing animals – the 'whole of creation'.[11]

And this fatherly God is 'in the heavens': not, for the *Catechism* a space but a way of being, specifically of aweful, transcendent being which enables the Godhead to be closer to us than we are to ourselves, though here is no metaphysics without morals since

---

[9] A. Nichols, O.P., *Byzantine Gospel. Maximus the Confessor in Modern Scholarship* (Edinburgh 1993), p. 68.
[10] Paragraph 2789.
[11] Paragraph 2793.

it is precisely because he is thrice-holy that he is so close to the humble and contrite heart.[12]

And since in the incarnate and ascended Lord, heaven and earth are reconciled and even fused, those who are in Christ by grace are raised, while still in this world, to the 'heavenly places' (Ephesians 2:6). Catching up a major theme of the *Catechism*'s ecclesiology, the Church is not wholly distinct from the Kingdom. In Andrew Pozzo's Baroque masterpiece, the ceiling of Sant' Ignazio in Rome:

> while the Church of heaven descends, the pilgrim Church ascends to her native land; or rather, both make their way to meet one another.[12]

And so finally to the *Pater*'s seven petitions.[13] Although the *Catechism* has presented the *Pater* as a practical lesson in how to ask for the new life of the gospel, this does not signify that its petitions are always self-regarding, albeit for our transfiguration. The gospel itself, after all, is thoroughly focussed on the Father's reign. It should not surprise us to learn, therefore, that the trio of petitions which open the septet of requests in the Lord's Prayer are themselves utterly theocentric.

> The first series of petitions carries us toward him, for his own sake: *thy* name, *thy* kingdom, *thy* will! It is characteristic of love to think first of the one whom we love. In none of the three petitions do we mention ourselves; the burning desire, even anguish, of the beloved Son for his Father's glory seizes us: 'hallowed be thy name, thy kingdom come, thy will be done ... These three supplications were already answered in the saving sacrifice of Christ, but they are henceforth directed in hope toward their final fulfilment, for God is not yet all in all.[14]

---

[12]C. Schönborn, *From Death to Life. The Christian Journey* (E.t. San Francisco 1995), p. 67.

[13]For an anthology of comments on the petitions from patristic, mediaeval and later authors, see N. Ayo, C.S.C., *The Lord's Prayer. A Survey, Theological and Literary* (Notre Dame, IN 1994).

[14]Paragraph 2804.

On the *first* petition, while recognising that the plea for the hallowing of God's Name can be regarded as a prayer of sheer adoration and blessing, the *Catechism* prefers the view, supported by august patristic testimony, that what is at stake here is, rather, the manifestation of God's glory by the accomplishment of his sanctifying work in the world.

> Our Father calls us to holiness in the whole of our life, and since 'he is the source of [our] life in Christ Jesus, who became for us wisdom from God and ... sanctification', both his glory and our life depend on the hallowing of his name in us and by us. Such is the urgency of our first petition.[15]

In the *second* petition, we pray for the Parousia, the final and definitive coming of the reign of God through the return of Christ for the consummation of the Son's creative and redemptive work. And though this will include the vindication of his own, summed up in the martyrs of the Apocalypse who cry out from beneath the altar 'How long?' (6:9), more fundamentally, and comprehensively, it is the Son's handing over of the Kingdom to the Father, so that God may be all in all (I Corinthians 15:24–28). But here too there are consequences for us: we are so to affirm the world – which God made in the beginning 'very good' – as to open it to Paradise and eternity. It is this eschatological dimension to incarnational humanism which gives the gospel its bite, and verve. And in the *third* of the theocentric petitions, the 'will' of the Father which we ask may be done on earth as it is in heaven can only be, for the *Catechism*, his universal will to *save.* And again, while this prayer displaces our interests from their centrality to make the focus God himself who alone is fully and efficaciously philanthropic, the Lover of mankind, it does not exonerate us from making our contribution.

> We ask our Father to unite our will to his Son's, in order to fulfil his will, his plan of salvation for the life of the world. We are radically incapable of this, but united with

[15]Paragraph 2813, with an internal citation of I Corinthians 1:30.

Jesus and with the power of his Holy Spirit, we can surrender our will to him and decide to choose what his Son has always chosen: to do what is pleasing to the Father.[16]

Still, it is only when we reach the remaining quartet of petitions 'give us ... forgive us ... lead us not ... deliver us' that the *Pater* moves into a mode which is anthropocentric. Here we ask that we may be nourished, healed of the sickness of sin, and come through victorious in the spiritual combat which is at once our life and our prayer. In the *fourth* petition we ask, in the *Catechism*'s cool phrase, for 'all appropriate goods and blessings, both material and spiritual'.[17] What counts as 'appropriateness' here will vary greatly. The grace before meals of the abbé Pierre (Henri Groués, founder of the *Compagnons d'Emmaus* for the homeless) is, 'Lord, give bread to those who are hungry, give hunger to those who have bread.' The physical needs of others may be my spiritual needs. Yet there is a famine in the land bleaker even than that of the maldistribution of the basic necessities of life. The *daily* bread for which we are to pray is a highly ambivalent matter. The word itself, in Greek *epiousios*, is a *hapax legomenon*, a 'one off' affair in the New Testament writings. How, then, are we to understand it? Just as the classical method of reading Scripture in the patristic and mediaeval periods involved the identification of a fourfold meaning in the biblical text, so too does the *Catechism* here, though its quadrilateral is differently constructed from that of a Cassian or a Hugh of St Victor.

Taken in a temporal sense, this word is a pedagogical repetition of 'this day', to confirm us in trust 'without reservation'. Taken in the qualitative sense, it signifies what is necessary for life, and more broadly every good thing sufficient for subsistence. Taken literally (*epi-ousios*: 'super-essential'), it refers directly to the Bread of Life, the Body of Christ, the 'medicine of immortality', without which we have no life within us. Finally in this connection,

---

[16]Paragraph 2825.
[17]Paragraph 2830.

its heavenly meaning is evident: 'this day' is the Day of the Lord, the day of the Feast of the Kingdom, anticipated in the Eucharist that is already the foretaste of the Kingdom to come. For this reason it is fitting for the Eucharistic liturgy to be celebrated each day.[18]

The *fifth* petition seeks our own forgiveness, for, clothed in the baptismal garment of that divine holiness with which the petitions of the *Pater* started, we have turned our festal robe into filthy rags by our sins. Like the prodigal and the publican we must recognise our fault. The *Great Canon* of St Andrew of Crete is the Church's sustained statement of this.

> Like the Thief, I cry out the 'Remember me',
> Weep bitterly like Peter, and cry like the Publican,
> 'Release me, Saviour': I shed tears like the Harlot:
> Accept my crying after Thee, as once Thou didst the
> Canaanite.
> Have mercy upon me, O God, have mercy upon me.

> Heal, O my Saviour, the putrefaction
> Of my soul abased, Thou only Physician:
> Lay a plaster on me, pouring in oil and wine –
> Works of repentance, compunction with tears.
> Have mercy upon me, O God, have mercy upon me.

> I too, following the Canaanite woman,
> Cry to Thee, 'Have mercy on me, Thou Son of David'.
> I touch Thy hem, like the woman with the issue.
> I weep, like Martha and Mary for Lazarus.
> Have mercy upon me, O God, have mercy upon me.

> The alabaster box of my tears,
> Saviour, I empty upon Thy head for ointment:
> Like the Harlot I cry to Thee, seeking Thy mercy,
> Bring Thee my prayer, and ask to receive forgiveness.
> Have mercy upon me, O God, have mercy upon me.[19]

---

[18]Paragraph 2837, citing (on the 'medicine of immortality') Ignatius of Antioch's *Letter to the Ephesians* 20, 2.

[19]*The Great Canon. A Poem of St Andrew of Crete* (London 1957), p. 39.

And if this prayer is directed to Christ rather than to the Father, we must bear in mind with the *Catechism* that our hope is only firm because in the Father's Son we 'have redemption, the forgiveness of sins'.[20] Such forgiveness will not be forthcoming, however, unless we also forgive those who have trespassed against *us*. This is not so much a forensic condition laid down by the divine Lawgiver as it is an existential condition of our receiving his healing touch.

> This outpouring of mercy cannot penetrate our hearts as long as we have not forgive those who have trespassed against us.[21]

But conversely, we cannot bring ourselves to forgive others (often) unless our heart participates in the merciful love of God. This is not a vicious circle: it is the circle, or rather the *spiral* of grace, which creates the conditions for our freedom increasingly to receive grace's ever fuller measure, in a process of lifting up and opening our hearts to God and neighbour that has no end.

The *sixth* petition strikes at the twist in the will which strangles its bent toward the good: 'lead us not into temptation'. As the *Catechism* interprets, the *Pater* prays here for 'the Spirit of discernment and strength'.[22] In an important distinction it sets apart wheat from tares in the field of our moral experience when it writes:

> The Holy Spirit makes us discern between trials, which are necessary for the growth of the inner man, and temptation, which leads to sin and death.[23]

But to know the distinction is not necessarily to practise it in doing the good (this was the mistake of Socrates). And the same is true for the other kinds of discernment the *Catechism*

---

[20]Colossians 1:14, cited Paragraph 2839.
[21]Paragraph 2840.
[22]Paragraph 2846.
[23]Paragraph 2847.

notes as pertinent to the case: distinguishing between
experiencing temptation and succumbing to it, even interiorly,
and between the apparent good it offers and the good of
reality. We need, then, not simply discernment or spiritual
judgment, but strength – and that kind of strength of which
Jesus remarks that it overcomes only through prayer (and
fasting: Matthew 17:21). It was by prayer that the Saviour
vanquished the angelic Tempter both at the outset of his
public ministry, in the wilderness, and at its climax, as his hour
struck in the garden. It will be by prayer likewise that we shall
overcome in our final battle, at the hour of our death.

In the *seventh and last* petition the *Pater*'s span extends to the
whole of a world that is not merely in the travail of perpetual
becoming but grievously endangered by the power of evil.

> When we ask to be delivered from the Evil One, we pray
> as well to be freed from all evils, present, past and future,
> of which he is the author or instigator. In this final
> petition, the Church brings before the Father all the
> distress of the world.[24]

The *Catechism* knows perfectly well of the collusion we can offer
Satan. Though Satan has no city to counterpose to the City of
God, for evil, not least in its angelic archetype, is essentially
divisive and disintegrative, there can be nonetheless an inter-
dependence in sin and death. The effect of Christ's victory is
to turn that tangled skein of misdeed, lying word, malicious
thought, into the solidarity of the Body of Christ, the
communion of saints.[25] But, as Hans Urs von Balthasar shows
so forcefully in the closing volumes of his theological dramatics,
spiritual experiment would appear to verify a law in the physics
of the spirit whereby the more God manifests his love and that
of his incarnate Son the greater the resistance of the world.
Only when heaven is thrown wide open does hell yawn visibly
at our feet. Because the messianic people in the person of
Mary, figure of the Church, Woman of the Apocalypse, is

[24]Paragraph 2854.
[25]Paragraph 2850.

caught up to God and crowned with stars, the diabolic warfare against the 'rest of her offspring' (Apocalypse 12:17), the sisters and brothers of her Son, grows *more* lethal, not less. The Church of all the ages does not underestimate, as do some foolish moderns, those principalities and powers. The beasts of the Apocalypse are realities in history: in the words of Gerontius' angel in Newman's poem, they

> In a deep hideous purring have their life
> And an incessant pacing too and fro.[26]

It is the prayer of *faith*, not optimism, which allows the Church to pray for the ingathering of all good, safe and sound, with the Parousia of him who holds the keys of death and hell.

For, in a Byzantine addition to the Lord's Prayer taken up in the Mass of Paul VI: 'thine is the kingdom and the power and the glory', and this is our only hope. In the midst of the slaughter on the world stage, the Church offers this prayer of sheer thanksgiving, adoring God's loveable majesty even in such a world of bloody conflict as ours. From the centre of history, the incarnate and crucified Logos both reigns and fights, that he may rule universally.

> Through the name of Christ and the reign of his Holy Spirit our Father accomplishes his plan of salvation, for us and for the whole world.[27]

Our final 'Amen' is to that.[28] The Amen should not be one of intellectual assent only but of the prayer of the heart – for the *Catechism* and above all its treatise on prayer with the commentary on the *Pater* as its *finale*, can itself be prayed – meditated on in *lectio divina* and turned into dialogue with God, and entrance into union with him.[28] What better could one say in its authors' praise?

[26]J. H. Newman, *The Dream of Gerontius* (London 1905), p. 31.
[27]Paragraph 2806.
[28]A. Cunningham, 'Praying the *Catechism*', *Communio* XXI, 3 (1994), pp. 473–486.

XVII

Critical Conclusion

The *Catechism* of John Paul II is taking its place in history among the great teaching instruments of the Catholic religion. To signal a pontificate so rich in its legacy of documents – encyclicals and apostolic exhortations, the Codes of Canon Law for the Western and Eastern Churches, the definitive clarification of the relation of Order to gender – Church historians may need to coin a word: since it could scarcely avoid allusion to the pope himself, perhaps 'Johanno-Pauline' might do the trick. The Johanno-Pauline 'moment' is one of stabilisation, following close on the heels of a period likened by one ecclesiastical historian to the flight of a runaway horse. It is typical of those epochs when the Church pauses to take stock of her faith in a ruminative way that they leave behind evidence of catechetical consolidation. A proto-Catechism, or the fully fledged article, does not, however, simply 'mark the spot'. Rather is it a vital reappropriation of the Church's tradition which injects fresh energy into that tradition's self-transmission in the future.

Catechesis is an institution supported by a text. At first the text in question might 'only' be the Creed, but the Creed represents a triumph of the Church's mind in decanting the content of the Scriptures in the light of the 'rule of faith', the expression by explicitation of the apostolic preaching. Along with a rudimentary moral teaching, the Creed would be 'handed over' to the catechumen of the patristic age in ceremonies at once didactic and mystagogic, the whole process coming to its climax with the rite of Baptism, on Easter Night, the feast of the

Lord's Passover. The Johanno-Pauline *Catechism* reproduces
after its own fashion this fourfold pattern from the Church of
the Fathers: for its credal section (Book I) is joined to its ethical
segment (Book III) by the bond of the Liturgy (Book III),
which, however, is not complete without the dimension (Book
IV) of personal prayer.

By the later patristic period, people realised that a fuller
doctrinal scheme than the Creed's, carefully crafted, would
greatly assist comprehension. Augustine of Hippo's *How to
Catechize Beginners* set forth the first catechetical plan for the
communication of the Church's teaching: it corresponds to
the outline of a draft catechism which the working party
summoned into existence by the Synod of Catholic Bishops
meeting in 1985 at Rome for the twentieth anniversary of the
Second Vatican Council's closure.

Although the *Catechism* eventually produced does not follow
the question-and-answer scheme which the post-patristic Latin
church introduced in the age of Charlemagne – this is a source
book for teachers of the faith, not a primer for little ones – the
crucial element of memorisation, vital to the learning process
as this is, receives due weight in its numerous pithy 'summaries'
of material.

On the eve of the Reformation, the lacunae in the doctrinal,
liturgical, moral and spiritual formation of the Church's faithful
(which, however, be it noted, will always remain after some
fashion, unless the *Catholica* is to deny her universal nature and
dwindle to a sect of the pure), led a Catholic reformer like Jean
Gerson, Chancellor of the University of Paris, to pin his hopes
on a new generation through the better catechesis of children.
The collapse of doctrinal formation – and so of all else that
flows from it – in local churches whose membership had
hitherto been well-instructed (above all in Western Europe
and North America), in the ecclesiastically and culturally
disorienting 1960s was likewise the chief stimulus to the
production of the *Catechism* of Pope John Paul II.

Much could be, and was, learned likewise from the Protestant
Reformers where the formal act of catechising (as distinct from
its material substance) is concerned. Luther's *Large Catechism*
was a teachers' book which provided a cue for the production

of similarly comprehensive works by Catholics, mid-sixteenth century archetypes, so far as *genre* is concerned, for the papally promulgated work of 1992.

But despite the excellence of the books of the Dominican Bartolomé Carranza de Miranda, and the Jesuits Edmond Auger and Peter Canisius (especially the latter), the Council of Trent felt an evident unease at the notion of a *Catholic* catechism authored by a single individual, or even by the members of a single civil society or nationality. Trent built in a deliberate internationalism to the drafting commission it established, entrusting the treatment of the *Pater* to the Louvain doctors and the French, and that of the Creed to Spaniards as theologians 'most sure in the faith'. (In the event, a Dalmatian archbishop and two Italian Dominicans in episcopal orders did most of the work!). The same desire not to render a catechism destined for the whole Church tributary to one nation led the present Prefect of the Congregation for the Doctrine of the Faith, Cardinal Joseph Ratzinger, to seek out from the Old World a Frenchman and an Englishman, a Spaniard and an Italian, with an Austrian to act as editorial secretary; from the New World two Latin Americans, one of Slav extraction, and a citizen of the United States to write the index. Finally, from the ancient churches of the East came a Lebanese priest of French origin to author the draft of the treatise on prayer.

These, then, are some of the ways in which the *Catechism* considered in this two-part commentary stands in a great tradition. It remains to consider the practical questions of the (prior) need for the *Catechism*, and its (subsequent) reception in the Church. As already suggested, the *Catechism* was brought into existence as the result of a widespread perception that Catholics below a certain age were, in many parts of the world, ill-informed and confused about their faith. In reaction against a sometimes dessicated Christian scholasticism, it was forgotten that Truth can hardly be had without truths. But the articulation of the truth in well-formulated propositions is a chief glory of the human mind, and a principal means whereby the Spirit of God brings us to salvation. The discovery that divine revelation is, at the deepest level, the self-communication of God in the personal reality of his own triune life, was allowed to obscure the fact that without the medium of germane truths this wonder could never be brought home to us. The bell whereby St Francis de Sales called together the children of the towns of his diocese, accompanying the words 'To Christian doctrine, to Christian doctrine, which will teach you the way to salvation', was ceasing to peal.[1] Yet a creedless Catechism is, as an American educationalist has pointed out, a contradiction in terms.[2] More than sixty years ago, the English Dominican philosopher-theologian Thomas Gilby was attacking the rote-learning of abstract formulae not yet understood as 'psittacism', and the schemes of religious education that fostered it as 'obsolescent parrots'. Yet he immediately went on to add:

> Religious teaching … must not stop at a stock of stories or visual images, any more than it must merely strive to inject a collection of verbal images. Its main object must be to give the child a sufficient knowledge of dogmatic truth, or divine truth expressed in human words.[3]

And in point of fact, the catechisms of the Catholic Reformation, weighted though they were to memorisation, sought the assistance of the imagination through adaptation into verse, pictures and music, as with Peter Canisius' graduated study programme through the steps of the *Minimus, Minor* and *Maior Catechismus*. But those responsible would have considered it a travesty to make of catechesis a 'happy hour' of children's entertainment, or an exploration of the child's own experience, something which could only guarantee the enclosure of revelation within a moralistic frame of reference. But *they* did not have to cope with the dominance of an educational method for which the priority of *savoir* had been displaced by that of *sujet*.

It was the realisation of a number of bishops, more percipient, or willing to 'trouble-shoot', than the rest, that not all was well

---

[1] Cited in R. de Vos, *Saint François de Sales par les témoins de sa vie* (Annecy 1967), p. 192.

[2] M. J. Wrenn, *Catechisms and Controversies. Religious Education in the Post-Conciliar Years* (San Francisco 1991), p. 29.

[3] T. Gilby, O.P., 'The Obsolescent Parrot', *Blackfriars* XII, 135 (1931), p. 365.

in the 'official' schools of catechesis that finally alerted Rome to the problem. The hypertrophy of method over against content; the excessive privileging of immediate experience *vis-à-vis* wider knowing-about; the predominance of the anecdotal over the essential; the deliberate non-directivity: these weaknesses bred disillusion among many laity and clergy but also a determination by some that the faith deserved better.

Inevitably, the resulting *Catechism* was something of a hostage to fortune. As Mgr F. D. Kelly, a consultant to the *Catechism's* editorial committee, has put it:

> The contemporary glorification of pluralism obviously creates a difficulty for the transmission of Christian truth, which is oriented towards leading people precisely to 'the obedience of faith'.[4]

And if the reception of the *Catechism* has been a bumpier ride in the Anglo-Saxon world than anywhere else, the reason may not be unconnected with the relative predominance, in that English-speaking Catholic Church, of the United States of America. For the ethos of intellectual life in America is deeply unsympathetic to what the *Catechism* represents. As one Orthodox writer has remarked:

> All the elements of American society agree on one thing: sacramentality, hierarchy, tradition, and asceticism are 'out'; pluralism, relativism, egalitarianism, democracy, self-realization, progress, and individualism are 'in'.[5]

The 'inculturation' of faith, in such a climate, will tend towards the subjective and selective unless the *sensus fidei* can assert itself vigorously in this unpropitious environment.[6] A catechism of its nature, however, will always aim at the

---

[4] F. D. Kelly, 'The Catechism in Context', *The Sower* (September 1994), p. 34.

[5] F. Schaeffer, *Letters to Father Aristotle. A Journey through Contemporary American Orthodoxy* (Salisbury, MA 1995), cited in extract in *The Christian Activist* 7 (1995), p. 10.

[6] See for an analysis of one such attempt – namely, R. A. Lucker, P. J. Brennan and M. Leach (eds.), *The People's Catechism. Catholic Faith for Adults* (New York 1995); M. J. Wrenn and K. D. Whitehead, *Flawed Expectations. The Reception of the Catechism of the Catholic Church* (San Francisco 1996).

objective and comprehensive, hence the mismatch between expectations in such a culture and the reality of our text. The instinct of the drafters of the *Catechism* to make it as universal as possible is the more truly Catholic, since the vocation of a particular or regional church should always be the refraction of the universal whole ('catholic' *means* 'according to the whole', *kat' holon*) via the prism of its own life. As Father David McLoughlin of St Mary's College, Oscott, has written:

> The *Catechism* attempts a blending of Western rationalism and Eastern aesthetics and spirituality which if it were to become normative would augur well for the future of catechetics and theology in a renewed world Church. The Latin tradition has tended to emphasise the Word, and so the verbal and rational aspect of revelation. But revelation is full of the visual, of image, of glory, of the beauty of the Lord. The Catechism opens up the liturgy and spirituality of the Eastern Church in a way rich with potential for the West.[7]

It goes without saying that the *Catechism* could have been improved. Who would maintain that not a line in even the greatest works of Racine, Shakespeare, Dostoevsky, could have been more incisive, more mellifluous, more terrible? But all tales must be brought to an end somewhere. Those who deny the need for a universal Catechism, or perhaps for any formal catechism; or who regard the attempt to gather up all the Church's teaching, whether defined or non-defined in a single organic whole, as misplaced; or who cannot see that the specifically ecclesial understanding of Scripture will inevitably go beyond the deliverances of the historical-critical (or any other secular) method, would not have been content, we can rest assured, with any book so devised as to stand in palpable continuity with what I have called above the great catechetical tradition. It is, unfortunately, the case that influential sections of the theological and catechetical departments and agencies of educational and administrative institutions in the Catholic

[7]D. McLoughlin, 'The Treasure House of Faith', *The Tablet*, 28 May 1994, p. 655.

world today are out of sympathy with the *Catechism*'s project. The existence of such titles as, for the German-speaking world, *Der Weltkatechismus. Therapie oder Symptom einer kranken Kirche?*[8] or, for the French, *Le nouveau Catéchisme. Veut-il tuer l'Eglise?*[9] is evidence enough that the problem is not confined to Anglo-Saxons. The protracted 'silly season' which the Catholic Church has enjoyed or endured, not without journalistic stimulus, for over a generation is no more at an end in Paris or Paderborn than it is in Philadelphia. There will, of course, always be contrary individuals so long as the human race lasts. What is alarming about a strongly worded yet fully documented survey of the commentary literature emerging from the United States is that catechists and pastoral ministers *trained under Church auspices* are learning *from this very training* that (in the vigorous if unlovely idiom of America):

> the *Catechism* is really no big deal, and ... anybody who is really 'with it' in religious education will want to continue looking elsewhere for the 'answers' (if there are any 'answers').[10]

The at best *de haut en bas*, at worst quite destructive tone of much of this literature appears clearly enough in the reporting, replete with judicious citation, in Wrenn and Whitehead. Fortunately, there are works available (even apart from this one!) of different stamp,[11] and perhaps the serene exposition of the content of a *Catechism* that is, well, *Catholic* is a better

[8]H. J. Verwyen, *Der Weltkatechismus. Therapie oder Symptom einer kranken Kirche?* (Düsseldorf 1993).

[9]*Le nouveau Catéchisme. Veut-il tuer l'Eglise? Des catholiques parlent à André Bercoff* (Paris 1993).

[10]Wrenn and Whitehead, *Flawed Expectations*, p. 329.

[11]For example, A. McBride, O. Praem, *Essentials of the Faith. A Guide to the 'Catechism of the Catholic Church'* (Huntingdon, IN 1994); J. Tolhurst, *A Concise Companion and Commentary for the New Catholic Catechism* (Leominster 1994). For those who have the language there is R. Fisichella (ed.), *Commento teologico al 'Catechismo della Chiesa Cattolica'* (Casale Monferrato 1993). Other edited essay collections whose overall view is somewhat jaundiced contain, of course, outstanding individual articles. Two issues of journals whose contents can be unreservedly recommended as studies of the *Catechism* are: *Communio. International Catholic Review* XXI, 3 (1994); *The Sower* 16, 1 (1994).

answer to critics than scholastic refutation, though some of the latter is needed as well.

Yet institutions are not run on seminars, and the outcome of such struggles, crucial as it is to the shape of the Church to come, cannot rely on the pen alone. The formation of fresh cadres of catechists is, therefore, a major priority. As Calvin realised, one might have the best Catechism in the world but without provision of a determinate rôle in Church organisation it will be but a sounding brass and a tinkling cymbal. That was why, at Geneva, his *Formulaire* was to be communicated to children Sunday by Sunday until they were sufficiently instructed to confess the faith in the presence of the gathered church. The Catholic response of the same period was the institution of new religious brotherhoods and sisterhoods whose members – the men of the Congregation of Christian Doctrine, or the Ursuline nuns – created a context in which the texts (most frequently St Robert Bellarmine's construal of the Tridentine Catechism in his *Dottrina cristiana breve* of 1597 and the *Dichiarazione più copiosa della dottrina cristiana* of 1598)[12] could enjoy efficacy. Some equivalent is surely needed today.

Such a foundation would meet a crying need in Western Europe and North America in general. But after making some critical animadversions of the state of things across both Atlantic and Channel, it would be foolish to pretend that all is well in Albion's sceptred isle. The publication by the National Project of Catechesis and Religious Education in the years 1987–1988 of a framework for such education in Catholic secondary schools of *Weaving the Web* echoed the American

---

[12]Important for English Catholics because of its influence on the *Doway Catechism – recte*, Henry Turberville's *Abridgement of Christian Doctrine* of c. 1649, which, in turn, simplified as *A Short Abridgement of Christian Doctrine for the Instruction of Beginners* (1745), was revised and enlarged by Bishop Richard Challenor to form his *Abridgement of Christian Doctrine* of 1759. This 'Penny Catechism', revised at various points in the nineteenth century, had its finest hour bibliographically speaking, in the publication of the 1931 Ditchling edition, by H. D. C. Pepler, with angular iconography by Philip Hagreen. For the complex history of the text, see M. Heinmann, *Catholic Devotion in Victorian England* (Oxford 1995), pp. 105–118. With all the resources of iconography in reproduction available today, it should not be impossible to create an English 'Minor Catechism', based on the new Great Catechism, by taking an iconic leaf from the St Dominic's Press book.

experience. Here too was a guide for the development of the school curriculum widely criticised for an aversion to doctrine and an incipient religious indifferentism. Though the defence has been offered that religious education belongs to the school, catechesis to the parish (and the home), that distinction simply does not correspond to anything so far recognisable as the mind of the Church. Thus less than ten years previously, the combined efforts of synodal and curial drafting led, via Pope John Paul II's Apostolic Exhortation *Catechesi tradendae*, to the contrary statement:

> Education in the faith ... especially the teaching of Christian doctrine ... should be imparted in an organic and systematic way.[13]

As one recent chronicler of the decline of the Catholic school system in England and Wales *when that system be viewed as an instrument of an evangelical and Catholic mission* has noted:

> The use of the phrase 'religious education' by the National Project in a non-confessional sense has led to ambiguity, and out of this ambiguity has grown misunderstanding and confusion about the aims of Catholic education.[14]

Against this background it is exceptionally encouraging to read *What Are We to Teach?*, a short but serviceable and accurate summary of the *Catechism of the Catholic Church* launched with a preface by the Cardinal-Archbishop of Westminster and an introduction by the Bishop of Menevia precisely as 'foundations for religious teaching' in the *Catechism*'s light.[15] This may be the turning of the 'ebbing tide': the beginnings of a recovery of Catholic Christianity's mighty ocean-voice in England.

[13] *Catechesi tradendae*, 18–19.
[14] J. Arthur, *The Ebbing Tide. Policy and Principles of Catholic Education* (Leominster 1995), p. 67.
[15] Bishops' Conference of England and Wales, *What Are We to Teach? Foundations for Religious Teaching in the Light of the 'Catechism of the Catholic Church'* (London 1994).

Catechesis, however, is not only for children, or adolescents; it is for adults too. I hope that this bipartite commentary on the *Catechism* will make some small contribution to the irradiation, among an older generation than those now at school, of the 'splendour of doctrine', in the 'service of glory'.

Appendix: The Catechism's Images

The *Catechism* (in its official version, I am not speaking of unilateral changes made to, for instance, the English translation) makes use of five visual images. The first, in the simplified form appropriate to a 'logo', acts as the symbol of the *Catechism*'s entire enterprise, figuring therefore on its cover and title-page. The rest serve to introduce – a lowly yet essential task – each of the four 'books' of the *Catechism* dealing as these do with, as we have now seen in detail, professing the faith in the Creed; celebrating the Christian mystery in the sacraments; life in Christ, and notably in its ethical dimension; and Christian prayer. As the short explanation of the iconology of each image already given with the text of the *Catechism* shows, these five artworks (or details of artworks) have been chosen with very great care.

The cover image, from a Christian tomb in the (third-century) catacombs of Domitilla, depicts a shepherd, guarding with his crook a single, presumably representative, sheep, which he entertains by pipeplaying as he takes his rest beneath the overhanging branches of a convenient tree. It derives from the pastoral tradition of ancient poetry and art, as that emerged in a largely agricultural society in southern Europe, where climate would lead one to associate repose with shade from a too powerful sun. In funerary art, such an image, borrowed from pagan culture and used in a new context by Christians, symbolised the 'refreshment and peace' which the Roman Canon seeks for the departed souls of the faithful.[1] By a process analogous with the reception of elements of pagan philosophy

---

[1] Good Shepherd images are peculiarly plentiful in this extensive catacomb. A number depict the *orante* figure, – symbol of the praying soul of the Church's faithful – behind each sheep, thus confirming that the proper context of interpretation of such images is Christian eschatology.

in the Church, Christian artists appropriated items in a pre-existing repertoire of images, and used them for the iconographic, rather than conceptual, articulation of the new faith. The early Church 'filled existing forms with a new content which gradually called forth its own proper stylistic expression'.[2] The *kriophoros* – a shepherd carrying home his sheep – is an 'age-old'[3] motif, while the freedom with which Christians felt able to draw on the iconic resources of paganism is shown by its occasional interchange with Orpheus[4] (and the presence of the musical instrument in the hands of the *Catechism*'s own shepherd may point towards this extra-biblical metaphor for the bringer of peace, security, eternal life).

As the authors point out, the shepherd of the catacomb of Domitilla can stand for the 'global meaning' of the *Catechism* itself. The shepherd is, evidently, the Good (or Beautiful, *kalos*) Shepherd of the Fourth Gospel, leading and protecting his faithful flock with his staff, the symbol of his legitimate authority. He draws them to himself, or keeps them by his side, through the melodiousness of his music, that is, his symphonic truth (there is a covert reference here, in the theological explanation of the iconography, to a favourite notion of Balthasar's).[5] Finally, Christ gives his faithful people a place where they can take their rest, in the all-sheltering shadow of the redemptive cross, the tree of life, as so much Christian art would have it, making Paradise real again.

The image introducing the first sub-book of the *Catechism*, on the Creed, comes from another Roman burial-ground of the early patristic period, the catacomb of Priscilla. A fragment of fresco from the early third century (the Shepherd Christ of the cover-image is usually dated a few decades later) gives us

---

[2] Nichols, *The Art of God Incarnate*, p. 51.

[3] E. Kitzinger, 'Christian Imagery: Growth and Impact', in K. Weitzmann (ed.), *Age of Spirituality. A Symposium* (New York 1980), p. 142.

[4] H. Stern, 'Orphée dans l'art paléochrétien', *Cahiers archéologiques* XIII (1974), pp. 1–16; and, more generally, K. Weitzmann, 'The Survival of Mythological Representations in Early Christian and Byzantine Art and their Impact on Christian Iconography', *Dumbarton Oaks Papers* XIV (1960), pp. 46–68.

[5] H. U. von Balthasar, *Truth is Symphonic. Aspects of Christian Pluralism* (E.t. San Francisco 1987). The theme is originally Irenaean, as Balthasar shows in *The Glory of the Lord. A Theological Aesthetics* II (E.t. Edinburgh 1984), pp. 72–73.

the first known representation of the Virgin and Child. Though modest in execution, it is, as the initial member of a series which includes the Madonna and Child of the greatest Christian artists from Cimabue to Sutherland, one of the glories of Christian Rome. As the *Catechism* remarks, in being a visual evocation of the mystery of the incarnation, the image makes manifest in painterly terms the very centre of the Christian faith. For the Creed finds its centre – even in the straightforward literary sense of the mid-point of its exposition – in its account of the Son who is at once revealer of the Father and giver of the Spirit.

More specifically, the Mother and Child of the catacomb of Priscilla evokes the Saviour as the divine answer to the human hope for redemption. The figure of a man pointing to a star hovering over Mary's head has with good reason suggested to art-historians[6] the prophecy of Balaam in Numbers 24:17:

> I see him, but not now;
> I behold him, but not nigh;
> a star shall come forth out of Jacob,
> and a sceptre shall rise out of Israel.

This messianic prophecy, embedded in the text of the Pentateuch, is made by the lips of a *pagan* seer, and so the *Catechism* can interpret the Priscilla image as an expression not only of the hope of Israel, the 'expectant' attitude of the Old Testament, but also of the less focussed, and often inarticulate, yet still very real aspirations of fallen humanity for some kind of Redeemer.

The *Catechism* treats the prophecy of Balaam as fulfilled in the birth of Mary's Child, conceived as he was by the Holy Spirit. Though in St Matthew's Gospel there is a more specific fulfilment still in the star which guides pagan astrologers, the representatives of the nations beyond Israel, to the manger at Bethlehem.[7] Yet on both occasions, Christmas and Epiphany,

[6]And originally to E. Kirschbaum, 'Der Prophet Balaam und die Anbetung der Weisen', *Römische Quartalschrift* 49 (1954), pp. 157–171. Prior to Kirschbaum, the prophet had more commonly been identified with Isaiah, and the whole image cast as an evocation of the fulfilment of his oracle, 'Behold a young woman shall conceive and bear a son, and shall call his name Immanuel' (7:14).

[7]In point of fact, three figures, generally interpreted as Matthew's images, appear on the archway of the so-called 'Greek chapel', or *cubiculum* of the *fractio*

it is the Virgin Mother who shows the Child – to the shepherds, to the magi – justifying the *Catechism*'s comment on this fresco that here Mary gives Jesus to the world, and gives him to men. In the God-bearer's rôle, we see the personification – in the literal sense of that word – of what the Church is called to be.

The second sub-book of the *Catechism*, its presentation of the Liturgy of the sacraments and the other rites of the Church, is prefaced by an image of Jesus with the *haemorhissa*, the haemorrhaging woman of Mark 5. A much better defined image than its predecessor it comes from a slightly later hand; the fresco is early fourth century, and its provenance the catacomb of St Peter and St Marcellinus. It is a touching play on gestures, where the outstretched arm of the sick woman, furtively yet reverently plucking the hem of Jesus' garment, is answered by the Lord's own signal, as he motions towards her by way of acknowledgement and acceptance of what she had done hiddenly and (as a pagan) in fear of rejection.

Given the quasi-liturgical setting of all the images of the catacombs, the *Catechism* is not necessarily practising 'eisegesis' when it finds in this scene an expression of the power of the Son of God, precisely through his sacraments, to touch the human person and make them whole. The divine power, flowing out through the humanity of Christ, not least in the sacraments, which are its continuing signs in the age of the Church, 'saves the human person in their totality, spirit and body'. The *Catechism*'s iconological commentary speaks of the sacraments in Leonine terms as the extended manifestation of the deeds worked by Christ in his flesh. It also adds a more ecclesiocentric remark: the sacraments are mediated by Christ's *Church*-body, to ends both recuperative and transformative – they heal the wounds of sin, and give new life in Christ, both by way of originating such life and in the form of giving it growth.

The catacomb of Peter and Marcellinus, cheek by jowl as it was with the private necropolis of the *equites singulares*, the emperor's guards, had housed numerous martyrs of the Diocletianic persecution, and these, when not anonymous,

---

panis, not far from the Mother and Child: F. Mancinelli, *Catecombe e basiliche. I primi cristiani a Roma* (Florence 1981), p. 28.

were all males. But the cubiculum of Nicephorus, where the *haemorhissa* still reaches out in the confidence of faith to the Saviour's person, boasts a series of scenes featuring women. Probably this portion of the catacomb was a woman's burial place: fittingly, given the *Catechism*'s emphasis on the femininity of the Church, as Bride of Christ and Mother of the faithful, a woman stands here for the sacramental Church, which, healed and houselled by Christ can nurture spiritually in her turn.

The *Catechism*'s book on Christian ethics understood as 'life in Christ' boasts the only one of the entire text's images to be precisely dated. Beneath the altar of the 'confession' (that is, of the place of the prince of the apostles' last testimony as a martyr) in St Peter's Basilica at Rome there stands the sarcophagus of a Christian gentleman, Junius Bassus, bearing the date 359. Conveniently for the *Catechism*'s purposes, it shows Christ in the act of giving his New Law to the apostles Peter and Paul, the co-founders of the Roman church. The glorified Christ is depicted on his throne, enjoying the full authority over human destiny which the Son acquires through his incarnation, and saving death and resurrection. Beneath his feet, holding a footstool for him, there stands a truncated and slightly disgruntled looking figure of the pagan god of heaven, Uranus. John Milton had known enough of the patristic tradition to present the moment of the incarnation as the depotentiation of paganism: 'the chill Marble seems to sweat, / While each peculiar power forgoes his wonted seat'.[8] But it is above all through his pascal victory that Christ reigns and 'must reign until he has put all his enemies under his feet' (I Corinthians 15:25), enemies which include pagan misconstruals of cosmic order that, at times, led men astray.

But if the gods of pagan antiquity have ceased to compete with the true God, that does not mean that the Lord of all is left in splendid isolation. Rather is he accompanied by his human disciples, whom he called not servants but friends. The sarcophagus image presents this youthful Christ-figure

[8]J. Milton, 'Hymn on the Morning of Christ's Nativity'.

(youthful because, in his everlasting creativity, God is permanently young) as handing the rolls of his New Law to a Peter and Paul who flank him in conversational intimacy. Moreover, as the *Catechism* interprets matters, the New Law in question is 'law' in a somewhat Pickwickian sense. If the law of the Christian covenant is truly the law of the 'new and everlasting covenant' foreseen by the prophets and which, at the Last Supper, Jesus declared himself to be constituting in his blood, then it must be first and foremost an *interior* law, brought about without alienating heteronomy, through the grace of the Holy Spirit. The iconological comment treats the rolls – one furled, the other unfurled – as metaphorical objects: this is not a law written on some medium comparable with the stone tablets of Sinai. It is inscribed on believers' hearts by the Spirit of God. Alternatively or complementarily, Christ here gives the Church, summed up in her apostolic heads, the power to live out the new life which he inaugurates. What he has commanded (for he is, in Matthew, a new Moses, and in John, the giver of a 'new commandment'), that he enables, 'for our good'. In the art of late antiquity, the function of the gesture was, often enough, to concentrate attention on the *words* of the person speaking.[9] Yet the word of Christ, as the very word of God is not simply ethical instruction, but possesses a unique efficacy as an active, transforming word which

> shall not return to me empty
> but shall accomplish that which I purpose
> and prosper in the thing for which I sent it –

thus spoke the prophet Isaiah (56:11).

The ancient Christian image-type of the *traditio legis*, of which the Junius Bassus sarcophagus is an excellent example, expresses both the continuity and the discontinuity which hold between

[9]H. Pfeiffer, *L'Immagine di Cristo nell' Arte* (Rome 1986), p. 16. Father Pfeiffer refers the reader to A. Quacquarelli's *Retorica e liturgia antenicena* (Rome 1960), and R. Brilliant, *Gesture and Rank in Roman Art* (New Haven, CT 1963), as well as to the monumental study by J. Wilpert, *Die römischen Mosaiken und Malerein der kirchlichen Bauten vom IV. bis zum XIII. Jahrhundert* (Freiburg 1917²), p. 121.

Jesus and the Torah. The *Catechism* itself does well when it speaks of Jesus explaining the Sinaitic Law of the Elder Covenant in the light of the grace of the New Covenant which is its successor.[10] In Peter and Paul we see the unity of the 'Church from the Circumcision', in its genetic descent from Abraham, and the 'Church from the Gentiles', born of the universalising of the covenant with the coming of the Messiah, not only in the drama of their chequered collaboration at Antioch and the message of their letters but also finally by their dying which sealed the faith of the Roman church in their blood.

The *Catechism*'s final image, the blazon of its book on prayer, is the only one of non-Roman provenance. An eleventh-century miniature in a lectionary from a Constantinopolitan workshop, now in the monastery of Dionysiou on Mount Athos, it is, as this description alone might show, resolutely Oriental. Appropriately, it ushers the reader into the space of the most Eastern section of the *Catechism*, its commentary on the Our Father. In iridescent gold and blue, it portrays Christ praying on a stylised hillside to the Father, aureoled in a nimbus in the top right hand corner of the page, while on the far left the disciples look on, attentive but respectfully distant.[11] The authors of the *Catechism*, in their comment, take the image to be one painter's exegesis of the request made by the disciples to Jesus as recorded in Luke: 'Lord, teach us to pray' (11:1). This is the very request which, in the Third Gospel, precedes the giving of the Our Father, the Christian prayer *par excellence*, with which the *Catechism* will conclude not only its euchology but its entire enterprise.

---

[10]Paragraph 577.

[11]Such is the lectionary's richness that one can well believe Kurt Weitzmann's claim, based on a detailed analysis, that it is an *imperial* lectionary — and more precisely a gift of the emperor Isaac I Comnenos to the Studios monastery in the great City. After the City's fall, it passed into the possession of the gospodars of Wallachia who presented it to Dionysiou. Thus K. Weitzmann, 'An Imperial Lectionary in the Monastery of Dionysiou. Its Origins and its Wanderings', in idem., *Byzantine Liturgical Psalters and Gospels* (London 1980), pp. 239–253.

Bibliography

Papal and curial statements:

'*Catechism* is sure norm of doctrine' = 'Letter of the Holy Father Pope John Paul II to Priests for Holy Thursday 1993', *L'Osservatore Romano*, English edition, 31 March 1993, p. 1.

'Communion must inspire catechists' = 'Allocution of Pope John Paul II to Presidents of the Episcopal Conference Commissions for Catechesis and Others', 29 April 1993, in ibid., 12 May 1993, p. 5.

'*Catechism of the Catholic Church* must serve as a model and exemplar for local catechisms' = 'Report of Archbishop Crescenzio Sepe, Secretary of the Congregation for the Clergy, to Seminar on the *Catechism of the Catholic Church* and the Catechetical Apostolate', 29 April 1993, in ibid., 12 May 1993, p. 6.

A helpful series of essays appeared in *L'Osservatore Romano* in the wake of the *Catechism*'s publication. They are cited here according to the English edition, where they received the general title 'Reflections on the *Catechism of the Catholic Church*':

1. Cardinal Jozef Tomko, '*Catechism* shows God's salvific will requires Church to be missionary', 3 March 1993, p. 7.
2. Archbishop Jan P. Schotte, '*Catechism*'s origin and content reflect episcopal collegiality', 10 March 1993, pp. 8–9.
3. (Bishop) Christoph Schönborn, O.P., 'The divine economy woven through new catechetical work', 17 March 1993, pp. 4, 9.
4. (Archimandrite) Guy-Paul Noujeim, 'Eastern tradition reflected in new *Catechism*'s spirituality', 24 March 1993, p. 10.

5. Cardinal Carlo M. Martini, S.J., '*Catechism* responds to desire and needs of Church today', 31 March 1993, p. 9.
6. Fr Max Thurian, '*Catechism* offers prospects for ecumenical reflection', 7 April 1993, p. 4.
7. Cardinal José T. Sánchez, 'Inculturation of *Catechism* at the local level is necessary', 14 April 1993, pp. 4, 7.
8. (Bishop) Alessandro Maggiolini, 'Introduction to new *Catechism* highlights the centrality of faith', 21 April 1993, pp. 8–9.
9. (Archbishop) Estanislao Esteban Karlic, '*Catechism* beautifully illustrates the nature of liturgical action', 28 April 1993, pp. 9–10.
10. (Bishop) Jorge Medina Estévez, '*Catechism* highlights centrality of sacraments in Christian life', 5 May 1993, pp. 9–10.
11. (Archbishop) Jean Honoré, '*Catechism* presents morality as a lived experience of faith in Christ', 12 May 1993, p. 10.
12. (Bishop) David Every Konstant, 'The Ten Commandments provide a positive framework for life in Christ', 19 May 1993, p. 9.
13. Fr Jean Corbon, 'In the name of Jesus we have confident access to the Father', 26 May 1993, p. 10.
14. J. Castellano Cervera, O.C.D., '*Our Father* offers the Christian a complete synthesis of prayer', 2 June 1993, p. 10.
15. Fr Giuseppe Segalla, '*Catechism* presents Scripture as revelation of God's salvific plan', 9 June 1993, pp. 9–10.
16. Lila B. Archideo, '*Catechism* points to Mary as the mother and example of the faithful', 16 June 1993, pp. 4, 6.
17. Monsignor Raffaello Martinelli, 'Formulas should be adapted to needs and capacity of audience', 23 June 1993, pp. 10, 13.
18. Ana Ofelia Fernández, 'Historical prespective sheds new light on most recent *Catechism*', 30 June 1993, pp. 10–11.
19. Fr Raúl Lanzetti, 'The new *Catechism* compared to the *Roman Catechism* of Trent', 7 July 1993, pp. 9, 11.
20. Fr Albert Chapelle, S.J., 'New *Catechism* presents essential elements of papal social teaching', 14 July 1993, pp. 9–10.
21. Anna Maria Cànopl, O.S.B., 'Man and woman are loved by the Lord and desired for one another', 21 July 1993, pp. 10–11.

Background studies:

Gautier, F., O.S.B., 'Transmettre le foi selon le Cardinal Ratzinger', *Revue Thomiste* 33, 3 (1983), pp. 430–444.

Soulages, G., *Dossier sur le problème de la catéchèse* (Paris 1977).

Transmettre la foi. La catéchèse dans l'Eglise, = *QuatreFleuves* 11 (1980).

Wackenheim, C., *La Catéchèse* (Paris 1983).

Wrenn, Msgr Michael J., *Catechism and Controversies. Religious Education in the Post Conciliar Years* (San Francisco 1992).

Idem., with K. D. Whitehead, *Flawed Expectations. The Reception of the Catechism of the Catholic Church* (San Francisco 1996).

The Making of the Catechism

Mastroeni, Anthony (ed.), *The Church and the Universal Catechism. Proceedings from the Fifteenth Convention of the Fellowship of Catholic Scholars, Pittsburgh,* Ohio (Steubenville, Ohio, 1992).

Ratzinger, Cardinal Joseph, '*The Catechism of the Catholic Church* and the Optimism of the Redeemed', *Communio* XX, 3 (1993), pp. 469–484.

Ratzinger, Cardinal Joseph with Christoph Schönborn, *Introduction to 'The Catechism of the Catholic Church'* (E.t. San Francisco 1994).

Reese, Thomas J., S.J. (ed.), *The Universal Catechism Reader. Reflections and Responses* (San Francisco 1990). Largely negative essays on the *Catechism* in its draft form, as circulated (confidentially!) to bishops for comment.

Schönborn, C., 'Les critères de rédaction du *Catéchisme de l'Eglise Catholique*', *Nouvelle Revue Théologique* 115.2 (1993) pp. 161–168.

Study aids:

The Companion to the 'Catechism of the Catholic Church'. A Compendium of Texts Referred to in the 'Catechism of the Catholic Church' (San Francisco 1994).

Läpple, A., *Arbeitsbuch zum 'Katechismus der Katholischen Kirche'* (Munich 1993). Provides relevant texts from Scripture, Church doctrine and Liturgy, and an anthology of what it terms 'impulses for thought and faith' drawn from ancient and modern authors.

On the Catechism's images:

Deichmann, F. W., *Repertorium der christlichen-antiken Sarkophage* I (Wiesbaden 1967).

Fasola, U., *La basilica dei SS. Nereo e Achilleo e la catacomba di Domitilla* (Rome 1965);

———— *Pietro e Paolo a Roma. Orme sulla roccia* (Rome 1980).

Mancinelli, F., *Catacombe e basiliche. I primi cristiani a Roma* (Florence 1981).

Millet, G., *Recherches sur l'iconographie de l'Evangile* (Paris 1916).

Nestori, A., *Repertorio topografico delle pitture delle catacombe romane* (Rome 1975).

Styger, P., *Die altchristliche Grabeskunst* (Munich 1927).

Testini, P., *Le catacombe e gli antichi cimiteri cristiani a Roma* (Bologna 1966).

Weis-Liebersdorf, J. E., *Christus und Apostelbilder* (Freiburg 1902).

Weitzmann, K. (ed.), *Age of Spirituality. A Symposium* (New York 1980).

———— *Byzantine Liturgical Psalters and Gospels* (London 1980).

Wilpert, J., *Le pitture delle catacombe romane* (Rome 1903).

———— *Die römischen Mosaiken und Malerein der IV bis zum XIII Jahrhundert* I (Freiburg 1917²).

Index

II. Subject

Adversus Haereses (Irenaeus) 29
affectivity 211
agnosticism 193
America, intellectual life 279
anamnesis 15, 16
ancien régime and the French
    monarchy 155
Ancrene Riwle and the Real
    Presence 61
angels, ministry 160
animal welfare 216
Anointing of the Sick 76–8, 98
Annunciation (Fra Angelico) 32
Apocalypse 273–274
Apocalypse of St John 14–15
Apologia pro Vita Sua (John
    Henry Newman) 220
Apology of the Prophet David
    (Ambrose) 19
apostles 236, 237
Apostolic Constitution (Paul
    VI) on Confirmation 51
Apostolic Exhortation on
    Marriage and Family
    (*Familiaris consortio*, John
    Paul II) 94
apostolic ministry *see*
    priesthood
apostolic succession 12
Apostolic Tradition 53
art and truth 221–223
artifical contraception 214
artificial procreation 214
asceticism 167, 178
Asperges 98
atheism 193
Augustine, Rule of St 143
authority in society 153–154
Ave Maria 250–251

Baptism (*see also* sacraments)
    20, 21, 138, 171, 173
    administration 44–47

and Confirmation 45, 50–51
and ecumenism 50
effects 48–50
foundations in the Church 49
recipients 45–46
and sacramentals 98
and second conversion 68
significance 43–44
use of God's Name in 196–197
Bassus, Junius, sarcophagus
    289–290
beatitude 120–125
Beatitudes 121, 166
believers, relationship with God 6
Benediction 37–38
Bertram, Edmund, views on
    faith and morals in
    Mansfield Park 107–108
bishops 85
    and Anointing of the Sick 78
    and initiation of priesthood 88
    magisterium 179–180, 181
    pastoral role 83
    role in Confirmation 52, 53
blasphemy 147, 196
Blessing, theology 8–10
Book of Blessings 10

calumny 219
Cana, wedding at 240
Canterbury, Council of the
    Province of (1222) and
    the Real Presence 61
capital punishment 205, 206
Catechesi tradendae (John Paul
    II) 283
Catechism of the Council of Trent
    189
Catechisms, development 276–
    279, 282–283
Catholic action 52
Catholic Bishops, Synod of 276
celebrants, identity 28

310 *The Service of Glory*

and prayer 229–30, 239–240,
  249, 266–267
redemptive activity 3–4
as reflected in family life 201
and sacraments 26
and society 150
truth 218
union with 173
truth
  offences against 219–220
  restrictions on disclosure 220
  and the Ten Commandments
    218–223
the two *'ways'* 115

unbaptised, salvation 47–48
unjust wages, payment 216
Ursuline nuns 282

Vatican II
  Ad Gentes, on mission 45, 83
  Constitution on the Sacred
    Liturgy 23, 32, 54, 57, 92,
    97
  Dogmatic Constitution 3, 78,
    177, 245
  on the *imago Dei* 118
  Lumen Gentium 51
  on priesthood 87
  and religious freedom 191–192
  and salvation of the
    unbaptised 47
Veni Sancte Spiritus 249
venial sin 147

vices and virtues, contrast 147
Virgin Mary 27, 33, 60, 194, 195
  and the Apocalypse 273–274
  in Christian art 287–288
  as the Church 171
  holiness 179
  invocation 36
  and prayer 101–102, 240,
    249–251, 255
virginity 91
virtues
  cardinal virtues 135–137
  development in man 134–
    135
  theological virtues 137–143,
    189–190, 247
  and vices, contrast 147

Weaving the Web, National
    Project of Catechesis and
    Religious Education 282–
    283
*Der Weltkatechismus. Therapie oder
    Symptom einer Kranken
    Kiche?* 281
What are we to Teach? 282
Wisdom literature, on idolatry
    194
Woman of Samaria 228
world development 217–218

YHWH 232

Zen Buddhism 259